THE
Temperature
—— OF ——
Death

DAVID BARRAT

Orsam Books
www.orsam.co.uk
First edition published 2023

David Barrat asserts his moral rights to be identified as the author of this work.

All rights reserved. No significant part of this publication may be reproduced in any form without the prior permission of the publisher (the author).

ISBN: 978-0-9570917-3-3

CONTENTS

Acknowledgements v
Preface vii

Chapter One   The Coldness of Death 1
Chapter Two   The Death of Elizabeth Gardner 35
Chapter Three   Trial 59
Chapter Four   Uproar 81
Chapter Five   Experiments 99
Chapter Six   Australia 125
Chapter Seven   1864-1873 133
Chapter Eight   The West Haddon Controversy 145
Chapter Nine   1875-1887 165
Chapter Ten   The Year of The Ripper 185
Chapter Eleven   1889-1960s 199
Chapter Twelve   1960s-Present 229

Conclusion 243
Appendix A 249
Appendix B 255

ACKNOWLEDGEMENTS

Many thanks to my proofreading team of Sidney, Jenita and Rachel.

PREFACE

Whether from a lifetime diet of book, film and television crime-detective dramas or otherwise, most people would probably expect a medical examiner, following a murder or suspected murder, to be able to provide the investigating authorities with an accurate estimate of the time of death. But can they do it? How do they do it? How has it been done historically? Those are the questions that this book attempts to answer, albeit that the focus is on how the time of death has been estimated based on the temperature of the corpse. That's because, traditionally, it's the main way it's been done for nearly two hundred years.

You will notice that I used the expression 'medical examiner'. Unfortunately, for much of the period under discussion in this book, a medical examiner was always, without exception, a man, due to women not being allowed to participate in the profession. For the most part, unless referring to a specific individual, I have tried to avoid making reference to a 'medical man' but it is inevitable that there will be some mentions of this, especially in direct quotes, which is an unfortunate reflection of historic gender inequality.

Another tricky linguistic issue is with the fact that the correct form of address for a surgeon is not 'Dr' but 'Mr'. I think we can all have sympathy with someone who spends five years studying medicine, and then a further number of years training, only to end up with the same title with which they started; a title, furthermore, which I, like every other adult male, is entitled to use, despite never having set foot in a medical college. For the purposes of this book, it makes no difference whether any particular medical examiner is a surgeon or a physician – we are dealing with the examination of dead bodies after all – and, for the purpose of clarity, in order to make clear their profession, I've tended to refer to surgeons as 'Dr so and so'. During the nineteenth century they were, in fact, often, or at least occasionally, referred to as such in newspaper reports of the period, so it's not entirely unhistorical to do so.

You will have noticed that I said that I have never set foot in a medical college. More than this, I have never examined, touched or even seen a dead body. Nothing in this book, therefore, should be taken as being first-hand information, coming from someone with medical knowledge, and I have no *personal* wisdom to impart. What you are reading is a purely curatorial exercise whereby I have extracted everything I know about the subject from newspaper reports, official reports, archived files of inquest and other legal proceedings, medical journals and textbooks. It should, nevertheless, be accurate and, taken as a whole, may even provide more information than is currently known to the medical community. Indeed, I'm not sure that an exercise of this nature has ever been attempted before. It's true that some expert writers in the field, such as Professor Bernard Knight, have written histories of the *medical* literature on the subject of estimating time of death but such histories never been properly set against the context of what was happening in the wider world. I suspect that some of what I have found in my research will be surprising even to medical experts who are unaware of the reasons and thinking behind certain historical experiments and papers.

So why am I, without any medical qualifications, writing a book about the estimation of time of death? Well, although I had long been aware of the difficulty in establishing time of death, I first became interested in the subject when writing my 2014 book *The Camden Town Murder Mystery* in which the estimated time of death was a crucial factor in the case. I found the book *Time of Death: The True Story of the Search for Death's Stopwatch* by Jessica Snyder Sachs which confirmed what I had already thought, namely that there was no accurate way of doing it. From reading various online discussions, mainly relating to issues surrounding the 'Jack the Ripper' murders, I realized that there was a general lack of knowledge regarding the abilities or otherwise of a medical examiner to accurately estimate time of death and, indeed, regarding the entire science behind such estimates. That was what started me looking at both published medical papers relating to time of death (especially from the nineteenth century to work out what the state of knowledge was in 1888) as well as newspaper reports relating to earlier estimates in order to try and assess their accuracy from the known facts in murder cases.

The purpose of this book is to share the results of what I discovered in my research into the subject.[1]

Let's start in 1862.

---

[1] A quick note on sources. I have occasionally transcribed evidence from witnesses as reported in newspapers from the third person to the first person for clarity. Where I cite evidence from trials at the Old Bailey, this has been taken in all cases from the official proceedings of the Central Criminal Court available online at www.oldbaileyonline.org.

CHAPTER ONE

The Coldness of Death

Henry Sequeira was in his surgery at 1 Jewry Street, Aldgate, shortly before 8am on Monday, 15 September 1862, when a young woman he knew as the servant to the wife of a local chimney sweep came rushing in, holding a two-year-old child in her arms. The young woman, who seemed to be in an agitated state, said in a desperate tone, 'Oh do come quickly, Mrs Gardner has cut her throat. Please come immediately, or you shall not find her alive.'[2] As requested, Dr Sequeira followed the servant, nineteen-year-old Elizabeth Humbler, to a house at 1 Northumberland Alley, a short walk of some two minutes from his surgery.

In a room on the first floor of the house, Sequeira saw the dead body of a woman he recognised as Elizabeth, the wife of Samuel Gardner, lying on the floor next to her bed, with her throat cut. She was wearing only a flannel vest and chemise. The medical examiner immediately placed his hand on her thigh 'and found that it was quite cold'. The upper part of the trunk, around the shoulders, was also 'quite cold' but the lower part of the trunk 'was warm'. This brief inspection by touch was to prove critical in the official investigation of Mrs Gardner's death. But what conclusions could properly be drawn as to the time of death from her abdomen being warm to the touch and her thigh and upper trunk being cold? This was a question which was to prove highly controversial in the world of Victorian

---

[2] *Times*, 8 October 1862. Cited as 'Do come directly, or she will be dead before we get back' in *News of the World*, 12 October 1862.

forensic pathology, and, moreover, a man's life and liberty would literally depend on how it was answered.

During the early part of the nineteenth century, when medical examiners were asked if they could estimate how long a body, which was found to be 'cold,' and thus exhibiting *algor mortis,* or 'the coldness of death', had been dead, the usual answer would be something like 'some hours' or 'several hours', while a warm body would be said to have 'not long been dead', 'recently deceased' or similar. Rarely would they be more specific than this. If, however, they *were* sufficiently bold as to offer a precise number of hours since death, it would invariably conflict with estimates provided by others. Some might say a cold body must have been dead one hour, some would say two or three hours, others would say even longer. For the most part, though, it didn't much matter. In cases of natural death or suicide, or even murder, nothing would *usually* rest on how long someone had been dead. Occasionally it might be necessary for the purpose of recording *the date* of death to establish if death had occurred before or after midnight on a particular day but, in almost all cases, including murder cases, the time of death was rarely of great importance.

Just occasionally, though, it was crucial because it might eliminate or implicate a particular suspect.

In the medical literature of the period there wasn't much reliable guidance as to precisely how long it took for a warm body to feel cold after death. The first priority for the Victorian medical examiner at the scene of an assumed death was to check that death genuinely *had* occurred and that a living person wasn't about to be buried, or dissected during an autopsy. The second priority, both at the scene and during any subsequent examination, was to attempt to establish the cause of death and to ascertain if there were any suspicious circumstances suggesting that a crime had occurred or, alternatively, if death was due to a natural cause, disease or suicide (albeit that suicide was considered a crime). This placed the medical examiner in the role of detective, whose skills were heavily relied upon by both the police and the courts in cases of unexpected deaths to determine whether a crime had been committed. In consequence of this, a new academic field of so-called 'medical jurisprudence' was created, with publication of 'medico-legal' books by experts to assist examiners. At the start of the century, however, working out precisely when death had occurred was either low on the list of tasks for a medical examiner or not on the list at all.

The first medico-legal textbook, *Elements of Medical Jurisprudence*, was published in 1788 by Dr Samuel Farr, who stated that the examination of a dead body should be carried out 'as soon as possible after death' but, he said, should not be performed where the body was found. While Farr advised that, during such an examination, 'The external habit of the body is to be inspected with the greatest accuracy and inspection', this was only to discover if death had been 'induced by poisonous substances'. He didn't consider it part of the job of a medical examiner to take temperature into account when examining a dead body, or to estimate the time of death by any means.

Despite this, the general public at large was happily making assumptions about what it meant for a dead body to be cold. During the night of 26 March 1784, some of the local populace of the town of Bickley, near Tiverton, Devonshire, were awoken by one of their neighbours, Thomas Smart, calling for help. Smart claimed that he had fled his house after having been disturbed by thieves and was afraid for the safety of his companion, Thomas Ewings, who he'd left behind in the house. Arming themselves with whatever weapons were to hand, the neighbours rushed to the house to find Ewings lying on the floor, covered with blood, his head smashed in, as if by the thieves. Suspicions were raised, however, by the fact that, 'though they had gone immediately on the alarm, they found the blood congealed on the floor, and the body quite cold, which could not reasonably have been expected in the time.'[3] This was quite a nifty piece of early forensic deduction by lay people, and their suspicions about Smart were confirmed by a plethora of evidence which proved beyond any doubt that he had committed the murder with a cleaver, and stolen money from his dead companion. Smart was found guilty of the offence at the City of Exeter Quarter Sessions and executed by hanging on 7 August 1784.

Given that it was known, or assumed, by members of the public that a body very recently murdered should not be cold (not to mention that blood shouldn't be congealed), it is perhaps somewhat surprising that Dr Farr didn't even consider the issue of body temperature in estimating time

---

[3] *Hampshire Chronicle*, 29 March 1784.

of death when discussing the examination of a dead body for the benefit of his medical peers.

Dr George Edward Male, in his 1816 treatise, *An Epitome of Juridical or Forensic Medicine*, described by Professor Sydney Smith as 'the first creditable book on forensic medicine in English'[4] did consider that, from the state of a dead body, 'we should endeavour to ascertain how long the deceased had been dead' but he didn't mention using the temperature of the body as a way of doing this, or indeed, any other method, so it wasn't clear what he was saying. Prudently, he added, 'we should also inquire by whom he was last seen', which, considering that he appeared to be unable to advise precisely how one should go about ascertaining how long the deceased had been dead from the state of the body, was almost certainly the more reliable way of doing it.

In his second edition, published two years later, Male said of the examination of a dead body, 'We should be careful to ascertain what time has elapsed since his death', but this comment related exclusively to an estimate based on the development or otherwise of putrefaction, thus only allowing a conclusion as to whether death had occurred 'several days' earlier or not. Dr Male only mentioned the coldness of a dead body in the context of establishing whether the person being examined was, in fact, dead. He had said in his first edition that one of the true signs by which death was manifested was 'coldness and rigidity of the body' but, by the time of the second edition, he didn't even seem sure of this, noting that two German authorities had, in the interim, concluded that those signs were 'not infallible'. The question of surviving body warmth after death was only mentioned in the context of a discussion about the effects of carbonic acid gas whereby Male said that, in cases of death caused by exposure to this gas, 'the body is supposed to retain its heat longer than when life has been destroyed by other means'. As Male never explained how long a body not poisoned to death by carbonic acid gas was supposed to retain its heat, it wasn't terribly helpful for the reader or student.

Dr John Gordon Smith, whose *Principles of Forensic Medicine* was published in 1821, wasn't at all interested in advising medical examiners to estimate time of death. In the context of attempting to establish whether

---

[4] Sydney Smith, 'The History and Development of Forensic Medicine', *British Medical Journal*, 24 March 1951.

death had occurred or not, he noted that one of the universal signs of death was 'coldness, accompanied by rigidity of the muscles'. However, he acknowledged that, 'Warmth frequently continues about dead bodies for hours and even days' while also noting that, occasionally, 'rigidity of the limbs does not occur at all'. He said nothing about using the temperature (or, for that matter, rigidity) of a dead body to work out when someone had died.

A three volume work called *Medical Jurisprudence* by Dr John Ayrton Paris, a prominent physician, assisted by John Samuel Martin Fonblanque, a barrister, published in 1823, merely stated that, 'Under ordinary circumstances, the body loses its vital heat in a very short space of time'. To this was added that, 'there are many circumstances that appear capable of controlling and modifying this general result; the heat of the body is not only abstracted with different degrees of celerity in different situations, but even in the same situation, in death from different causes.' Paris and Fonblanque didn't provide any advice as to what conclusion, in terms of the number of hours since death, could, or should, be drawn from a cold body, or from a warm one, but nevertheless noted, somewhat unhelpfully in those circumstances, that, 'The determining as accurately as possible, the length of time an individual has been dead, is…important in cases of murder'.

A year after the publication of Paris and Fonblanque's book, evidence about the rate of body cooling after death was given in Edinburgh during the belated trial of Margaret Boug for the murder of Elizabeth Low whose dead body had been found in her room, with her head fractured, six years earlier, in February 1818. Dr Peter Martin, who had been called to examine the body, noted in court on 19 January 1824 that putrefaction hadn't taken place at the time of his examination so that, he said, the murder must have occurred within the previous 72 hours but, at the same time, 'the body was cold, which probably would not have been the case in less than 12 hours.' Nothing turned on the time of death and the charge of murder was not proven but Boug was found guilty of stealing articles belonging to Low after her death and sentenced to transportation. Was it true, though, that it took at least twelve hours for a dead body to become cold? There didn't seem to be any authority for the claim.

Later in the same year, on 26 November 1824, a surgeon, Thomas Brown, was called to a house in Blake Street, Liverpool, where Alison

Wilkin was lying dead in her bed. At the trial of her husband, Joseph, for her murder in March of the following year at Lancaster Assizes, Brown said in his evidence that, when he arrived at the scene of the murder, 'I found the body quite cold and dead'. From that, he supposed, 'it must have been dead at least two or three hours'.[5] That was a bit of a difference from the twelve hours that Dr Martin had said earlier in the year was necessary for a dead body to turn cold.

In one of the leading textbooks of the age, *Elements of Medical Jurisprudence* by Dr Theodric Romeyn Beck, the second edition of which was published in 1825, it was noted that 'sudden death is not uncommon and...those who, at one moment, we see in the full enjoyment of life, may, at the next, be cold and inanimate', but that was merely by way of cautioning the medical examiner against jumping to the conclusion that a sudden death meant that murder had occurred. The advice given by Beck to the medical examiner conducting a scene-of-crime examination was to 'examine the colour of the skin, the temperature of the body, the rigidity or flexibility of the extremities, the state of the eyes...any fluid flowing from the nose, mouth, ears, sexual organs etc. and indeed every thing varying from the natural state'. Frustratingly, for anyone wondering what conclusions should be drawn from all these factors, Beck was completely silent.

Without any expert advice to guide them in published medical works, the state of knowledge about body cooling by medical examiners during this time can perhaps best be seen in evidence given at the Old Bailey during the 1832 trial of Bridget Culkin, accused but acquitted of murdering a six-year-old girl called Margaret Duffey. The young girl's body had been found in a privy in Hartshorn Court, in the City of London, at about 9.45pm on 3 December 1831. It was taken to the shop of a nearby apothecary, John Smith, who performed what he admitted was a very cursory examination, no doubt because he was distracted by an angry mob surrounding his shop seeking to lynch the child's unknown murderer. Under questioning later in court, Smith said of the girl's body: 'I felt it, and said it must have been dead for some little time...I should think it had been dead an hour or an hour and a half, but that opinion can only be formed by circumstances – its legs and arms were uncovered, and, of course, cold.'

---

[5] *Morning Herald*, 21 March 1825.

Under further questioning he added, 'I form my opinion from the degree of coldness of the body – it was comparatively uncovered, except the frock; it was not quite cold – it struck me it had been dead about that time'. Asked what factors could affect the rate of cooling, he responded, 'it depends on the temperature of the air.' To the judge, he said, 'as to the time it would take to cool - being in a cold exposed place would make a difference of perhaps an hour, and if she had been walking all the evening in the cold air, she would cool sooner'. Asked if he could form any decided opinion as to whether the child had been dead more than about half an hour, Smith replied simply, 'I could not'.

On the night the murder was discovered, Smith arranged for the child's body to be taken from his shop to Bunwell Row Police Station where, at about 10pm, it was examined by a surgeon, John Leeson, based in Chiswell Street. His belief as to what time would elapse between the death of a person and the coldness of their body was set out in his evidence in court when he said, 'That depends on circumstances; it would be a much longer time cooling than in a case of natural death – it might take four, five, or six hours; it depends on circumstances, and the situation where the person died – if exposed to cold when alive, and then remaining in the privy, it might be five or six hours becoming cold; it might take an hour or two longer if the person was under shelter.' In the specific case of Margaret Duffey, however, Leeson said that, 'the extremities were cold, and the body warm – I should suppose about eighty degrees, there was a considerable degree of warmth'. On the basis of this estimated temperature of eighty degrees Fahrenheit for the external surface of the little girl's body, he said, 'I formed a supposition that it had been dead about an hour.' At the same time, he accepted that he could 'very easily' have been mistaken by a full hour in his calculation. By this he appears to have meant that Duffey could have been dead for two hours, because he also said, 'I guessed the degree of heat by applying my hand, and may be mistaken; blood heat is 98 degrees – a body would be about two hours losing 18 degrees.'

Leaving aside that there was no scientific reason to suppose that the temperature of a dead body dropped by nine degrees an hour, as Leeson appears to have believed, guessing the degree of heat by applying one's hand, which even the surgeon admitted might have led him to a mistaken conclusion, wasn't entirely satisfactory to say the least; but this seems to be how it was done during the nineteenth century. While each individual medic would probably have had their own method of feeling a dead body to assess the warmth or otherwise of the skin – some using their fingers or palms – it would appear that the customary method, going back many years, was to use the back of the hand.[6] One nineteenth century doctor explained in court that, 'You feel the heat and cold much better with the back of your hands. That is the custom of the medical profession, and every common-sense person would do so.'[7] It was hardly ideal. Yet, the use of a thermometer at the scene of a murder to record either the surface or internal temperatures of dead bodies seems, on the whole, to have been spurned by Victorian medical examiners. As late as 1904, one surgeon said at the Old Bailey, in a major murder case, 'if anything important turns upon the temperature of a body, a thermometer would be more accurate, but it is not usually used'.[8]

In any case, in saying that 'blood heat' is 98 degrees Fahrenheit, Leeson was in error. The internal or core temperature of the human body – as opposed to 'blood heat' – is certainly around 98 degrees in a healthy living person, as measured by a thermometer placed in the one of the cavities, or under the armpit, but that doesn't mean that the surface skin temperature will be the same. In fact, it will usually be a few degrees lower than the core temperature in most places of the body, while the temperature at the extremities will be significantly lower than that. A modern study has shown that the average temperature of the male hand in normal conditions is 90 degrees while that of a woman is 87.2 degrees.[9] Outside, in the cold air, that could easily, and quickly, drop by another ten degrees or more.

---

[6] See *Time of Death: The True Story of the Search for Death's Stopwatch* by Jessica Snyder Sachs, 2003, Arrow Books (p.15), who says that in ancient times when it came to establishing if a person who died in their sleep had expired before or after midnight in order to correctly register the date of death, 'The official chronometer in such cases would have been the back of the coroner's hand held against the corpse to judge its warmth or lack of it.'

[7] Dr Charles Nugent Fox giving evidence in the Ramsgate murder case, *Thanet Advertiser*, 20 June 1893.

[8] Evidence of Augustus Joseph Pepper in case of murder of Emily Farmer, Old Bailey Proceedings, 14 November 1904.

[9] 'Cold hands, warm heart' by Han Kim, Clark Richardson, Jeanette Roberts, Lisa Green, Joseph L. Lyon, *The Lancet*, 1998, Vol 351, Issue 9114. The temperatures in this study were taken with infrared tympanic thermometers.

The face and feet are also often cooler than the rest of the body. The girl's legs and arms, which Leeson said felt cold, could easily have been less than 98 degrees while she was alive, especially on a cold winter's day in December, so that a calculation based on an assumption that they were at 98 degrees while she was alive, then guessing the temperature of those parts of her corpse by feeling them with one's hands, was not likely to be productive.

This leads us to an obvious problem with assessing time of death by simply feeling the body temperature of a corpse; one that was, perhaps, so obvious that it was hardly ever mentioned in the medical literature of the period. This is that a *living* body, just as much as a dead one, can feel cold on the surface. There are plenty of examples of this that could be cited but, to take an early one from the period, a story reported in the press in 1798 said that a thirteen-year-old girl called Ann Blake had attempted suicide by drowning herself in a tub of water for fifteen minutes and, when rescued by a medical man, 'She was to all appearance dead; there was no pulsation either in the temporal artery or at the wrist; her body was cold and motionless, and her face livid'. The muscles of her jaw were also rigid. A prolonged resuscitation had no effect but, after the administration of a solution of zinc oxide emetic, which ejected a large quantity of water from her stomach, the girl was brought back to life and, 'By the next morning she was quite recovered'.[10] A similar thing was reported by a Dr William Crane of Boston in 1816 who said that he once attended a case, 'where there was every appearance of death; the body felt cold, and was even rigid; but upon being put into bed, and proper means applied, the patient in a few hours recovered'.[11] A few years later, the *London Courier & Evening Gazette* of 29 September 1824 carried a story from Pennsylvania, USA, that a newspaper had prepared for publication the obituary of a local man, Mr J. Montgomery, believed dead, who was, however, 'restored to life, after, as every appearance indicated, it had been suspended for about two hours' although it had been stated that, 'his body was cold and that he had no pulse.' Less dramatically, any number of medical examiners would

---

[10] *Staffordshire Advertiser*, 10 November 1798, taken from an article signed by Charles Brown in the *Monthly Magazine*.
[11] *Stamford Mercury*, 29 April 1816.

describe their sick patients as being cold to the touch, even though they were alive.

One cold winter's day, a malnourished unemployed man called James Brook collapsed in the City of London and was carried by his friend into a nearby surgery where he was examined by a Dr Crosby who described his body as being 'as cold as ice' although he was still alive and conscious. He died a few minutes later from 'want of food, accelerated by the very low temperature then prevailing'.[12] Had Mr Brook been found dead in the street, instead of being carried to the surgery, an examination at the scene by a medical examiner would undoubtedly have revealed a body that was extremely cold to the touch, something which might have led to the conclusion that death had occurred some hours previously when, in fact, it might only have been a few minutes earlier. If Brook had, say, happened to have been robbed and killed, so that it was important to fix the time of his death, there would obviously have been a danger that a killer who had an alibi up to shortly before the time of the murder might have escaped justice, with an equal possibility that an innocent person, who had no alibi for that time, could have been wrongly convicted. It was a danger that was largely unrecognized in the medical literature of the nineteenth century and very few medical men who believed they had the ability to assess the time of death from external body temperature seem to have had it in their minds.

In the year after the Calkin trial, surgeon John Vincent Medhurst was called to examine the dead body of the 'wife' of William Rose, a pedlar and itinerant dealer in spice, who had been travelling through a small village in Hampshire and who had been found lying dead (murdered by Rose as it transpired) in a lane with marks of violence on her hands and face during the evening of 1 November 1833. Dr Medhurst, who had rushed to the scene of the murder, said in evidence at the subsequent inquest that, 'The extremities of the body were cold, but not the trunk, and it appeared to have been dead about two or three hours'.[13] So Medhurst had come up with a similar time of death for a body whose trunk was warm as Thomas Brown had done nine years earlier for a body which had been found quite cold, without *any* warmth.

---

[12] *Morning Herald*, 5 January 1867.
[13] *Salisbury and Winchester Journal*, 11 November 1833.

Another revealing case from this period occurred in April 1837 at the Old Bailey when James Greenacre and Sarah Gale were tried for, and found guilty of, the murder of Greenacre's fiancée, Hannah Brown, whose severed head had been found alongside Regent's Canal. Greenacre, who tried to hang himself in police custody, admitted to police that he had killed Hannah and cut off her head but claimed that her death had been an accident. Although the coldness or otherwise of Hannah's body was not an issue in the case, a question asked of the examining surgeon, John Birtwhistle, during the trial was how long blood could flow to the head after death. His dubious answer was that blood would flow as long as the body was warm. So the next question was: How long would the body be warm? To this, he answered, 'The average period of continuance of warmth in a body after death is from one hour to two'.[14] Asked what his personal experience of this was, he said, 'I have examined a good many bodies recently after death, but not immediately [after death].' This was undoubtedly the case for most medical examiners. It was rare to have the opportunity to be present to examine a body within an hour of death, especially in cases of murder where it might take some time for a body to be discovered and then for the medical man to be notified and reach the scene of the crime. For that reason, most examiners would not have much personal experience of what a body felt like an hour or two after a (violent) death. Was it going to feel cold or warm?

At the Old Bailey trial of Richard Gould for the murder of John Templeman, killed in his Islington cottage with a blow to the head during the night of 16th and 17th March 1840, Edward Roe, the surgeon who examined Templeman's dead body said in his evidence that, 'from the appearance of the body when I saw it, I should judge it had been dead five or six hours – it retained a little warmth about the region of the heart but the body was quite cold'. He explained that, 'the time in which a body gets cold depends occasionally on the kind of death the person meets with – a body has retained warmth occasionally two days after death – ten or eleven hours is not at all an unusual time'. During re-examination by the prosecution barrister, he conceded that Templeman 'might have been dead more than five or six hours.' It was he said, 'mere matter of opinion'. The judge then intervened to try and clarify the position, asking, 'It may

---

[14] *Globe*, 11 April 1837.

have been fifteen, ten, or five or six, but it must have been [at least] five or six, that is what you mean?' to which Dr Roe answered. 'Yes, it could not have been less than five or six – I do not know whether it might have been fifteen, it is a very difficult question to answer – I should rather not pledge myself to a few hours, more or less.'

The question was not an academic one. Templeman had retired to bed at 6pm on 16 March and been found dead by a neighbour at 8.30am the following morning. By the time Dr Roe arrived at the scene it was twenty minutes past eleven. His initial estimate of the time of death of five or six hours prior to 11.20am wasn't helpful to the prosecution because it would suggest that Roe had been murdered between 5.20 and 6.20am, when the prisoner, Gould, had an alibi. At some point between 2 and 4am, he had showed up at his lodgings, close to where Templeman had been murdered, and retired to bed for the night (the owners of the lodging house didn't have a clock so couldn't narrow the time down further), having been seen drinking at a local public house during the entire afternoon of 16 March up until midnight when the pub closed. His whereabouts for the hours immediately after midnight could not be accounted for, so that, if he had murdered Templeman, it must have been between 12 and 4am. A time of death later than this would have meant that he was innocent, so it was no wonder that prosecuting counsel attempted to extend the possible time of death back to ten hours or more prior to Roe's examination of the body. Although the evidence against Gould was overwhelming - he had, for example, told a number of people in advance that he was going to rob Templeman - he was inexplicably acquitted, so it's possible that the medical evidence in this case was a factor in his acquittal, albeit that it doesn't appear to have been mentioned by his barrister as a reason for his innocence in his closing speech.

In an extraordinary twist to this story, shortly after being freed from Newgate prison, Gould was arrested for the burglary at Templeman's cottage and, knowing that he couldn't be prosecuted again for the murder, was gulled by the police into making a confession (for the promise of a reward of £200 which he would never collect) in which he admitted that he and another man called Jarvis had broken into Templeman's cottage and murdered Templeman at some point between midnight and about 1am. After being convicted of the burglary on 22 June 1840, the judge, Mr

Baron Parke, made the surprising, but undoubtedly correct statement that, 'there could be very little doubt in the minds of all those who heard the trial, but that he was the person by whom the murder was perpetrated' and, to a round of applause in the Old Bailey, sentenced Gould to transportation for life, being 'the severest [sentence] short of death that the law allowed him to pronounce'.

In 1844, William Augustus Guy, a professor of Forensic Medicine, published *Principles of Forensic Medicine* in which he advised medical examiners performing a post-mortem examination to observe those appearances of a dead body, 'which serve to denote how long the party has been dead, viz. the presence or absence of animal heat, of cadaveric rigidity and of putrefaction'. His advice on the subject of determining how long life had been extinct from the presence or absence of animal heat was that, 'The extinction of animal heat is not a very sure means of determining the period at which death took place, for the body cools with very different degrees of rapidity in different modes of death, the period varying from two or three hours to fifteen or twenty, and if we may trust the authority of Foderé and Mahon, to upwards of four days.' It was quite a wide range, even if one didn't trust the authority of the latter two gentlemen. And, if Professor Guy was to be believed, a cold body could indicate one which had been dead for two hours or, alternatively, twenty. What was a medical examiner, asked to estimate time of death from a cold body alone, to do?

Guy noted that there were a number of factors which influenced the cooling of the body. The temperature and moisture of the surrounding air, the wind speed, whether the body was clothed or naked, whether the body was in water or in air, the condition of the body, whether overweight or emaciated, the age of the body and the mode of death. All these factors, he said, could affect the rate of cooling, but he didn't say precisely how they would do so.

Guy also pointed to the onset of rigidity or stiffness (otherwise known as *rigor mortis*) as being of assistance in pinpointing the time of death. Thus, he said, 'Though rigidity may make its appearance long before the animal heat has disappeared, it may be retarded by the application of warmth, or accelerated by exposure to cold.' He didn't, however, commit himself to say what an examiner should conclude as to time of death from a body that was rigid or one that was both cold *and* rigid.

In the same year as Guy published his book, a Scottish physician, Dr McKellar, gave evidence at the trial of Thomas Wilson for the murder of his wife by strangulation, saying that when he had examined the body of Mrs Wilson on 26 October 1843, 'She must have been dead about an hour, as she was cold; she was generally cold…not at the extremities only, but generally'.[15] Estimating death as having occurred only an hour earlier on the basis of a body being cold was unusual but it was sufficiently damning against Mr Wilson, who had given the impression that he had spoken to his wife shortly before Dr McKellar had examined his wife's body, the doctor having been visiting his house at the very time Mr Wilson said he found her dead body. However, another doctor, John Spiers, examined the body two hours later and felt that, 'The body was then warm'. In the end, the jury at Wilson's trial couldn't decide whether he had murdered his wife or whether she had committed suicide and produced a verdict of 'Not proven'.

Writing in the 11 April 1846 issue of the *Lancet*, in a paper entitled, 'On the Observance of Method in Conducting Post-Mortem Examinations, Especially when they are Intended for Legal Purposes', Dr Henry Letheby, lecturer of chemistry at the London Hospital, listed sixteen questions that a medical man should be asking himself when examining a dead body, the eleventh of which was, 'Can any opinion be formed as to the time which has elapsed since death?' Dr Letheby said that this was, 'an important question, and may involve an answer having a certain day, or even hour, for its limit'. He warned his readers, however, that 'the post-mortem signs are not by any means so constant in their occurrence, or so conclusive in their import, as to warrant us in making, on all occasions, such a positive reply'. As to the issue of looking for warmth in the body, Letheby admitted that he had 'not been able to get together very many facts connected with this sign'. Nevertheless, he revealed that he had personally made some observations from deceased individuals moved directly after death to a mortuary from the wards of a hospital (presumably the London Hospital) and that, from these observations, he had concluded that, 'the extremities lose their heat very rapidly, sinking to the temperature of the room in less than three hours, while the surface of the trunk has felt warm, even up to the twenty-fourth hour; and at this time a thermometer, placed either in the axilla or rectum, has generally stood at somewhere about 70°

---

[15] *Greenock Advertiser*, 19 March 1844.

Fahrenheit'. Those parts, he said, hardly ever lost the whole of their heat until after a lapse of thirty-six, or sometimes forty-eight hours. He added, however, that there were 'many circumstances which modify the order of things' such as the body cooling faster if it is exposed to cold air, or slower if it remained in bed or was well clothed.

As to rigor mortis, Letheby said that the limbs begin to stiffen in about two or three hours after death and that rigor is generally firm and complete after seven or eight hours. He noted, however, that there can be various exceptions to this, such as when there has been a violent convulsive action or prolonged muscular exertion before death which, he said, causes the living spasm to pass 'at once' into dead rigor. Letheby also advised the medical examiner to consider the condition of the cornea (in the eye), advising that in general it becomes slightly clouded about nine or ten hours after death, with certain other changes after sixteen, twenty-four and forty-eight hours.

By the time of publication of the sixth edition of his *Elements of Medical Jurisprudence*, in 1848, Dr Beck had evidently given some more thought as to what happened to a body immediately after death, commenting that, 'The earliest changes that take place in the body after life has departed, are coldness, stiffness and lividity', although he also said that the onset of coldness and stiffness was 'far from uniform'. Beck still didn't provide any advice himself as to estimating time of death from coldness or stiffness but included a footnote referring to the work of a French physician, Marie-Guillaume Alphonse Devergie, who had calculated that, if there was some heat remaining in the body with more or less relaxation of muscles, 'death may have occurred from two to twenty hours'. If the heat was gone and cadaveric rigidity, or stiffness, was present then death had occurred 'from ten hours to three days'. Beck did, however, add a caution that these rules were 'evidently only approximations, as many circumstances may interpose to delay their consecutive development.' Nevertheless, between Guy and Beck there were at least signs of some sort of consensus that a body would become cold between two and twenty hours after death, even though this kind of range would provide little or no assistance in identifying a murderer, or acquitting an innocent person, in most cases.

The other standard work of forensic medicine during the nineteenth century was Dr Alfred Swaine Taylor's *Medical Jurisprudence,* first published in November 1843, but his early editions avoided the subject of estimation of time of death entirely, save for a single remark that, 'In order to determine probable time of death, we should always notice whether there be any warmth about the body, whether it be rigid or in a state of decomposition, and to what degree this may have advanced'.[16] Like other writers, he didn't explain what conclusion in terms of time of death could be drawn from noticing or not noticing warmth in the body (or from rigidity or decomposition for that matter). He dealt with the subject in more detail, however, during a subsequent lecture at Guy's Hospital where he was Professor of Medical Jurisprudence.[17] In that lecture, while acknowledging that the cooling of the body after death will take place 'with varying degrees of rapidity' according to the manner of death and the physical conditions under which the body is exposed, he stated that the coldness of the body was 'rarely complete' until fifteen or twenty hours after death. Nevertheless, he conceded that, 'Sometimes it is true the body cools much more rapidly than this', and said that, where death was occasioned by violence to a person in perfect health, a body could be 'found cold' within eight or nine hours. Furthermore, in cases of death from chronic disease, bodies had been found 'quite cold on the surface within four or five hours after death' being at least as cold as those who had died fifteen or twenty hours earlier.

Despite referring to bodies being cold 'on the surface', Taylor was nevertheless critical in his lecture of one case where temperature of a body was estimated from touch alone, and said: 'It has to be regretted that in this case the heat was not accurately measured by the introduction of a thermometer into the mouth or rectum, as this would have been far more satisfactory than a mere conjecture from the feelings; which are always very uncertain guides of temperature'. In this respect, he noted that the temperature of the rectum, mouth, armpit and groins, 'will be found to contain a higher temperature than that of the surface'. It was the first warning to the medical profession not to rely on touch of the surface of the skin alone when assessing body temperature of a corpse but one which, like all others during the century, was almost completely ignored. The other warning given by Taylor, relating to the aforementioned case, was that, in

---

[16] Taken from the second edition, published in 1844.
[17] Reported in the *London Medical Gazette*, January 1846.

some circumstances, it seemed that a body could retain heat equivalent to the body heat of a normal living person for at least some eight or ten hours after death. He also noted that, from his own experience during a cholera outbreak of the early 1830s, some dead bodies could actually *increase* in temperature after death. This 'singular phenomena', he said, 'has received no adequate explanation.'

In the third edition of his book, published in 1848, Taylor didn't deal specifically with the issue of estimating time of death on the basis of body temperature but, in a section of the book about inferences to be drawn from the position of a body, he included an anecdotal story about a case from November 1847 in order to show how an assessment of time of death based on body temperature could help acquit an innocent person from a charge of murder. This was the case of an unnamed woman who, he said, had been found dead in her apartment with her throat cut. According to Taylor, 'it was ascertained that when first discovered the body was so warm as to render it highly probable that the crime must have been committed within an hour'. This observation, said Taylor, 'tended to prove the innocence of a person who was suspected of the murder, because it was known that he had been absent from the house for at least five hours'. Taylor gave no identifying details relating to this case but modern digital newspaper searches allow us to determine from the clues he provided that he must have been referring to the murder of a young and attractive Spanish maidservant called Josefa Martínez Mundo at the palace of Queen Christina (the Queen-mother) in Madrid.

Mundo's dead body was discovered by the Queen's chaplain, Don Jose Fulleda, at 5pm on 16 November 1847, after he had supposedly returned from a stroll at the Calle de Leon, on the opposite side of the town from the palace, where he had purchased some books. The poor maidservant had been virtually decapitated and was lying in a pool of her blood. Due to the fact that the murder was committed in a secure building, and because the murderer seemed very relaxed in the environment, having supposedly wiped his bloody hands on the victim's apron, washed them in the hand basin, dried them with a towel and then perfumed them with eau de Cologne, suspicion immediately fell on Fulleda who was placed under arrest. The surviving newspaper reports don't mention the warmth of the body but they do say that the evidence of the medical examiners tended to exculpate the chaplain because, 'when the room in which the body lay was forced open, not more than three-quarters of an hour could have elapsed since the murder; and it was shown, on the evidence of the porters, that the chaplain had been absent at least five hours'.[18] Another report, however, said he had been gone for four hours.[19] One assumes that the medical evidence suggesting a time of death of no earlier than 4.15pm was based on the warmth of the body but it didn't seem to totally exonerate the chaplain in the way Taylor's summary of the case suggests.

In January 1848, it was reported that, following two months of inquiries, the judge of the district had caused the chaplain to be charged for the murder. The preface of the third edition of Taylor's book was dated August 1848 which means that he couldn't possibly have known the final outcome of the proceedings whereby the chaplain was tried on 27 November of that year and acquitted, the Spanish newspapers praising the closing speech of his defence counsel for presenting irrefutable evidence of his innocence. Full details don't seem to be available, and it's quite possible that the victim's body warmth was part of the evidence which secured Fulleda's acquittal, but it obviously wasn't quite as cut and dried as Taylor presented it in his book given that this case was supposed to demonstrate how an innocent suspect was eliminated from police inquiries as a result of the unequivocal medical evidence relating to body temperature. Moreover, with Taylor having stated in his earlier lecture that a body could retain heat equivalent to the body heat of a normal living person for up to ten hours after death, how could it be said that the warmth of the body in the Mundo case exonerated the chaplain? Perhaps Taylor would have answered that the body of Mundo was found to have been so warm that it couldn't have been more than an hour after death but, if that's the case, it's strange that he didn't mention in his book for the benefit of medical practitioners that there is a period after death in which a body is so warm that one can say that it couldn't have been dead for more than an hour. In fact, Taylor didn't include in his 1848 book *any* information from his earlier lecture about assessing time of death from body temperature so perhaps he was himself uncertain about it.

---

[18] *Liverpool Mercury*, 30 November 1847.
[19] *Stamford Mercury*, 3 December 1847.

By this time, there had been very few scientific experiments on the subject of the cooling of the human body after death. For obvious reasons, it's no simple matter to secure access to the bodies of dead people who have recently died in order to take temperature readings and, even if one could, it isn't always possible to know the precise moment they passed away. Dr John Davy, however, had conducted some observations with a thermometer on the dead bodies of ten soldiers (who had died of various illnesses in a military hospital) in Malta during 1827, taking single temperature readings of various organs within the body such as the liver and heart. His findings, published in 1839, had caused some surprise, because they indicated that, contrary to accepted wisdom, albeit having been first observed by an Austrian doctor in the eighteenth century, body temperature could rise after death in some circumstances. Davy didn't, however, consider whether the bodies he was testing *felt* cold or warm because he was only concerned with recording the internal temperatures of his subjects. In addition, most of the bodies were first tested more than four hours after death and some more than ten hours. The soonest that a temperature was taken was two hours after death. Further observations on ten more soldiers during 1838 produced similar results.

Despite the limited number of examples of bodies tested, and a failure to provide any solid conclusions, Davy felt able to say in an 1839 book entitled *Researches, Physiological and Anatomical,* that his observations, 'may enable the inquirer, instituting similar thermometrical trials, and reasoning analogically, to arrive at a tolerably positive conclusion in doubtful cases of death, as to the time which may have elapsed, between the fatal event and the post mortem examination.' It's a little hard from reading his book to know how inquirers were supposed to do it with any degree of accuracy and, furthermore, he cautioned that, 'Much judgement…and nice discrimination may be requisite on the part of the medical man, in appreciating the circumstances likely to modify temperature, so as to enable him, when called on for his opinion, to give one which will be satisfactory to the legal officers, and to himself, on reflection.' Davy didn't seem to consider – or at least he didn't mention – that, if a body can become warmer after death, the usual rule of thumb that a warm body means that death must have occurred fairly recently might be unreliable.

Following Davy, Dr Bennett Dowler of New Orleans made observations on forty-three dead bodies in the morgue attached to the New Orleans Charity Hospital, and his results were included in an article called 'Experimental Researches upon Febrile Caloricity, both before and after death' published in *The Western Journal of Medicine and Surgery* in two parts in June and October 1844. He took more detailed thermometer readings than Davy at a number of areas of the body and concluded that, '...my observations show that there is an increase of heat after apparent death, a true *post-mortem* fever, hotter than is ever known during life...'. Dowler also noted that there was no correlation between an increase in heat after death and the rigidity of the body, saying that there was sometimes increase in heat when there was no rigidity while, at other times, the contrary applied. He didn't, however, suggest that his conclusions would lead to improvements in estimating time of death. Perhaps the most interesting part of his paper is when he speaks about the hardship experienced by medical researchers conducting experiments into post-mortem temperatures. 'Few' he said, 'except those who have gone over the same ground, can imagine the labour and irksomeness of these dismal researches along the frontiers of death. Silent, alone, sitting for hours on a coffin, among dead bodies bearing on their saddened faces the impress of the last agony, watching the wanings of a lingering vitality and the steady advances of the great annihilator, decomposition, with scalpel, pencil, book, and thermometer, like Sterne's prisoner in the dungeon, who etched down with a nail his diurnal history – these are circumstances that fiction cannot heighten'.

Another American doctor, Benjamin Hensley, conducted similar observations on nine dead bodies, taking two or three thermometer readings, at different times after death, in each case. He didn't offer any conclusions, however, in his short paper, 'Experiments on the Temperature of Bodies after Death', published in the *Philadelphia Medical Examiner* of March 1846, merely setting out the temperature readings without comment. He didn't seem to find any increases in temperature after death. Like Davy, he said nothing about the temperature at the surface of the body although he did take measurements under the armpit (axilla) and occasionally elsewhere on the skin. From the data provided, one commentator came to the conclusion that the cooling of the body after death was a slower process than generally imagined under normal circumstances.[20]

Another case mentioned by Taylor in his 1848 book - one in which he was an expert witness in the case (in respect of bloodstains) - was the trial of William Spicer who was convicted of murdering his wife, Elizabeth, at the Assizes for the Oxford Circuit in March of that year, the murder having occurred during the previous summer. Mrs Spicer's dead body was found at the bottom of the cellar steps of her home in Reading at 8pm on 8 August 1845, and the attending surgeon, Dr Frederick Blissett Hooper, said at the inquest into her death that he noted an hour later that the body was 'quite cold' so that 'life had been extinct some time'.[21] At the trial, however, he expanded on this a little by saying that the body was 'quite cold and rigid' and, as he believed that rigidity would not come on before eight hours after death at that time of year, he placed the time of death at no later than 1pm.

As it happens, the time of death in this case wasn't hard to establish from witness evidence. At shortly after 12.30pm, various neighbours of the Spicers heard what they described as 'a tremendous fall' and 'a very heavy noise' in the Spicer house which sounded like someone falling down the cellar steps. Looking out, one of the neighbours saw William Spicer looking down the cellar stairs and, thus, didn't investigate further. Half an hour later, a neighbour happened to enquire of Mr Spicer as to how his wife was and he said she was 'very poorly' and 'very giddy' to the extent that he was afraid she would fall down and kill herself. At shortly after four o'clock he mentioned to someone that he had been home to tea but couldn't find his wife and concluded that she had gone out. Thirty-five minutes later, two friends of his wife called at his house asking to see her but he told them that she had just stepped out. At 8pm, Spicer asked a male neighbour if he had seen his wife but must have been a little shocked when that neighbour asked in response if he hadn't heard her falling down the steps earlier that afternoon. It was at this point that Spicer looked in the cellar and found his wife dead, or so he claimed.

From those circumstances alone it wasn't difficult to work out that Spicer, who had a history of violence, had murdered his wife at about

---

[20] Dr J. Wilkie Burman in 'On the Rate of Cooling of the Human Body After Death', *Edinburgh Medical Review*, May 1880.
[21] *Reading Mercury*, 16 August 1845.

12.30pm. He hadn't pushed her down the stairs though. The medical evidence was that she had been hit on the head with a blunt instrument. After being convicted, Spicer confessed that he struck his wife with a poker after a quarrel and then threw her down the cellar stairs to try and make it look like she had fallen.[22]

Had the medical evidence about time of death been all that was relied on to convict Spicer, it's possible that there could have been a miscarriage of justice. The effect of Dr Hooper's evidence was that Spicer couldn't have seen his wife alive at shortly after 4.45pm, three hours and fifteen minutes prior to his examination, due to the rigidity of the body at shortly after 8pm. However, twenty-six years later, a French medical student, Paul Niderkorn, conducted tests on over one hundred dead bodies from which he noted that, in 14% of cases, rigor was complete within three hours after death and in 43% of cases it was complete within four hours.[23] While there is no doubt in the correctness of the jury's verdict in the Spicer case, from those figures alone, one would not want to have ruled out the possibility of Mrs Spicer having been killed after 4.45pm.

Estimating time of death in this case from body temperature or rigor wasn't the reason why Taylor mentioned the Spicer case in his book. For there was one more indication over and above rigor and body temperature which Taylor evidently found more interesting. This was the fact that Mrs Spicer's stomach contained only a small quantity of dark coloured mucus, but no food. At the time, it was understood that a healthy person would digest food in about four hours so that, as the digestive process is known for a fact to cease with the expiry of life, a body with an empty stomach couldn't have consumed food within four hours prior to their death. The assumption in this case appeared to be that, if Mrs Spicer had died after 4.45pm, when her husband said he last saw her alive, but before 8pm (when her body was found), she must have had her dinner prior to her death, so that there would have been food remaining in her stomach. The problem

---

[22] The *London Medical Gazette* didn't find this explanation convincing and suggested it was more likely that he had given his wife a couple of blows over the head with a stone (which had been found in the cellar), those blows knocking her backward down the steps. The stone apparently matched the marks on Mrs Spicer's head but it's difficult to see what advantage Spicer gained in lying about this.

[23] *Contribution à l'étude de quelques-uns des phénomènes de la rigidité cadavérique chez l'homme*, 1872.

here was that there was no evidence as to when she had eaten that day, so it doesn't appear to have been regarded as a conclusive factor in the trial.

In commenting on the case in his book, Taylor seems to have been confused about the evidence. He claimed that, 'The prisoner stated that after he and his wife had dinner, he heard a fall', whereas, said Taylor, the empty stomach meant that it was 'clear that this part of the prisoner's story was untrue, as, had the deceased died immediately after dinner, some portion of the undigested food would have been found in the organ.' The evidence at the trial, however, was that Spicer had said to a neighbour at 8pm that, 'I came home to my tea, and she was not at home. I can't think where she has got to.'[24] He never said *she* had eaten any food. After his wife's dead body had been discovered, he did tell a couple of neighbours that he had heard 'a noise' during dinner time but that could have been anything, not necessarily his wife falling down the stairs. The *London Medical Gazette* in commenting on this case, however, stated that, 'In a case of murder from wounds, it may often appear unnecessary to pay particular attention to the stomach or its contents; but the evidence on this trial shows that the observation may have some incidental importance'. It was, nevertheless, rare at this time for an analysis of stomach contents to assist in estimating time of death but, as we shall see later, it does appear to have been used as an important factor in one of the 'Jack the Ripper' murders in 1888.

One case which Professor Taylor might have mentioned in his 1848 book, but didn't, was the trial of a couple of Irish hawkers, Patrick Reid and Michael McCabe, both charged at York Assizes in December 1847 with the murder on 12 May of that year of a servant girl, Caroline Ellis. Two other people had been murdered at the same time as Ellis: her elderly employers James and Ann Wraith, killed in the Wraith's house in Mirfield. Reid had previously been tried but acquitted of Wraith's murder and this new trial was a device to finally convict him on the basis of some new evidence. Mr Wraith had last been seen alive at 11.30am on 12 May when he asked one of his nephews to come and do some work for him later in the day. When the nephew arrived at about 1.30pm he found a massacre. His uncle and aunt, along with the maid, had all been battered to death, their throats superfluously cut. From evidence found at the house, it was obvious that

---

[24] *Morning Post*, 6 March 1846.

the Wraiths had been disturbed while they were taking lunch, which they normally did at some point between midday and 1pm.

The medical examiner in the case was Henry John Watkinson who arrived at the scene of the massacre at 2.10pm. With reference to the body of Caroline Ellis, he said. 'The body was warm, and had probably been dead from half to three-quarters of an hour.' Cross-examined by Counsel for Reid, Watkinson said, 'The warmth of the weather would extend the animal heat of the bodies by half, or even three quarters of an hour; and this was a very warm day'. He confirmed in re-examination that he had taken this into account when speaking of the probable time of death. Watkinson can't have been quite right with his estimate because the evidence suggests that the murders couldn't have occurred any later than 1.10pm, a full hour before he arrived at the house, but it's difficult to see how it would have been possible to narrow the time of death down to such a specific time without relying on other evidence as to when the murder had likely occurred.

After both Reid and McCabe were convicted and sentenced to death, Reid confessed that he had committed the triple murders on his own and was solely responsible for them. He said he had murdered Ellis first at about 12.40pm, hitting her over the head with a soldering iron, while Mr and Mrs Wraith were despatched a few minutes later. It's possible that Ellis didn't actually die until her throat was cut by the razor, which must have been at about 1pm, but she gave the appearance of being dead from the blows. When Reid was executed in January 1848 he made a statement saying that McCabe was innocent of the crime. McCabe was subsequently reprieved but still transported to Australia, even though he appears to have been innocent of any involvement. He managed to return to England eventually.

A couple of years later, in October 1850, Professor Taylor, the author of *Medical Jurisprudence*, gave evidence at an inquest in Doddinghurst, Essex, into the death of a pregnant young woman, Jael Denny, whose dead body had been found in a field on a Sunday morning near where she had made an appointment to meet Thomas Drory, the father of her unborn baby, at 6.30pm the previous evening. The man who found the body said that, 'The arms and the legs were very cold and stiff'. However, when Ms Denny's mother took the body of her daughter home shortly after 8am on the Sunday morning, she found warmth in parts of the abdomen. When Professor Taylor was asked by the Coroner, 'How long does a human body retain heat after death?', Taylor replied, 'As a matter of medical experience, I have known a body retain heat from thirty to forty hours – that is, the trunk of the body. The extremities become cold much quicker than the more solid parts of the body.'[25] Asked how long it would take for a body to become cold and rigid 'in an ordinary case', Professor Taylor answered:

> This would depend very much upon circumstances – upon the age and health of the deceased, and upon what amount of clothing the body was enveloped in. It is a fact, however, that persons who die a sudden and violent death are more slow in becoming cool than other cases. The body of a person in strong health and full vigour of life will cool much more slowly than that of a very old or a very young person. Again, if the body be well covered up with clothes, it will take a much longer period than the average in becoming cold, and that average I would state to be, according to my observation, about fifteen or sixteen hours after death, for a person who judges by a touch on the outer skin; the inside warmth is much longer retained.

He added that a friend of his had told him of a case where, seven hours after death, a temperature of 104 degrees Fahrenheit was recorded by a thermometer placed into the abdomen. Professor Taylor also agreed that Jael Denny being nine months pregnant would 'tend to prolong the warmth of her remains after death'. The coroner asked Professor Taylor directly if, assuming Jael Denny had been murdered at 6.30pm on Saturday evening, her remains might be warm at 8am the following morning, to which the professor answered, 'To say it was not possible would be contrary to all practice. It is certainly a long time, thirteen hours and a half, but I should say that heat might be found in the abdomen after that time. It would, of course, depend in some measure upon who judged of the warmth.'

The evidence in the case was that Drory had left his house at 6.30pm and was next seen at a pub at 8pm. Without interruption, he should have arrived at the pub at 6.50pm, twenty minutes after leaving his house. He was known to have arranged to meet Denny in a field about five minutes

---

[25] *Morning Post*, 18 October 1850.

from his house to discuss their future. As a result, the murder couldn't have taken place later than 7.40pm. Drory was found guilty of the crime and executed on 25 March 1851.

Another important real-life case regarding body cooling occurred in December 1852, with a trial two months later, involving the killing of Sarah Parrott (known as 'Sally') by her husband, John.

Between seven and eight o'clock in the morning of 8 December 1852, lodgers living in the same house as the Parrotts in the East End of London heard loud screams from Mrs Parrott, including cries of 'murder!', while her husband shouted back at her. He went out for an hour but on his return Mrs Parrott was heard by everyone in the house to scream one last time at about ten o'clock followed by the noise of someone falling, after which her husband went back out. She wasn't heard from again after this time. At between five and six o'clock of the evening of the same day, John Parrott paid a visit to a nearby surgeon, Samuel Forest Leech, asking him to come and visit his wife who, he said, was very ill. He explained to the surgeon that she had told him only about ten minutes earlier that she didn't know where she was. Leech accompanied Parrott to his room where he found Parrott's wife dead, lying partially on a mattress and almost naked.

In his testimony at the Old Bailey, Leech said of Mrs Parrott that, 'in my judgment, she had been dead about three or four hours; the body was quite cold'. Leech then sent Parrott out to Dr John Blennerhast Godfrey, a physician who arrived at the scene a few minutes after 6pm. In his own evidence at the trial, Godfrey said, 'in my judgment she had been dead about four or five hours; that was only conjecture; that is still my opinion; the body was cold except over the region of the heart - that was where the covering was - there was warmth there, amounting to the natural warmth - the body was rigid'.

The two doctors weren't quite singing from the same hymn sheet but, together, were putting forward an estimated time of death within a range of three and five hours prior to about 5.30pm. The problem was that this would put the time of death at no earlier than 12.30pm, some two and a half hours after Mrs Parrott had emitted her last scream. If correct, though, it would still mean that Parrott was lying about having spoken to his wife shortly before he left to fetch Mr Leech.

During questioning by the judge, Dr Godfrey set out his understanding of the rate of body cooling after death, saying:

> I think an attenuated body of this description would get cold sooner than a more robust one - the time in which a body loses heat differs exceedingly - it depends so much upon the surrounding temperature, that it is impossible to say; I have seen rigidity and coldness of the body arise in two hours; I have seen bodies remain warm eight or nine days, and I have seen rigidity without coldness come on almost immediately after death – it is uncertain – it may depend upon internal causes, the circulation, the vital warmth of the body itself, the state of heat retained in the flesh and fat, and it may depend upon the external temperature – a body exposed to a draught will cool sooner than one not so exposed – there was nothing either in the nature of this body or in the place where it was, to make me suppose that warmth would last longer than usual – indeed, I should think a very attenuated body, in a garret without a fire, in the month of December, and with no clothes on, would get cold sooner than in an ordinary case.

The doctors didn't think that Mrs Parrott had died a natural death, although they couldn't entirely rule it out, but it was probably the evidence of the landlord's wife, Elizabeth Beer, which destroyed Parrott's defence. She told the court that she had seen Mrs Parrott shortly after 5pm when Parrott had asked her to come into his room because, he told her, his wife wasn't well. Mrs Beer testified, 'I went with him to his room, and saw the deceased there – she was lying on an old straw mattress in one corner of the garret – I went up to her and felt her; she was quite dead – I said, "My God! Mr. Parrott, she is dead, she is stiff and cold, you must have done this this morning before you went out" – he said, "Why, God bless you, woman, she spoke to me two minutes ago" – I said, "I am sure it is false, for I am sure she has been dead for hours" – he said that he had said to her, "Sally get up and let's have some tea" – and that she said, "I do not know where I am" – he said he had only been in about two minutes, and had just set light to the fire'. Mrs Beer, however, was not fooled and deduced from the appearance of the fire, 'that it had been lighted a long while – the coals were bright, and quite at the bottom of the stove'. She told Parrott that the death of his wife must have been the result of his fighting with her during the morning and, although Parrott denied this, it was the detective and indeed medical forensic skills of Mrs Beer which did for Parrott. With her added knowledge of when his wife was last heard to scream, she was able to pinpoint the likely time of death even more accurately than the two doctors. Although cleared of wilful murder, Parrott was convicted of manslaughter and sentenced to transportation for life.

An interesting observation was made by an Irish doctor at the proceedings of the Surgical Society of Ireland on 12 April 1856. One of the members of the society, Dr H. Kennedy, commented that, 'The heat of the body was also a subject well worthy of investigation; for it was a remarkable fact that one body would be as cold within an hour after death as another would be at the end of six.'[26] This remark, which appears to have gone unnoticed in the medical world in general, suggested that a dead body which felt cold to the touch might just as easily have died (or been murdered) one hour earlier as six hours earlier. If that was the case, making an estimate of time of death from touch alone was inevitably going to be problematic.

At an inquest held in December 1857 upon the bodies of Mary Smither and her two sons, all killed due to prussic acid, it was stated by the examining surgeon, Dr Bottomley, that when he came to the crime scene at 10am, 'The body was warm, but the body would retain warmth a considerable time. She might have been dead two hours.' Mr Carter, the coroner for East Surrey, chipped in to remark that 'he had known bodies to be cold within an hour after death, and yet warm on the following day.'[27] This is further evidence, corroborating what Dr Kenney had said during the previous year, that some bodies could be as cold within one hour after death as others would be after six hours.

Giving evidence at an inquest into the death of Prudence Parke, the wife of Captain Edwin Parke in Gloucester in December 1858, the examining surgeon, Dr Pratt, attempted to reassure the jury that Prudence had not been alive when he examined her, despite her body having been

---

[26] *Dublin Medical Press*, 23 April 1856.
[27] *London Daily News*, 16 December 1857.

warm twenty-four hours after he had pronounced her dead, by informing the coroner that, 'Bodies sometimes retained their warmth for several days', and that, 'It was a well known fact that some bodies retained their warmth as long as three days.'[28]

A year later, on 28 November 1859, the landlord of a house in Shoreditch was invited into the room of James Moore, one of his lodgers. On entering the room he saw the dead and naked body of his wife, Mary Ann, whose abdomen had been cut open. Her head had been removed and placed into a basin. Moore casually informed the landlord that he had only been released from a lunatic asylum a week earlier. The police were called and the officer who first arrived in the house at about 3.30pm said, 'I placed my hand on the body, and found it quite warm.' When John Bubbers Mather, a local surgeon, arrived about an hour later, he too felt the body which, he said 'was warm, especially internally.' Asked by the coroner at the inquest how long he thought Mrs Moore had been dead he said, 'Several hours. Very likely six or eight, even then the body would still be warm, if dead between two and three it would have been much warmer. Most probably death occurred at the more lengthened period.'[29] One can deduce that the murder probably occurred at 8am when the landlord's wife said she heard 'great screaming in the first floor front room' which was the room occupied by Mr and Mrs Moore. When asked why she didn't call for assistance or tell anyone about the screams, she replied, 'Because I did not suppose there was anything serious; our neighbourhood is very low, and we often hear screams of murder.' With a murder at 8am, this means that the surgeon's examination of the body occurred about eight or nine hours after the murder. If he knew that the landlord's wife had heard screaming at 8am, this might have influenced his estimate. Moore was found not guilty of the murder but only by reason of insanity and was detained at Her Majesty's pleasure.

Six months later, in May 1860, an elderly gentleman, William Hodgson Elstob, retired to bed in his Hartlepool lodgings at one o'clock in the afternoon for a nap after lunch. His landlady, Mrs Shields, heard him sleeping heavily at 3pm. When, at six o'clock, she went to his room to ask if he wanted tea, she found him lying on top of his bed and saw

---

[28] *Cardiff and Merthyr Guardian*, 4 December 1858.
[29] *Morning Advertiser*, 30 November 1860.

his hands were very pale. She fetched Dr Stamp who discovered that Mr Elstob had poisoned himself with hydrocyanic acid. At the inquest into his death, Dr Stamp stated that on seeing the deceased shortly after 6pm, 'he apparently had been dead two or three hours, his body being cold'.[30] Fixing on two or three hours seems to have been quite random in view of the wide range of time within which the authorities stated that a person's body could become cold after death.

The year 1861 saw the publication of the seventh edition of Professor Alfred Swaine Taylor's *Medical Jurisprudence.* There was still no section in the book on how to estimate the time of death based on the temperature of a corpse (or on rigidity) but, in the chapter dealing with the position and condition of a dead body, Taylor squeezed in a recent case relating to time of death which followed his mention of the 1847 case of Josefa Martínez Mundo. This was the case of Thomas Hopley, the principal of a private school in Eastbourne, who had been found guilty of the manslaughter of one of his young pupils, Reginald Channell Cancellor, who happened to be a nephew of Professor Taylor,[31] after severely beating him for being slow at his lessons. The beating, heard by witnesses, had occurred around midnight on Saturday 21 April 1860 (although Taylor placed it at 11.30pm when writing about it in his book) and the boy was found dead the next morning. Hopley had claimed that the boy must have died much later than the beating, which he said was a light one, so that his death was unconnected to that beating. This had been the original finding of the inquest in which it was concluded that Cancellor had died of a disease of the heart, a verdict which was challenged by the Cancellor family, leading to a post-mortem examination being carried out and the subsequent arrest of Hopley when that examination found evidence of the beatings. Taylor, who didn't mention in his book that Cancellor was his nephew, stated that Hopley had informed the coroner that he went into Cancellor's bedroom at 6am on Sunday, 22 April, when he found him dead, 'his body cold, and his arms stiffening.' On this basis, Taylor concluded that, 'there was a strong probability that deceased must have been dead at least six or seven hours, and, therefore, at a time when the prisoner was last known to be with him'.

---

[30] *Hartlepool Free Press and General Advertiser*, 26 May 1860.
[31] *Fatal Evidence: Professor Alfred Swaine Taylor and the Dawn of Forensic Science* by Helen Barrell, Pen & Sword, 2017 (p. 166).

Although Taylor had some personal knowledge of the case due to his family relationship with the victim, his summary of the evidence was not quite correct. At the inquest on 24 April, Hopley stated that when he entered the boy's bedroom at 6.30am, 'I put my hand on his forehead and found it was quite cold, as were his extremities. I moved his arm, and tried to bend it, and found it stiff, as if he had been dead some time. Some parts of his body were slightly warm.'[32] Part of the lesson which was supposed to be drawn from the case was that, 'Criminals sometimes unknowingly furnish important evidence in reference to the condition of a dead body' but, still, not only was Taylor here relying on a layman (and a layman accused of being responsible for the boy's death to boot) for evidence as to body temperature and rigidity, but Hopley was saying that *some of the body was warm*, yet that wasn't mentioned by Taylor or factored into his estimate as to the time of death. A medical man arrived at the school shortly before 9am but he didn't carry out any kind of examination of the body, so Hopley's evidence was all that was available.

During the trial of Hopley at the Lewes Autumn Assizes in July 1860, Prescott Hewitt, surgeon of St George's Hospital, who had participated in the post-mortem, was asked: 'Supposing that at half-past six, as stated by Mr Hopley...the arm was found stiff and he could not bend it, how long do you think that the boy would have been dead?' to which he replied, 'About six or seven hours. This would be the minimum time'. Dr Robert Willis, medical adviser to the Cancellor family, agreed, saying, 'Supposing the arm had been found rigid at six o'clock in the morning, death must have taken place six or seven hours previously.' Another surgeon at St George's Hospital, Timothy Holmes, 'fully concurred on this point' and said, 'There would be heat discoverable about the body six hours after death.'[33]

One might think it no coincidence that, with clear evidence of Hopley having severely beaten the boy with a thick stick and a skipping rope up to midnight, at which time the boy went silent, the medical men had managed, from the body temperature and stiffness alone, to calculate a period of almost exactly six hours back from 6am to place the boy's death at precisely that time. There is no doubt that Hopley had killed the boy.

---

[32] *Surrey Gazette*, 1 May 1860.
[33] *Brighton Gazette*, 26 July 1860.

He had dressed him in large stockings and gloves to hide the bruises and wounds he had inflicted upon him, ensuring that nothing was visible to the doctor who was called at 9am, other than the face. It's hard to avoid the thought that if Hopley had been heard at 2am beating the boy, who was then found cold and stiff (with some warmth) at 6am, the doctors would have said that death could have occurred about four hours earlier. On the other hand, had Hopley been heard beating the boy at 10pm they could equally have said, upon exactly the same medical evidence, that death had occurred about eight hours earlier. One may recall the advice given to medical practitioners by Dr Male in 1816 to make enquiries as to when (or by whom) a person was last seen alive, in order to estimate the time of death. It would seem that this was being followed by the doctors in this case.

Also in 1861, Professor Guy made some updates to the second edition of *Principles of Forensic Medicine* but his central conclusion on the subject of body cooling after death, namely that, 'the period of cooling may vary from two or three hours to fifteen or twenty, and may even extend upwards of four days', was essentially the same as he had written in 1844. Very little had evidently changed in seventeen years.

That was pretty much all the combined medical knowledge available to Henry Sequeira when he perceived that the dead body of Mrs Gardner was cold to the touch that morning in September 1862. Nevertheless, he regarded that coldness as sufficient to accurately estimate the time of death. When later questioned in court, he claimed to have had 'very great experience' in estimating the time it would take to produce coldness in a human body. As the medical officer of one of the poor law unions, he said he frequently had to examine dead bodies and he asserted that he was often asked by that poor law union how long it had been since the patient had died (although for what purpose was unclear).

So what did Sequeria make of the fact that parts of Mrs Gardner's body felt quite cold while the lower trunk felt warm? Well, in his mind, he thought this meant that she had been dead for some four hours. This would have placed the time of her death at around 4am, i.e. four hours before his examination at about 8am. It was a conclusion of some considerable importance because this was approximately the time her husband had left home that morning to go on his rounds as a chimney sweep. If she had died any later than this, he couldn't have had any responsibility for her death because he had an alibi for the entirety of the next four hours, carrying out his work at various locations in the City. As a coroner was soon to decide that the death of Mrs Gardner was a crime of murder, the precise time of her death would become a critical issue in the case.

CHAPTER TWO

The Death of Elizabeth Gardner

It was an early start for a chimney sweep in the 1860s. Samuel Gardner was roused from his slumber at a quarter past three on the morning of Monday, 15 September 1862, which was, as it happens, some fifteen minutes earlier than he had wanted to be woken up. In the absence of alarm clocks, the job of waking local residents in the middle of the night in London fell to police constables on their beat. This was known as 'calling up', or 'knocking up', and was a service provided by both Metropolitan and City police officers. Gardner had a system whereby he would chalk on his front door the time he would like to be 'knocked up' in the morning. On Sunday evening, before retiring to bed, he had chalked the time of 3.30 on his door but City Police Constable Cornelius Meagher, who had been performing the task during his night beat since almost the start of the year, somehow managed to get confused and rang Gardner's bell at 3.15. A sleepy Gardner answered the call by tapping on a window in his room on the first floor, thus letting the constable know that he had heard his call.

After dressing himself and collecting his chimney sweeping machine, Gardner left his house. He was a small man, barely more than five foot two inches in height, but he was strong and stout and carried his chimney sweeping machine on his shoulder. Monday morning was when he did his extra dirty work in the grimy chop houses in the City. Heading in that direction, he walked along Northumberland Alley and turned into Fenchurch Street. There he saw Constable Meagher who, acknowledging

• 35

his earlier mix-up, said apologetically, 'I called you before your time this morning, Mr Gardner'. Gardner, not halting his pace, replied, 'It makes no difference' and passed on.

Gardner probably had a lot on his mind. His living arrangements were unconventional to say the least, and the problems caused by those arrangements had come to a head over the weekend. One way or another they were responsible for the tragic occurrence that morning.

Samuel Gardner had been born in Shoreditch on 1 August 1824, the son of a master chimney sweeper, Robert Gardner, and was destined to follow the same occupation. On 19 February 1843, at the age of nineteen, when he was already working as a sweep, he married Elizabeth Dewis, eleven years his senior, in Bethnal Green. Dewis was a widow, born Elizabeth Evans (the illegitimate daughter of gunmaker Angel Byrne and Elizabeth Evans) who had previously married a chimney sweeper, Thomas Dewis, in 1832. That couple had three children, two boys and a girl, before Thomas died seven years later in 1839. Samuel's marriage to Elizabeth was childless but he became stepfather to Elizabeth's children from her earlier marriage. The marriage only lasted for seven years because, on 15 December 1850, Elizabeth died a horrible death after fifteen months suffering from a wasting disease followed by three weeks of chronic diarrhoea.

Elizabeth died at 10 Still Alley, a small alley off Bishopsgate, the scene of a notorious cesspool during the previous summer which, to loud complaints, had produced a highly unpleasant smell and had caused a number of local residents to become ill. On 27 August 1849, an unknown male sweep, aged 25, who lived at 10 Still Alley had died of cholera. The problem of the cesspool wasn't entirely resolved and a two-year-old boy died of cholera at 5 Still Alley on 19 September 1852. Henry Spencer, the registrar of St Botolph was quoted as saying at the time that, 'this is a close and crowded place, with little ventilation, and occupied by very poor persons; a drain is in the middle of it, which is frequently chocked up, and emits offensive effluvia'.[34]

At the time of the 1851 census, Samuel, now a widow, was still living at 10 Still Alley, with his three stepchildren, and with his older brother, also a Chimney Sweep, James, his wife, also called Elizabeth, and their seven-year-old son who was also called James. The senior James had married

---

[34] *Standard*, 29 September 1852.

Elizabeth Read in November 1847, more than three years *after* the birth of their son. Elizabeth was only a year older than Samuel and their close proximity within 10 Still Alley appears to have led to the occurrence of some extra-marital relations. Within a year of the census of 1851, Elizabeth was pregnant with Samuel's illegitimate daughter, although from the birth certificate, with Elizabeth correctly being stated to be Elizabeth Gardner, formerly 'Reed', it would have appeared that she was married to the man named as the father, Samuel, although she was still actually the wife of his brother. Their child, a girl unimaginatively named 'Elizabeth', although they called her 'Betsy', was born in February 1853. By this time, the Gardners had moved out from Still Alley to another alley, a small one off Fenchurch Street, called Hartshorn Alley.

Samuel and Elizabeth did marry in March 1855, albeit bigamously because Elizabeth was still married to Samuel's brother, but they used a clever ruse to enable them to do so. They temporarily moved, or at least claimed to have moved, to South London where they were not known and banns were posted announcing their pending nuptials in which both of them said to be 'of this parish', being the parish of St George the Martyr, Southwark. Elizabeth stated that she was the daughter of Thomas Cook, an Ivory Turner, although it appears that her father's name was, in fact, Thomas Henry Read.[35] Elizabeth's actual husband, James, appears to have accepted his fate and moved out. The story told by Samuel and Elizabeth was evidently that her husband, James, had died. This was, in fact, what the younger James Gardner, Samuel's nephew but now his stepson, later told police during the investigation into Elizabeth's death.

After the marriage, Samuel and Elizabeth, along with their daughter, Elizabeth, and stepson, James, moved to a larger house at 1 Northumberland Alley. Things seemed to be going well for the couple at this time and their relationship was strong but everything changed with the arrival into the household of the fifteen-year-old Elizabeth Clark in 1858. She had come

---

[35] Documents show that Elizabeth Read was born on 3 March 1823, the daughter of Thomas and Elizabeth Read and was baptized at St Leonard's Church on 16 November 1823. Intriguingly, however, an Elizabeth Cook, the daughter of Thomas and Elizabeth Cook was registered as being born in Mile End Town on 9 February 1824 and baptized in the parish of St George East on 17 April 1825. The second birth was presumably a different person but Elizabeth Read might have known her and used her identity for the purpose of her marriage to Samuel.

from Gravesend to live with the Gardners four years earlier at the age of eleven for a period of nine months when she had carried out some servant-type work for Gardner for which she was paid a shilling a week before she left to better herself with a situation paying sixpence more per week. Her father, John Joseph Clark, had, for a time, been a chimney sweep, while her mother, originally Ann Priestley, came from a large family of chimney sweeps, which presumably explains how she was introduced to Samuel Gardner. During the 1840s, however, John Clark and his wife ran a lodging house in Gravesend which operated as a brothel. In 1849, when Elizabeth was six years old, her father, who was known in the underworld as 'Turpin', had turned to crime – serious crime – and was arrested following a burglary with violence at an isolated farmhouse in Meopham, the plotting of which took place in Clark's lodging house.

Clark's gang, comprising six masked men in total, including 'four of the first-rate house breakers in the country', burst into the house of Augustus Munyard and terrorised him and his wife with bludgeons and an iron bar until they gave up their valuables.[36] The same gang had carried out similar violent burglaries in Totteridge and Farnham in the preceding months.[37] Clark was captured after the Meopham crime and, on being convicted of the offence of burglary with wounding, was sentenced to death at the Kent Assizes, a sentence which was subsequently commuted to transportation for life. He was sent to Bermuda on the *Sir Robert Seppings* convict-ship on 5 December 1850, arriving in late January 1851, but, due to the appalling conditions on board the floating hulks in Bermuda, which substituted for prisons, where epidemics such as cholera and yellow fever were rife, this turned out to be an actual death sentence for Clark. He became sick within a year of arrival, spending most of his time in hospital, and died on 8 October 1853.[38]

Returning to Northumberland Alley as a fifteen-year-old girl, the effect of Elizabeth Clark's appearance on the 34-year-old Samuel Gardner was deeply damaging to his relationship with his wife. He casually seduced

---

[36] *Canterbury Journal*, 28 July 1849.
[37] TNA: HO 45/3546.
[38] His wife, Ann, nevertheless, impossibly named her dead husband as the father of her son, William, born in the East End of London in September 1857, on the boy's birth certificate, thus avoiding the taint of illegitimacy.

her, and an extended sexual relationship between the pair began, despite Elizabeth Gardner becoming pregnant in about March 1859. This relationship was kept secret from the young girl's mother who remarried in May 1859 in St Phillip's Church, Bethnal Green, where Samuel Gardner and his wife were in attendance, being the two witnesses to the wedding, showing the closeness of the relationship between the Gardner and Clark families.[39] At this wedding, Ann Clark married a labourer called Francis Seymore, and the couple moved to Gravesend where Seymore joined the family business and became a chimney sweep himself.

In December 1859, Mrs Gardner gave birth to her second daughter with Samuel. They obviously couldn't call her 'Elizabeth' too so they decided to name her 'Eliza'.

There were whispers in the local neighbourhood of Northumberland Alley about the nature of Gardner's relationship with Elizabeth Clark which continued for two years up to early 1860. The whispers eventually travelled as far as Gravesend, to Elizabeth's mother, who 'came and broke the door open' and took Elizabeth's box (containing her personal possessions) away, forcing the young girl to leave the Gardner residence. Gardner whispered to Elizabeth to go home 'but not to remain long'. She did indeed return to Gravesend for a few weeks but was then lured back to London by Gardner who paid for her to live in a furnished room. We find her in the 1861 census, described as a seamstress, living as a lodger in a house in Shadwell. During October 1861, in a surprising development, she married John Humbler, a painter, in Gravesend, whom she had apparently known for three years, and they lived in a house near Liverpool Street, but, within three days of the marriage, she was back chasing after Samuel Gardner. One evening at that time, Gardner was leaving his club in Brick Lane when he heard a woman's voice calling 'Sam, Sam'. On turning round, he saw Elizabeth Clark, now Mrs Elizabeth Humbler. The two of them went for a drink, during which, according to Gardner's account, Humbler pulled out a knife from beneath her shawl and said, 'Sam, I thought you never intended speaking to me again and, if you had not made it up with me, I meant this for you, and then for myself.' In a moment of sadly typical cruelty, Gardner dragged Humbler to a brothel, left her there and went home. Despite this, Humbler separated from her husband in

---

[39] Elizabeth Gardner signed the wedding certificate as usual with a cross.

December 1861 and returned for a third time to Gardner's house in early 1862, once again to work for him as his servant. Although Mrs Gardner became pregnant again, the sexual relationship between Gardner and Humbler was resumed. We don't know much about their relationship but it is known that Gardner took Humbler for a day out at the Epsom races during June 1862, leaving his wife behind.

Elizabeth Gardner was already aware of the sexual relationship between her husband and Elizabeth Humbler. She must have worked it out by herself because she told her neighbours what was going on at around the time of the birth of Eliza. A few months later, in February 1860, she received some anonymous letters, known as 'valentines', which apparently set out the facts of the relationship between her husband and Humbler (or Clark as she then was) in some detail. During the nineteenth century, Valentine's Day afforded an opportunity not only for people to anonymously reveal their secret love but also to send gratuitous insults and messages of hate. Bizarre as it may seem today, stationers sold cards containing pre-printed insults in rhyme with accompanying colourful pictures, to which one was free to add one's own imaginative but anonymous abuse. The sending of hate valentines (which have since been referred to as 'vinegar valentines') was, bafflingly, as popular as the sending of love cards at the time, if not more so. The precise contents of the valentines received by Mrs Gardner are not known but they were said to be 'of a very offensive character and had reference to the [sexual] connection that existed between [Samuel] Gardner and Humbler'. The evidence as to whether Elizabeth Gardner could read or not is unclear but, if she could not, the valentines must have been read to her.[40] A few weeks before her death, they were found by her husband, presumably having been hidden in a drawer, and read out loud.

---

[40] The reported evidence of Humbler concerning Elizabeth Gardner at Samuel Gardner's trial was that, 'She could not read or write'. This is entirely consistent with all official documents (i.e. marriage, birth and death certificates) which she always signed with a cross, indicating that she was illiterate. However, in the official report of the proceedings at the Old Bailey, as well as in the judge's notes of the trial, Humbler is only recorded as stating that she, *Humbler*, could not read or write (which is also consistent with official documents) and, in addition, she apparently said of the valentines that, 'Mrs Gardner read some of them'. Furthermore, Humbler said that on the Sunday before her death, Mrs Gardner read the newspaper to her while her husband had gone out for a walk.

On the night before her death, Humbler found a letter by the door of the Gardner residence. She gave it to Gardner but Gardner refused to read it out and would not reveal its contents to her or his wife.

According to Humbler, there were problems in the relationship between Gardner and his wife, which is hardly surprising. She said that, one Wednesday night in August 1862, Gardner returned home late from his club in Brick Lane, probably drunk, and began rowing with his wife until half-past-one in the morning. The argument must have been about Humbler's presence. Humbler claimed that an angry Gardner yelled that he was fed up with the two women and that both she (Humbler) and his wife should leave the house and he would have it to himself. Humbler then supposedly said to Gardner as he was going to bed, 'I would rather go than Mrs Gardner', to which Gardner replied, 'You mind your own business, I believe I am master', adding that he would do whatever he liked.

It seems that Gardner, a horrible brute of a man, had also beaten his wife to the extent that she sported black eyes. According to Mary Bywater, the wife of a fishmonger, Mrs Gardner came into her husband's fishmongery in the Minories on Saturday, 13 September, and told her that she had fallen down some stairs and hurt her elbow. She also described herself as feeling 'very bad', believing that she had no option but to go for help at the Bow Union. Mrs Bywater also thought that Mrs Gardner, who was a regular customer to the shop, 'always appeared very deep in trouble.' At this stage, she was also seven months pregnant with her fourth child, Gardner's third.

During the weekend before she died – 13 and 14 September – everything seemed to come to a climax. Humbler had taken to annoying and teasing Mrs Gardner and this caused a row to erupt between Gardner and his wife who insisted that Humbler should be told to leave. Samuel spoke to Humbler about the way she was treating his wife but she just laughed and sang aloud some kind of song in response. He had already warned her about her behaviour and told her she would have to leave the house on Monday. Mrs Gardner, who referred to Humbler as 'the creature', had told her the same thing. Humbler had responded defiantly that she would never leave, a remark that was heard by Mrs Gardner's son, James. Gardner told her that he would kick her all the way home to Gravesend if she didn't go voluntarily but it didn't seem to have any effect. On the

Sunday evening, in Samuel's presence, she continued to laugh and jeer at Mrs Gardner who told her husband, 'When your back is turned it is worse than that'. Gardner said, 'There shall be an end to it'. He told Humbler that tomorrow (Monday) they would have a few words to settle the matter and that he would 'not put up with such nonsense'. He also accused her of placing the anonymous letter by the door, which she denied. Humbler began to cry but, according to Humbler, Gardner told her he would break her jaw if she didn't hold her tongue. Upset and tearful, Humbler retired to her room early at seven o'clock, some two or three hours earlier than her normal time of going to bed. By her own admission, she brooded on what Gardner had said to her and the injustice of it all.

Gardner and his wife remained up for a short time and subsequently went to bed together. 'We were friends then' he would later say. After being woken by Constable Meagher at quarter past three, Gardner looked at his watch and found it was too early to get dressed so he returned to bed. According to Gardner's account, his wife then said to him, 'Did you hear that creature up and down in the night?' Gardner had slept soundly and hadn't heard anything. His wife explained, 'I heard her at one o'clock come down from the top room, go to the bottom room, and then come into this room and take the candle off the table, and go down into the kitchen, and then up to the top room, and then come back and place the candle on the table where she took it from'. Gardner claimed that in response he told her, 'Oh! Well, don't bother, it will be decided to-day; we will have no more of the girl's nonsense'. He then got out of bed at about quarter to four, dressed himself and left the house at what must have been shortly before four o'clock. At the time, his wife was lying in bed on her right side with baby Eliza beside her. His eldest daughter had been sent out to the country, presumably because she was ill, and his stepson, James, no longer lived at home.

When Gardner left his home that morning he pulled the door to so that it locked. His wife and Humbler were the only two adults inside.

Gardner walked up Northumberland Avenue and turned left into Fenchurch Street, going down Fenchurch Street and up through Lombard Street before turning left into Change Alley where he arrived, as he always did at four o'clock on Monday mornings, at Baker's Coffee House, which was also a restaurant or chop house. George Davis, the porter, let him in as the clock struck 4am and he swept the chimney for an hour-and-a-half, leaving at 5.30am.[41] He then walked up Change Alley into Cornhill, to the premises of Messrs Purssell, confectioners, where he met the watchman, John Graham. At this establishment, Gardner quickly cleaned the hothouse but left the chimneys which didn't require sweeping. He moved on to Ned's Chop House at 19 Finch Street, off Cornhill, arriving at 5.45am precisely, according to the manager, Robert William Flanders.[42]

While he was there, cleaning the chimneys, a constable of the West India Docks, George Blanchard, was passing through Northumberland Avenue at a little after 6am when he heard a peculiar scream coming from the first floor of the house at number one, which he knew was Samuel Gardner's house. At the time he was only four or five yards away from the house and he could see that one blind was up and one was down on the first floor. He thought the scream was peculiar because it sounded either like a hysterical scream or a child laughing but he couldn't quite tell which. The sound was so unusual that Blanchard retraced his steps and waited to hear if it was repeated. Hearing nothing more he continued on his beat. He knew that children lived in the house (although he was unaware that the Gardners' nine-year-old daughter, who was the only child likely to have been laughing, wasn't there that morning) and assumed that's what he'd heard.

Back at Ned's Chop House, Samuel Gardner finished cleaning the chimneys and left at about 6.30 for his last appointment of the morning at Reeves' Chop House in nearby Pope's Head Alley.[43] He arrived about ten minutes later and was let in by the manager, Walter James Cathie. He remained there, cleaning the restaurant's six chimneys, for over an hour

---

[41] At least, it was Davis' evidence at the trial of Gardner that the clock struck 4am but Gardner himself would say that he *left his house* as the clock struck 4am and arrived at Baker's six or seven minutes later. It's possible, of course, that they were both correct but that their respective clocks were inaccurate.

[42] The Official Proceedings of the Old Bailey transcribe the name as Lake's Chop House but the correct name can be found in the Post Office Directory for 1862-3.

[43] This must have been connected with the City Arms Tavern, at 3-5 Pope's Head Alley, the landlord of which was George Reeves. Newspapers reported the name as either 'Read's Chop House' or 'Reed's Chop House'. The judge's notes also have it has 'Read's Chop House' while the Official Proceedings record the name as 'Reeve's Chop House'. Samuel Gardner later referred to it as 'the premises of Mr Reeves', confirming that it must correctly have been 'Reeves' Chop House'.

and left at about ten minutes to eight, being observed the whole time by one of the employees, George Alexander Galloway.

As Gardner was walking back home from Pope's Head Alley, Elizabeth Humbler must have been on her way to fetch Henry Sequeira from his surgery and lead him to Northumberland Alley. Gardner might even have returned before them but he first went to the cellar in order to store his chimney sweeping apparatus. As Humbler was asking the doctor if he wanted a candle, she heard Gardner coughing in the cellar. She cried out 'Good God, Sam, come upstairs!' It's not clear if Gardner heard this call. He would later say he was alerted by the sound of footsteps treading hastily through the room on the ground floor and, knowing his wife was in an advanced state of pregnancy, thought that she had been taken ill. Finding no one in the room on the ground floor, he walked upstairs and entered the room in which his wife was lying, only a few seconds after Dr Sequeira who was kneeling at her feet. The doctor hadn't noticed the knife in Elizabeth's right hand but Gardner did. He saw she was holding it upside down, by the blade, with her hand partially bent across her breast. Gardner then did something which would later raise suspicion, although it wasn't questioned at the time. Crying out, 'What is this?', he ran over to where Elizabeth was lying and grabbed the knife from her hand. As he would later explain, he didn't at first think she was dead and wanted to protect her from any further injury.

But as soon as he realized his wife's throat had been cut, and she wasn't alive, he immediately accused Humbler of murdering her. 'Oh, you wretch,' he shouted, 'you have done this.' Humbler protested her innocence, saying she knew nothing about it but Gardner said, 'We will see about that. She has never done it herself. Do not move from here until I give you in charge'. Dr Sequeira took the knife from Gardner and instructed the two of them not to move anything until the police arrived. At this, Humber fell to her knees crying, 'Good God, show mercy on my innocence'.

Gardner went out to fetch a policeman, informing P.C. Temple that his wife was dead. Constable Temple passed the information to Sergeant William Mobbs, on duty in Fenchurch Street, who promptly made his way to Gardner's house. Meanwhile the Ward Beadle, Thomas Pallet, had been informed of what had happened and he was there by half-past eight.

At the same time, Gardner took his two-year-old daughter round to a neighbour, Mary Spencer, and asked her to have her own daughter look after her. He then invited Mrs Spencer to accompany him round to his house without telling her why. He brought her upstairs into the room where Mrs Gardner was lying dead.[44] Humbler, who was now crying, said, 'Oh, Mrs Spencer, Mrs Gardner has cut her throat and Mr Gardner says I have done it.' Mrs Spencer asked Gardner if she could offer any assistance but was told, 'Not just now.' Meanwhile, Humbler continued crying and said, 'What a shocking thing; what a wicked man to accuse me of such a thing'. Gardner ignored her.

An examination of the area surrounding where Mrs Gardner's body was lying revealed that there was more to the incident than originally met the eye. Carefully lined up on a chair at the foot of the bed was Mrs Gardner's wedding ring, a brooch containing a portrait of Samuel Gardner, the insulting valentines and some unopened letters. They had obviously been deliberately placed there. Was it Elizabeth Gardner who had done this, collecting together the items that reminded her of her husband, and his infidelity, before taking her own life? Or had her murderer cunningly lined them up to make it look like she had committed suicide in a mood of sadness about her relationship?

On close inspection, the injuries on Elizabeth Gardner's body certainly gave the appearance of foul play. She had cuts across the fingers of her left hand. On the middle finger, one cut had sliced through the bone while those on the other fingers were slighter, only grazing the external cuticle. She also had six slight and irregular cuts on the palm of her right hand and five cuts on the palm of her left. It wasn't entirely clear if the cuts were defensive wounds, as if Elizabeth had been protecting herself from an attacker, or if they had been made while she grasped the blade of the knife. It would have been difficult, however, if not impossible, for Mrs

---

[44] In the *Times* report of the police court hearing on 25 September, which was also published in the *Morning Herald*, Mrs Spencer is quoted as saying that Mrs Gardner, 'was not then quite dead, and I thought she was being taken to hospital.' This is quite odd because Dr Sequira had already pronounced her dead and no other reports of her evidence from that hearing contain the suggestion that Mrs Spencer thought that Mrs Gardner was alive. Furthermore, at the trial, Mrs Spencer unambiguously stated that, when she went into the room, she 'saw Mrs Gardner lying dead at my feet'. The *Times* reporter must have been mistaken in what he thought he heard.

Gardner to have cut through to the bone herself by simply clenching the sharp end of the knife, even if she had been in agonizing pain at the time. When Dr Sequeira examined the body (at a later stage), he noticed that on the inside of Mrs Gardner's thigh there was a bloody impress of a large and broad palm revealing a distinct thumb print. There was also the mark of a sooty hand on the left arm above the wrist and a small sooty patch above the elbow but these sooty marks could have been made by Gardner, fresh from cleaning chimneys, when he removed the knife from Mrs Gardner's hand and touched her left arm with one of his sooty hands in doing so (although Sequeira would state in evidence that there was no contact at the time). The insides of her hands also looked like they had been wiped because they were free from running blood, being merely stained whereas the backs of the hands were very bloody. There was also blood on the upper part of Elizabeth's chest. According to Gardner, her long hair was also immersed in blood.

As for the neck wound, the knife had cut deep through the centre of the throat into the cartilage of the larynx but the carotid artery wasn't severed, so that Mrs Gardner must have died an agonizing death through suffocation as the blood flowed into her larynx causing her to be unable to breathe.

After Sergeant Mobbs arrived at the house, Dr Sequeira handed him the bloody knife. The sergeant could see that it was a small, sharp, white-handled carving knife covered with marks of blood. Sequeira told him that it had been taken from the right hand of the deceased by Gardner. In the presence of Sergeant Mobbs, Gardner repeated his accusation that Humbler was responsible, saying, 'You wretch; you are the cause of this, you have done this'. Humbler replied, 'Oh my God! Gardner how can you say that?' Sergeant Mobbs told him that he was charging the girl with a serious offence and that he needed to be careful with what he was saying. He asked Gardner what his reasons for suspecting Humbler were. Gardner's disarming answer was: 'Because I have been in the habit of having intercourse with her; there was a dispute and she was aware that she had to leave.'

Mobbs took Humbler, who was in an excited state and 'hardly knew what she was about', out of the Gardners' bedroom and up into her own room on the second floor where he carefully examined all her clothes, including those she was wearing, to see if there was any blood on them but found none. At the same time, he noticed that her hands and face were 'begrimed with dirt' and it appeared that she hadn't washed for a long time. Coming back down from the second floor, he then examined Gardner's clothes which, while dirty with soot, had no blood on them and there was also no blood on Gardner's hands or face. He next examined the Gardners' bedroom and found no marks of blood on the wall apart from a little splash above where the head of Mrs Gardner was lying. He examined the bedstead, and a cornice which formed part of the bed, but found no marks of blood on them. He then went down to the room on the ground floor. He noticed that the fire in that room was alight but the bars were cool suggesting that it hadn't been alight for a sufficient time to warm them. He didn't see any marks of blood in any part of the room. He couldn't find a cloth in the house on which someone could have wiped their bloody hands.

The police officers continued to search the house, including Humbler's room, but found nothing to incriminate her. Despite Gardner's suspicions, based on what Dr Sequeira told them the police officers appear to have concluded at this stage that Elizabeth Gardner had committed suicide. It seems that the doctor hadn't yet carried out a thorough examination of the body which was still lying where it had been found, squeezed between the wall and the bed, and hadn't noticed the deep cut to the middle finger of Mrs Gardner's left hand, let alone the bloody palm mark on the thigh. He said to Sergeant Mobbs, 'I don't think it's murder, I think it's suicide'. That being so, Gardner was asked by one of the officers what he thought should be done with Humbler. He replied, 'She shan't remain here', to which Humbler responded, 'I am willing to go wherever he likes to send me.' It was decided that she would stay with Mrs Spencer for the time being.

According to Gardner, at about nine o'clock that morning, Dr Sequeira asked him to collect together the bloody bedclothes and help move the body from the floor onto the bed. Gardner would later complain that some of the blood could have transferred to his clothes at any time which could easily have incriminated him. He said, 'I stood at the foot of the bedstead, pulling the bedclothes together in a bunch, throwing them round my left shoulder, casting them partly behind me.' The body was then placed on a board which was laid upon the mattress of Gardner's ornate four poster bed. Sequeira left the house at about a quarter to ten followed by the police soon afterwards. After they departed, Gardner was visited by friends and relations who had heard the tragic news. One of them was Eleanor Buckstone, a friend of Elizabeth's, who had rushed over from her home at Sussex Place, near Liverpool Street. When she arrived she found a pool of blood under the carpet where Mrs Gardner's body, which was now on the mattress, had been lying. She saw Gardner examining the cuts to the fingers of his dead wife and thought he looked upset while he remarked that the hands were so badly cut that it couldn't have been suicide. 'She never done it herself' he said, and, in any case, she was 'too weak in the nerves'. Buxton herself had never heard Elizabeth say that she meant to take her own life. To all the visitors to his house that morning, Gardner displayed the body, raising the left arm by the wrist and pointing out the severe cut at the first joint of the middle finger.

The Ward Beadle, Thomas Pallet, who had attended in the morning, showed up again at the house during the evening at about half-past-six and told Gardner he could have everything washed and cleaned. Gardner himself washed up the blood with a bucket of water and house flannel. According to Gardner, Dr Sequeira returned to 1 Northumberland Alley by arrangement the next morning at eight o'clock to conduct a post-mortem examination, asking again for Gardner's help to lift the board upon which the body rested from the bed to be balanced on four chairs into a position where there was sufficient light for the doctor to be able to see the body clearly. It would appear to be the case that it was during this examination that Sequeira noticed both the deep cut to the finger and the bloody palm print on the thigh for, according to Gardner, after leaving his house at shortly before ten o'clock that morning, the surgeon went straight to Tower Hill Police Station in Scathing Lane and laid a charge of murder against Gardner, although the police took no action at this stage.

Dr Sequeira, however, appears to have been uncertain about whether Mrs Gardner could have inflicted the wound to her own throat and therefore called for the assistance of Dr John Comley, an older and more experienced surgeon, formerly the resident Medical Officer of the Eastern Dispensary, who resided in Whitechapel High Street, in order to conduct a further post-mortem examination. The two men arrived at Gardner's house for this purpose at about eight o'clock that evening. Gardner would later complain that Comley was in his house for only a few minutes and that the examination was concluded very quickly.

It's not known if the two doctors discussed the time of death based on Dr Sequira having found most of the body to have been cold in the morning of the previous day, but Dr Comley had given evidence about such a thing at an inquest in February 1861. Charles Souter Laidlaw had been found dead in his room in Islington by his landlady having, apparently, leaned backwards in his chair which caused him to accidentally strangle himself. The time of death in this case was, therefore, of little relevance but *Lloyds Weekly News* of 24 February 1861 reported that, 'Mr Comley, surgeon, of High-street, Whitechapel, said that when he was called to see deceased, he found that the body was cold, and death must have taken place some hours previously'. A vague estimate of 'some hours' wasn't quite as specific as the four hours that Dr Sequeira had already decided upon in the Gardner case.

On Wednesday, 17 September 1862, an inquest into Elizabeth Gardner's death was opened in the Saracen's Head Tavern in Northumberland Alley, presided over by the deputy coroner for the City, William Payne. At this inquest, the deposition of Samuel Gardner was taken. He said the following:

> I am willing to tell all I know about the matter. Deceased has been my wife for seven years. We lived together before marriage. We lived comfortably together for some years after marriage. Elizabeth Clark first came to my house five or six years ago, as a servant. Three years after that we cohabited together. When the deceased found it out she was very disagreeable to it, and Clark had to leave the house. She has been away several times. She lived with me and the deceased. Clark then married a man named Humbler. I knew that she was married to Humbler. Deceased said the girl was worse after marriage than before. On Sunday morning I went out at 11 o'clock, and returned at 2 o'clock. Elizabeth Humbler and my wife were both there. I did not go out again after 2 o'clock. On Sunday evening, from 5 to 7, I and the girl had words together; deceased was there also. The girl was annoying and teasing my wife, and I spoke to her about it. She kept on laughing and singing. Deceased said to me, "When your back is turned it is worse than that"

I then said, "There shall be an end to it." I then spoke to the girl, and said that next day I should have a few words to settle the matter; that I should not put up with such nonsense. The girl went to bed at 7 o'clock. I and deceased remained up. We slept together. We were friends then. At half-past 3 on Monday morning the police called me, as I wished. I looked at my watch, and found it was too early to get up, and I went to bed again. Deceased then said to me, "Did you hear that creature up and down in the night?" I said, "No." Deceased said, "I heard her at one o'clock come down from the top room, go to the bottom room, and then come into this room and take the candle off the table, and go down into the kitchen, and then up to the top room, and then come back and place the candle on the table where she took it from." I said, "Oh! well, don't bother, it will be decided to-day; we will have no more of it." I meant the girl's nonsense. That was all that passed between us. I got up at twenty minutes to 4, left the room at a quarter to 4, and dressed myself downstairs, and left the house at 4 o'clock. When I left the room, deceased was lying in bed, on her right side. She was awake. She had our child, three years old, with her. I covered deceased up with the bedclothes. I did not see the girl Humbler before I left. I went to sweep chimneys at Pope's Head-alley, Change-alley, and Purssell's. I went home at 8 o'clock, and then I found the doctor there. I never heard the girl threaten the deceased. The brooch found on the chair contains my likeness. It was locked up in the desk on Sunday. The key of the desk was kept in my trousers' pocket. Deceased had her wedding-ring on on Sunday night when we went to bed. I can't tell who wrote the letters produced. Deceased often spoke about them. They were kept in the top drawer. When I got up on Monday morning I saw them and the brooch, and the ring, on the chair. I swear that I took the knife out of deceased's right hand. I did not put it there. I have not spoken to the girl since about it. I did say to her on the Monday morning, "You've done this." I thought they had been quarrelling, and that she had done it; that she had killed her. I fancy I heard the knife drawer rattle on the Sunday night; I am almost certain that I did. I never had any quarrel with Humbler's husband. When I left home on Monday morning I pulled the door to, and no one could have got in without a key. It is a lock, not a mere latch. I washed the floor of the room next day. Deceased was not left-handed.

Gardner's evidence as to the time he left his house was corroborated by Constable Meagher (the officer who had woken Gardner at 3.15am) who said he saw him leaving Northumberland Alley at about four o'clock.

Humbler, who, by now, was staying with a cousin in South London, was also deposed. We don't have a full version of her deposition but it was reported in one newspaper[45] which allows us to reconstruct it as follows:

> I am a married woman, and the wife of John Humbler. I lived with Samuel Gardner before I got married. I had been living with my husband for three years, but had left him to lodge in the same house as the Gardners. On Monday week I got up at half-past seven o'clock but could only find one lucifer match. I then went to the Gardners' room to procure the box. Having taken the matches, I was about returning downstairs with them, when I stepped on something, and on looking down on the floor found it was blood. I then noticed Mrs Gardner lying on the floor, with her throat cut, and her little child at her feet. I immediately ran off and called in a surgeon, who arrived, and pronounced life extinct. I had never heard the deceased threaten to destroy herself.

This was the first time Humbler had provided a full account of how she found Mrs Gardner's body and the first time she had mentioned stepping in blood. After the hearing concluded, she was asked by the coroner to give her stockings to Sergeant Mobbs who could find no trace of blood on them. As he would later say, 'I saw no trace of anything on them - they were very dirty - we inspected them minutely, but we could see no trace of any blood upon them - we could have seen it on the leg if there had been any there, but on the sole of the foot the dirt was too thick - she had been running in the dirt with them, there is no doubt.'

It was reported that Dr Sequeira gave evidence at the hearing on 24 September but the nature of his evidence wasn't reported and, curiously, it didn't seem to implicate Gardner who remained at liberty while the

---

[45] *Daily Telegraph*, 25 September 1862.

inquest was adjourned until the following Wednesday. After the hearing, Humbler went back to Gravesend to live with her mother, having received three shillings from Gardner to enable her to pay for her journey and other expenses.

On the same day as the inquest hearing, Gardner spoke to his sister, Sarah Reeves, telling her that he had thought at first that his wife had taken her own life but had then dismissed the idea saying, 'To tell you the truth, I don't think that she could have done it herself, as she was so weak minded'. He described how 'one finger was nearly cut off and it appeared as if she had struggled for her life.' He told her that he would like to know whether Betsy Humbler murdered her or not but he also said about Humbler, 'I know she has taken her life away, because she was going away'. He also mentioned that he had heard the dresser-drawer opened on Sunday night by his wife but said that if she had taken up the knife he did not think she would do anything to herself.

During the evening, Eleanor Buckstone and a couple of other local women came over to wash Mrs Gardner's body which was then placed in a coffin.

Over the next couple of days, Sergeant Mobbs, Detective Monger and the Ward Beadle returned to Gardner's house and conducted further searches of the premises but found nothing.[46] Detective Monger lifted the lid of the coffin into which the body of Mrs Gardner had been placed. A gruesome sight presented itself because Mrs Gardner's face had turned black. Gardner, who was standing next to Monger, began to cry and said, 'My poor wife has been murdered.' Monger asked why he thought it was murder and Gardner said that Elizabeth was too feeble and nervous to have committed suicide and he was sure it was murder because of the way his dead wife's hands were cut. The detective then asked if he suspected anyone in particular of having committed the crime to which Gardner instantly replied, 'Yes, Elizabeth Humbler' explaining that she had known

---

[46] There are some serious and irreconcilable contradictions in the police evidence throughout the legal proceedings as to precisely when the searches of the house occurred, the sequence in which they were carried out and which officers were present. As Gardner's legal team don't appear to have taken any point on the inconsistencies, so that they may not be significant, I will gloss over them but this could and should have been the basis of some close cross-examination during Gardner's trial.

that she had to leave the house on the day of the murder. He told the officer that he had several times seen Humbler sharpening knives on the doorstep of his house and on the sink-stone in the cellar. He also said he had found knives in her bedroom on several occasions. He once found a knife sticking in the wainscotting as if Humber had been imagining that she was stabbing someone. When he had asked her why she had done this, she told him that she had intended to take her own life. On another occasion, she had told him that the reason she had a knife was 'To take your life and then my own.'

During the search, Gardner directed the attention of the officers to a slight bloodstain on the white curtain of the window in the room on the ground floor and a bloody fingerprint on the inside of one of the shutters which, at that time, was shut. Gardner said, 'She opened the window that morning', apparently meaning Humbler but not naming her. Mobbs told him that he was positive that those blood marks hadn't been there when he examined the room on Monday. According to Mobbs, Gardner 'made no answer.' In the Gardners' bedroom on the first floor, the officers saw a large splash of blood at the foot of the bed and several spots of blood at the head of the bed and at the side of the bed and on the wall. Part of the bedstead had the appearance of having had a wet bloody cloth drawn across it and, on the cornice of the bed, there was a splash of blood which wasn't quite dry. Mobbs again said that none of this blood had been there on Monday. Gardner suggested the spots of blood might have been caused by the wet cloth with which the body of his wife had been washed.

A mystery during these searches was that Sergeant Mobbs found a copy of the works of Aristotle in the top room, Humbler's room, which, he said, hadn't been there when he searched before. How it had got into the room of someone who was supposed to be illiterate, or what its sudden appearance meant, was never explained.

On Saturday, 20 September, Detective Monger and Sergeant Mobbs travelled to Gravesend at the request of the coroner and saw Humbler, who was asked to change out of her clothes, the officers having brought a spare set of clothes from London for this purpose. She was then cautioned and questioned. She denied Gardner's tales of her sharpening knives but admitted that he had spoken to her about sharpening knives once, not to chide her for doing so but to suggest that the only reason she was doing it on the doorstep was so that she would be seen by the neighbours in order to make it clear that she was living with Gardner. She repeated some of what she had told the coroner, saying that on the Monday morning she didn't leave her room until half-past seven when she went downstairs to light the fire. She said that she went into Mrs Gardner's room for a match and, having found one, she saw Mrs Gardner 'lying dead' on the floor and, picking up young Eliza who was at her mother's feet, immediately went for a doctor.

After the funeral of Mrs Gardner on Sunday, 21 September, at Bow Cemetery, the adjourned inquest resumed on Wednesday, 24 September. Dr Sequeira was reported to have told the coroner that, 'since the inquest was commenced I have carefully examined the body externally and internally'. This was odd bearing in mind that the post-mortem examination was conducted on the day before the inquest had commenced, after which Mrs Gardner's body had been placed into a coffin so that it's difficult to see when any further examination could have been carried out. In any event, he informed the coroner that, 'Taking all things into consideration, I am inclined to think that the female did not do the deed herself, unless with the left hand, and that seems improbable'. He also mentioned that when he and an unnamed assistant lifted the body on the morning of the murder, presumably at some time after 9am, 'it was quite stiff'.[47] Although an indication of rigor mortis, and thus potentially of significance to the time of death, this evidence was never repeated by Sequeira. Dr Comley told the coroner that the cut through the finger bone 'could never have been caused by clasping a knife'. Asked if he believed the wounds were self-inflicted, he said: 'I do not think that the deceased could have placed herself placidly down after having cut her own throat'. Neither medical man was asked to estimate the time of death, and neither of them gave any evidence about Mrs Gardner's body temperature, but from the evidence of Constable Blanchard, who heard the 'hysterical screams' coming from Mrs Gardner's room, an observer would have understood that the murder must have occurred at six o'clock in the morning. Although no direct evidence was presented against them, at the conclusion of the hearing, which was adjourned to the following Monday, the coroner said that, 'considering the serious aspect which the case has assumed', he would

---

[47] *Daily News*, 25 September 1862.

order the inspector in charge of the case for the City of London police to arrest Elizabeth Humbler and Samuel Gardner. While being transported to prison, Gardner told the inspector that he was glad to be taken into custody and that he hoped something would come out.

Now officially announced as a murder, the case became a sensation in the London newspapers, being called 'The Mysterious Murder in the City' or such like. The very next day, Gardner and Humbler were brought before the Lord Mayor, who was the magistrate at Mansion House Police Court, and were formally charged with the murder of Elizabeth Gardner. Dr Sequeira couldn't be present at this hearing but Dr Comley told the Lord Mayor that, 'The conclusion which Mr. Sequeira and I came to was that death could not have been caused by her own hand, and I am still of that opinion.' Comley, who didn't see the body of Mrs Gardner until the day after her death, couldn't say anything about her body temperature on the Monday but Sergeant Mobbs stated that the body was cold when he first arrived. He also confirmed that the only blood he saw in the house was where the body was found. At the end of the hearing, both prisoners were remanded into custody. Gardner rather optimistically applied to be admitted to bail but the Lord Mayor declined even to consider his application.

The publicity arising from the remand hearing appears to have led some new witnesses to contact the police. At the resumption of the inquest on Monday, 30 September, three men who had known Gardner for a number of years all said they had seen him in the vicinity of Northumberland Alley at times he claimed to have been sweeping chimneys in the City on the morning of the murder. George Goulbourn, a lamplighter, testified that he saw Gardner in Leadenhall Street, heading in the direction of Cornhill, at about a quarter to five in morning of Monday, 15 September. He claimed that he said 'Good morning' to him and that Gardner returned the greeting. John Maguire, a photographic artist, said that he saw Gardner between Jewry Street and the Minories, near the premises of a firm called Moses & Sons, walking towards Northumberland Alley, at about five minutes to seven on the same morning, holding his sweeping machine and carrying a bag over his shoulder which appeared to be empty. Like Goulbourn, he recalled exchanging pleasantries with Gardner. He said that he then saw him again twenty-five minutes later in Fenchurch Street sitting on a rail at the King's Head, a public house near the corner of Star Alley. Between these supposed sightings, Thomas Raffield, a carpenter, said that he saw Gardner carrying his sweeping machine in Fenchurch Street at almost exactly seven o'clock in the morning, walking as if he had just turned out of Northumberland Alley. He also said that he exchanged pleasantries with Gardner. The first of these witnesses said that he saw Gardner again later that morning, after being told about the murder by Constable Temple, who had asked him to fetch his brother officer, and he tried to enter his house, but Gardner told him that there were quite enough people in already.

Following the testimony given by these three witnesses, Constable Meagher, the City policeman who had woken Gardner up at 3.15am and who had previously told the coroner that he saw Gardner leaving his house at 'about four o'clock', now changed his evidence to inform the Lord Mayor that he believed he saw Gardner leaving his house at between 4.30 and 5am. He hadn't seen the time anywhere but he recalled that it was light enough to see Gardner walk up the alley which, on reflection, he thought, meant it must have been much later than 4am.

If we assume that Gardner wasn't really sweeping chimneys all morning, the evidence of these witnesses is quite confusing. One can understand that Gardner might have left his house significantly later than four o'clock because he had murdered his wife, possibly following an argument, after being woken up by Constable Meagher at a quarter past three, so that his being spotted by both Goulbourn and Constable Meagher at the top of Northumberland Alley at a quarter to five would be understandable. But the next two sightings are confusing and inconsistent. The effect of their testimony was that he was walking towards Northumberland Alley at shortly before 7am and then, a few minutes later, walking away from it. That doesn't really make sense. Presumably he didn't pop back home to murder his wife. Was he just supposed to have been hanging around the area all morning, not doing any work, after having committed the murder?

Nevertheless, the inconsistency in timings was held against Gardner at the inquest. The coroner pointed out to the jury in his summing up that the evidence of those three witnesses, 'tended to throw grave doubt on the truth of the statement which Gardner had made as to his movements on the morning of Mrs Gardner's death'. He pointed out that there was a motive for Gardner and Humbler to have conspired to get rid of Mrs Gardner. The jury members were reminded of evidence given by Dr Sequeira, repeated that day, that, while it was not impossible for Mrs Gardner to have stabbed herself in the throat with her left hand, it was 'highly improbable'. On this basis, after deliberating for thirty minutes, the jury returned a verdict of wilful murder against both Samuel Gardner and Elizabeth Humbler. Both prisoners were then committed to Newgate to await trial.

In the meantime, there was a further remand hearing before the Lord Mayor on 7 October. Both prisoners now had legal representation. On behalf of Humbler, William Campbell Sleigh said that there was no evidence against her. He was pushing at an open door because the Lord Mayor said that he was of the same opinion. In addressing the Lord Mayor on behalf of Gardner, Mr Lewis of Lewis & Lewis solicitors said that Gardner could not have committed the murder bearing in mind that a scream was heard at six o'clock in the morning when Gardner was sweeping chimneys in the City. The Lord Mayor said that he was of the view that the sound must have been that of children laughing but Mr Lewis produced evidence showing that the only child in the house was the two-year-old Eliza. Nevertheless, the Lord Mayor said that he was of the opinion that the evidence against Gardner was sufficiently strong to commit him for trial, which he did. Regarding Humbler he said he had heard nothing to incriminate her and that if it was in his power he would discharge her, but, as the coroner's jury had sent her for trial, she could not be released.

The Temperature of Death • 57

CHAPTER THREE

Trial

The trial of Samuel Gardner and Elizabeth Humbler for the murder of Elizabeth Gardner commenced at the Old Bailey on 30 October 1862 before Sir Frederick Pollock, the Lord Chief Baron, an elderly judge, aged seventy-nine years old. The indictment was rather interesting because, to the uninitiated, it would appear that three women had been murdered. Samuel and Elizabeth were charged with no less than *three* counts of murder, the first count being the murder of Elizabeth Gardner, the second count being the murder of Elizabeth Reed Gardner and the third being the murder of Elizabeth Cook. This reflected the different maiden names used by Elizabeth and the fact that her marriage to Samuel was bigamous.

The trial was obviously going to present a challenge to the prosecution which was conducted by Henry Bodkin Poland on behalf of the Corporation of London. If the case for the prosecution was that Gardner and Humbler had jointly conspired to murder Mrs Gardner, why did Gardner instantly accuse Humbler of having committed the crime? Such an accusation would surely have been self-defeating because there would have been a huge risk of Humbler then either accusing Gardner or, worse, admitting that they were both involved in killing her. And, if they *were* both involved, why did Humbler not retaliate when Gardner very publicly and unexpectedly accused her of murdering his wife in front of the doctor and police officers? The coroner's jury, however, had found a verdict of wilful murder against both of them and the prosecution was bound by that decision.

When opening the case, Mr Poland admitted that the evidence against Humbler was 'very slight', at which point the judge surprised Gardner's defence team by interjecting that the proper course was for Mr Poland to offer no evidence against her and for the jury to be instructed to return a not guilty verdict in her favour, in which event she could appear as a prosecution witness against Gardner and be cross-examined. Mr Poland demurred, saying that he didn't think he would be justified in allowing the jury to return such a verdict before all the facts were known but the Lord Chief Baron, after consulting his colleagues outside of the courtroom, ruled firmly that no evidence was to be offered against Humbler and she was duly declared not guilty by the obedient jury.

Gardner was now alone and in a virtually impossible position if he wanted to argue that Humbler had murdered his wife. She had been formally acquitted and thus, in the eyes of the law, couldn't possibly have done it. His Counsel, Mr William Ribton, of Elm Court Chambers in the Temple, also hadn't had much time to prepare for the important cross-examination of Elizabeth Humbler, something that he wasn't expecting to happen but would have to do that very day.

The prosecution's case as to when the murder occurred seemed confused from the outset. P.C. George Blanchard's firm recollection of hearing a scream coming from the Gardners' bedroom at 6am was part of the prosecution evidence, thus apparently placing the murder at that time. But the evidence of George Goulbourn and P.C. Meagher, also called by the prosecution, was to the effect that Gardner had left his house at somewhere around 4.45am that morning which, being about forty-five minutes later than he had claimed in his deposition, suggested that he was lying for some reason which could only be that he had already murdered his wife before that time. Yet, with the evidence of Thomas Matthew and John McQuire, both prosecution witnesses, placing Gardner in the area of Northumberland Alley at 7am, perhaps the suggestion was that Gardner had returned to his house at 6am and committed the crime then.

However, when the medical men gave their evidence, they firmly contradicted the notion that Constable Blanchard could have heard Mrs Gardner screaming. Dr Sequeira said that, when he examined the body at about 8am, he thought that 'she had been dead four hours'. This was on the basis that, while the lower part of the trunk was warm, the upper part of the body and the thigh was cold. If he was correct, it would have meant that Mrs Gardner had been murdered at about 4am so that the peculiar and mysterious scream heard by P.C. Blanchard two hours later couldn't have had anything to do with the case.

Dr Sequeira was extensively cross examined on his conclusion as to the time of death by Mr Ribton. The doctor's somewhat confused answers under cross-examination were recorded in the official proceedings of the Old Bailey as follows:

> I say the body had been dead about four hours; it is impossible for anyone to say — it may have been longer than that, but I should say it was quite as long — I think it could not have been shorter — I will not swear that it may not have been half an hour shorter, but I should think it was more likely to be rather more than four hours than under, very much more likely — I will say that it could not have been an hour under; it is quite impossible that it could have been three instead of four; that is my opinion — I swear it is impossible that it could have been three hours instead of four — I won't swear as to the impossibility of three hours and a half — I think it is impossible it could only have been three hours.

He was then asked by Mr Ribton if he had had much experience of examining dead bodies. His answer was that he treated about five thousand patients during the course of a year and 'a great many of them unfortunately die.' This wasn't terribly helpful and the judge intervened to ask if he had the type of experience which enabled him to know what time it would take 'to produce coldness in the human frame after death'. Sequeira's response to this was to say: 'I have had very great experience, being connected with a public charity; I am medical officer to one of the poor law unions — I frequently have occasion to examine dead bodies — I am frequently not sent for till after death, and then they wish to say how long the patient has been dead.' Mr Ribton asked him when this had last happened; his answer was vague and unconvincing:

> I cannot say; perhaps not more than a month ago — I do not mean a case of this kind, but a case in which a person died,

and I was called upon to give my opinion how long the patient had been dead — I was called in and shown a dead body, and I was asked to give my opinion how long it had been dead, and I did so; I forget now the time I said — I forget the case but I know it was within a month ago — I say I cannot remember the case — they asked my opinion on it, which had been frequently done before — they did not themselves know how long the body had been dead — nothing that I am aware of occurred in that case to test the accuracy of my opinion — there have been many other cases where it has been tested afterwards — I cannot tell you any without referring to my books — I could if I had my books, but without them I cannot — there may have been six, eight, ten, or a dozen cases where my opinion has been proved to be accurate — cases have often occurred in which I have been called in and asked my opinion as to the time the body had been dead, and I have found what I have said was correct — I have found that from the circumstances that have transpired; perhaps one party may have been absent at the time, and when he has come home he has said, "I left so and so" — there was one case in particular, I remember; that was perhaps twelve months ago; a neighbour called on me to come and see so and so; I found the person was dead; I pronounced an opinion as to how long the person had been dead; my opinion was about three or four hours; I found the body almost cold — that was proved by circumstances to be correct, by the man, whose wife it was, being out, and they imagined he went out to work and left his wife dead in bed — when he came home of course I inquired of him, and he told me — it was in the morning that I was called in to see her — I cannot say exactly the time now, but I recollect those circumstances—the man told me he left his wife dead when he went out in the morning — he did not tell me the time — he told me the time he went out in the morning, but I forget now what time it was — I neither recollect the time he told me, nor the time I was called in to see her — I recollect it was in the morning — my opinion was proved to be correct by the man's own statement — I cannot recollect any other instances.

In short, it would seem that the only example Sequeira could provide of having previously estimated a time of death which, in his mind, proved to be correct, was one where he found a body 'almost cold' and estimated the time of death as having been three or four hours earlier, although he couldn't satisfactorily explain how this was proved to be correct.

The final question and answer on the subject should have disposed of the matter. Mr Ribton asked Sequeira, 'Can you tell me any scientific principle by reason of which you would be able to tell the length of time a body has been dead?' causing the witness to admit, 'I think it is impossible to say positively'. The *Times* recorded his answer as being: 'There is no particular scientific theory with regard to the period at which a body becomes cold after death'.

Had it been left there, perhaps the notion of time of death having been at 4am would itself have died a quick death. But Dr Comley provided support to Sequeira's estimate, despite not having viewed the body until more than twenty-four hours after it had been found. He did so when answering questions from the judge. The first answer didn't seem promising for the prosecution, as the judge asked, 'Is it part of a medical man's duty to be acquainted with the period of death upon examining the body a very short time after?' to which Comley replied, frankly, 'No, it is not', adding somewhat cryptically, 'it depends upon the rigid state of the body'. The judge then followed up by asking: 'Is it any part of a medical man's scientific, or medical, or physiological learning, if a body is shown to him with a certain degree of warmth in it, to form an opinion how long that body has been dead?'. In view of his previous answer, Comley's answer to this question seems to be contradictory because he said: 'Yes, it is — I think, from the nature of the case, as described, and the woman being with child, which would keep up partial heat, that the body would not have got cold so quickly as it would otherwise.' It will be recalled that Elizabeth Gardner was seven months pregnant and Dr Comley was saying here that the unborn child would account for why there was some warmth in the lower trunk despite the body being cold elsewhere.

Having accepted that a medical man could form an opinion as to how long a body had been dead, the judge next asked Comley a question as if he was giving evidence as an expert witness (which he was not) rather than as a witness of fact (which he was supposed to be). 'The woman was found at 8 o'clock with her feet and shoulders cold, and the lower part of the trunk warm,' he said, 'can you form any opinion from that, according to your experience, how long she had been dead?' Comley obliged with an answer that corroborated his colleague's evidence, saying: 'I should say about four or five hours'. He justified this opinion by explaining, 'I have been called in to a number of deaths at the police-station — it is sometimes of importance to ascertain from the state of a body how long the person has been dead — it is a matter of ordinary surgical and medical skill to be acquainted with that, and to form an opinion upon it.' It will be noted here that, while Comley said that he had been called to a number of deaths for which it was important to ascertain the time of death, he didn't say whether or how he had managed to successfully ascertain it on these occasions.

This line of questioning by the judge brought Mr Ribton to his feet. 'It is a remarkable fact', he observed, 'that Dr Taylor's celebrated work on medical jurisprudence does not say anything upon this point.' As we've seen, the seventh edition of Taylor's *Medical Jurisprudence* published in 1861, which was the current edition at the time of the trial, did not include a section on estimating time of death from body temperature and did no more than refer in vague terms to the 1847 murder of Josefa Martínez Mundo in Spain (which was said to demonstrate that a body would still be warm one hour after death) and the 1860 manslaughter of his pupil by Thomas Hopley (which was said to demonstrate that a cold and rigid body covered with bedclothes in a reasonably warm room must have been dead for six or seven hours) neither of which cases could have been said to apply to the Gardner case. Ribton suggested that, while the absence of anything about establishing time of death through body temperature in Taylor might be because it was very seldom of material importance, 'it undoubtedly is so in the present case'. Despite the absence of any textbook authority supporting the views of doctors Sequeira and Comley, the idea seems to have stuck that the medical evidence proved that the murder had occurred no later than 4am, thus implicating Gardner.

The other crucial medical evidence in the trial went to the question of whether Elizabeth Gardner could have committed suicide. The two medical men were united on this. Dr Sequeira said that it was impossible for her to have inflicted the throat wound on herself with her right hand but he accepted it wasn't impossible if she had used her left hand. His logic was hard to follow and he admitted that he didn't have much experience examining throat wounds. The more experienced Dr Comley initially insisted that it couldn't have been done by either hand, saying, 'The nature of the wound was deep backwards, and turned inwards, going to divide the thyroid artery, muscle, and cartilage, into the larynx, which could not have been done by a person's own hand.' He backtracked slightly under cross-examination, however, saying, 'it is possible the left hand might, but the right hand, I am sure, could not — the left hand might have done it, but it was a sort of edging wound, not a regular clear cut — the right hand could not have done it, from this circumstance, it went digging downwards and inwards — it was an incised wound — it came down, and went backwards, and then inwards — I say, the left hand might have done it, because it could have turned in so easily, whereas the right could not — she could not have got the right hand round as to make the wound — that is my opinion — I think it is most improbable'. But, he added, 'hardly anything is impossible at the present day.' The idea that someone would be physically unable to cut their own throat with their right hand in a way in which is possible with their left hand seems strange and hard to understand.

Another factor which influenced Dr Sequeira in his conclusion was the fact that Gardner was able to remove the knife from his wife's hand so easily. He felt that if Elizabeth had committed suicide it should have been grasped firmly in her hand and would have needed some force to be removed. In cross-examination, Mr Ribton focused on the fact that Sequeira's deposition from the inquest referred to the knife having been 'clutched' in the deceased's hand and also that it was 'clenched'. Sequeira denied having used the word 'clutched', although he admitted to 'clenched', but Mr Ribton didn't get to the bottom of the rather more important question as to precisely why it couldn't have been loose in her hand if she had committed suicide.

Had he turned to the most recent edition of Taylor's *Medical Jurisprudence,* he would have found reference to a case cited by Taylor from his own knowledge in which an unnamed woman had cut her throat with a razor which had been found under her left shoulder. It transpired that it had fallen into this position when the surgeon who had been first called to the scene had turned the body over without noticing the razor.

Taylor said, 'We must remember that it is quite compatible with suicide that a weapon may be found at some distance, or in a concealed situation; but it is much more frequently either grasped in the hand, or lying by the side of the deceased.' Where a weapon is found firmly grasped in the hand of the deceased, he went on, 'no better circumstantial evidence of suicide can, perhaps, be offered.' This grasping, he explained, was thought to be due to a muscular spasm persisting after death known as a cadaveric spasm and it was something that couldn't be imitated in a murder case. It was one thing, however, for a firmly grasped weapon to prove a suicide but quite another for a loosely grasped one to mean that a murder had been committed and the weapon placed in the victim's hand by the murderer. It doesn't seem to follow but Taylor cited the case of the murder of Anne Saville in the village of Colwick, near Nottingham, in May 1844 for which her husband, William, was arrested, convicted and executed.[48] Along with her three children, Mrs Saville had been found lying dead in a small area of trees and bushes with her throat cut and the razor loose in her hand. There was no blood upon the hand which held the razor and, said Taylor, 'this, together with the fact of its being quite loose, rendered it certain that it must have been placed there by the prisoner after having cut the wife's throat'.

While that summary of the facts is true enough, Taylor omitted to mention that, prior to the discovery of his wife's body, William Saville had already been suspected of murdering her (by drowning) due to statements he had made following her disappearance and also due to the fact that he had a clear motive for killing her because he wanted to marry another woman with whom he was in an adulterous relationship. In fact, according to the *Times*, a large mob had surrounded his house and, 'if the man had not been taken into custody, he would probably have received rough treatment at the hands of the populace'. It was only after this that the body of Mrs Saville was discovered with her throat cut. The fact that the knife was loose, and there was no blood on her hands, only added to the case against the prisoner rather than having created it.

There was other evidence too. Spots of blood were found on William Saville's trousers, his razor case was empty and suicide was ruled out due

---

[48] At Saville's execution on 8 August 1844, the crowd was so large that twelve people died and a further twenty-one were seriously injured in a crush.

to traces of Mrs Saville having been dragged along the grass.[49] Saville had also been seen where the body was found, together with his wife and three children, the day prior to the discovery, after which they hadn't been seen alive again. In time honoured fashion he also supposedly made a confession to a fellow inmate in his cell.[50] At the trial, the key fact stressed by the medical practitioners was not so much that the razor was loose in Mrs Saville's hand but that there was no blood on her hand that was holding the razor, or along her arm. This was also emphasised by Taylor in his book, so that if Dr Sequeira was relying simply on the knife being loose in Mrs Gardner's hand as evidence that she had been murdered, he might well have led himself astray in his thinking. Mrs Gardner's hands were, of course, stained with blood and, although, as we have seen, Dr Sequeira thought that the insides of her hands, which were free from running blood, had been wiped, he also said that the backs of the hands were 'very bloody'.

Three years after the Gardner case, Professor Taylor updated his section on suicide to say that 'the mere fact of a weapon found loose, should not be taken as evidence of murder unless other circumstances – such as the nature of the wound, the freedom of the hand from blood, the position of the body etc. concur to prove the act was one of suicide.' This doesn't mean that he thought that the doctors in the Gardner case had made a mistake for he also said that in the Gardner case, the weapon had been placed in the wrong hand by her murderer. This was based on the medical evidence that Mrs Gardner could only have killed herself with her left hand but the knife was in her right hand. Clearly he thought that the nature of the wound and the position of the body meant that the looseness of the weapon *could* be taken as evidence of murder in the Gardner case. As we will see in the next chapter, Professor Taylor had other observations to make on the Gardner case.

The way that Mrs Gardner was holding the knife in her hand wasn't something that Dr Comley could have given evidence about, not having been present when the knife was removed (although even Sequeira admitted that he only had a momentary view of it before Gardner took it) but both doctors were insistent that Mrs Gardner could not have cut her own finger through to the bone simply by holding the knife tightly in

---

[49] *Times*, 25 May 1844.
[50] *Times*, 27 July 1844.

her death throes after having inflicted the wound in her neck. 'It would have been impossible to cut through the bone of the finger', Dr Sequeira said, 'because no one could possibly clutch or clench the fist sufficiently to cut through bone'. Pressed further by Mr Ribton, however, this turned into, 'It is not impossible, but most improbable'. He also admitted that it was possible that 'a person in the agony of suffocation, in the convulsive struggles accompanying suffocation, might have clutched the blade of the knife in the left hand, and then seized it, and pulled it out by the right.' If that *had* happened, of course, it would explain why Mrs Gardner had been found with cuts on both hands.

The fact that there was a broad mark of a bloody hand (including a thumb print) on the inside of Mrs Gardner's right thigh was regarded as another important piece of medical evidence. Dr Sequeira said that the mark was broader than his own hand which suggested that it wasn't made by the hand of a female. Mr Ribton wondered if Sequeira himself might have left the mark with his own hand, bloodied from examining Mrs Gardner's body, but he denied it. Perhaps of less importance were the sooty marks on the body which, considering that Mrs Gardner was married to a chimney sweep, could easily have occurred at some time prior to her death. Dr Sequeira was cross-examined on the basis that Gardner had put one hand on his dead wife's wrist and elbow when removing the knife with his other hand, but Sequeira denied that this had happened.

The final factor that caused the doctors to think that there had been foul play was the appearance of the blood on the palms of the hands which looked as if they had been wiped, thus smearing the blood. In cross-examination, however, Dr Comley accepted that the smearing could have been caused naturally if Mrs Gardner's hand had been slightly stained with fresh blood and had then grasped the handle of the knife. A supposed bruise on one of the thighs that Dr Comley had referred to when giving evidence to the coroner, and which suggested to him that someone had held Mrs Gardner down before murdering her, did not feature in his evidence during the trial which presumably means that he had concluded that it wasn't a bruise after all.

While their evidence might have been somewhat undermined during cross-examination, it was clear that the doctors believed, nay insisted, that Mrs Gardner had been murdered. In which case who had murdered her? After the medical men gave evidence, Elizabeth Humbler took to the witness stand. Her account of how she found the body of Mrs Gardner, according to the official proceedings of the Old Bailey was as follows:

> I got up about half-past 7 on the Monday morning — the first I heard was Mr. Spencer's saw-mills, that was what woke me up — when I left my room in the morning I went straight down to the bottom room — that was about twenty-five minutes or half-past 7 — I never left my room during the night — when I went down stairs I went into the room on the ground floor — I can't be positive whether the shutters were shut — I looked up at the clock and saw that it was half-past 7 — I went to the cupboard and took some wood out and placed it in the fire — I looked on the mantel-piece for some lucifers, and I only saw one on the mantel-piece — I set light to the paper with that, but it did not seem to catch, and I was afraid it would go out — I knew that the remainder of the lucifers were upstairs, because Mr. Gardner took the lucifers upstairs every night, and a candle too — he used to have lucifers there every night because of getting up early in the morning — I went upstairs and opened the door, and the round table was before the door — I took the lucifers off the table, and in turning round I saw Mrs. Gardner lying on the floor — I dropped the lucifers and saw the child at its mother's feet — I took hold of the child and rushed immediately for Mr. Sequeira, the doctor — I had taken hold of the lucifers before I saw Mrs. Gardner on the floor — the hinges of the door are on the left hand side going in — the moment I opened the door there was the body on the right hand — I dropped the lucifers on the floor and took hold of the child; it had a little frock on that it slept in — the child was not quiet — I had heard the child cry before I came downstairs, while I was dressing — I went for Mr. Sequeira, and took the child with me — it is two years and nine months old — I fetched Mr. Sequeira, and he came back with me.

It will be noted that, in this account, Humbler omitted to state that she was alerted to Mrs Gardner's dead body by the fact that she trod in some blood, as she had told the coroner. As we have seen, she said in her deposition at the inquest that, 'I stepped on something, and on looking down on the floor found it was blood'. This supposedly led her to notice the body of Mrs Gardner. During cross examination at the trial, she confirmed that she was only wearing stockings at the time and said, 'when I went upstairs and opened the door I trod in something — it was blood, but I did not know what it was till I went for the doctor — I trod on it as I was passing through the door with my stockings…it was wet and cold'. She initially said that she didn't know if the stockings were stained with blood but then said that, after she returned from the doctor's, she saw blood on the stockings and that they were 'damp with blood'. That, of course, is rather different from her claim that, after stepping in something, she looked down and immediately saw blood. It is also a curious feature of the case that there was no blood seen anywhere else in the house by any of the police officers (or anyone else) on Monday morning, yet if Humbler had stepped in some blood with her stockinged foot she would presumably have transferred at least some of it around the house when running for the doctor. Furthermore, if the blood was still in a liquid state, and hadn't dried, it would suggest that Mrs Gardner had died more recently than four hours earlier. It is also noteworthy that no blood was noticed on the stockings when Humbler gave them over to the police two days after the murder. Unfortunately, Sergeant Mobbs said that he didn't examine Humbler's feet during his search on the day the body was discovered. At this stage Humbler, due to her excited state, hadn't been asked to explain how she found the body so he didn't know that she was claiming (or would claim in the future) to have trodden in some blood.

Due to her confusing answers in the witness box, Mr Ribton tried again to get an answer about the blood on the stockings, asking Humbler, 'Did you, after you had trod in the blood, ever see blood on your stockings?' She replied, 'I never noticed my stockings; I never looked — I put on my old shoes — I know that I trod in something wet and cold — and when I returned with Mr. Sequeira, I thought it was blood I had trod in, by the blood being at the door — I never looked at my stockings to see if there was blood on them — I gave them to Sergeant Mobbs'. This seemed to contradict her earlier answers in which she had said that she had seen the blood on returning home with the doctor. She was pressed further and her final answer was: 'I do not know whether it was a pool of blood that I trod in — I did not stop to examine the blood — I do not know that I slipped in it — I trod in something wet and cold as I was passing through the door — I felt it cold and wet through the stockings.' To say her answers about this blood were suspicious would be an understatement. At the same time, the evidence of Sergeant Mobbs did offer a partial explanation for her account in that he said that, when he arrived at the house, blood had soaked into the carpet which caused 'a moisture and dampness' so that if Humbler had trodden on such a patch in the carpet it might have felt cold and wet without her actually stepping in a pool of blood.

There were two parts of Humbler's evidence which conflicted with what Gardner had told the police. The first related to whether she was aware that she was supposed to leave the Gardners' house on the Monday, the day Mrs Gardner was found dead. She denied that she had ever been told this. 'Mr Gardner never hinted such a thing to me', she said, 'he never told me that I was to leave on the Monday — he did not tell me until he accused me of the murder, and then he said, "You knew you had to leave to-day" — he said that in the room upstairs, in the presence of Mr. Sequeira — I said, "I did not know I had to leave to-day;" and I did not — he said, "I intended you to leave to-day" — I will swear that I said, "I did not know I was to leave".' Her evidence on this, however, was contradicted by Elizabeth Gardner's son, James (Samuel's stepson), a witness for the prosecution, who said in his evidence, 'I know the girl Humbler — I have heard her laughing and jeering at my mother, and annoying her very much — I was at the house about two or three weeks before the death — I heard that Humbler had got express directions to leave — I heard the directions given to her by my mother — she was to leave on the Monday — I heard Humbler on one occasion say, once there, she would never leave the house.' Humbler was recalled after this evidence but she remained adamant that she had made no such statement.

The second part of Humbler's evidence which conflicted with what Gardner had told the police (although it didn't form part of the evidence in his deposition) was in respect of the knives. While she admitted to having sharpened a knife, and being seen by Gardner in doing so, she said she was doing it on the instructions of Mrs Gardner and only did so outside, on the doorstep of the house, not in her bedroom as Gardner had suggested to the police. A bit later in her evidence she said, 'I sharpened several knives'. However, she said that Gardner had never taken a knife from her bedroom and she never sharpened a knife at eleven o'clock at night. She also denied telling Gardner that she would stick him with a knife unless he was nicer to her. 'I never said such a thing', she protested, 'I never threatened anything of the kind', adding cryptically, 'it had been more him threatened it to me.' Somewhat surprisingly Mr Poland did not ask her to elaborate on that allegation.

The alleged murder weapon was a bit of a mystery because it had supposedly been brought into the house by a neighbour's child, charmingly known as 'Tinkey' Lewis, on the very day before Mrs Gardner's death, having been found abandoned by the boy. According to Humbler, 'I never saw that knife in use until Sunday, dinner-time. I do not know where it came from…Mrs Gardner said Sunday morning that a basin, and two plates and a knife and fork had been brought in by little Tinkey Lewis, that had been left on a ledge by some of the men at work.' With Mrs Gardner being dead, it would appear that there was only Humbler's word that Tinkey Lewis had brought the knife into the house. Amelia Cox, a sister of Gardner's, had given evidence at the inquest on 24 September that, 'I know nothing further about the knife than that it had been left on some wood in the court', but it wasn't clear where her understanding of this came from or when she learnt it.

Upon the close of the prosecution's case, it was clear that there wasn't any direct evidence against Gardner to implicate him in the murder of Mrs Gardner but the argument against him was, to a large extent, one of logic rather than evidence. On the basis that the unqualified opinion of the medical men was that Mrs Gardner was murdered, if Humbler didn't do it (and she had already been acquitted), by a simple process of elimination, as the only other adult with access to the house, it *must* have been Gardner. *Quod Est Demonstrandum.* True, he didn't seem to have had a motive bearing in mind that he evidently didn't have any interest in living with Humbler, as shown by him accusing her of the murder, but he might have had an argument with his wife that morning and murdered her in a fit of passion or rage. The precise time of the murder wasn't clear but the medical evidence that it must have happened at about 4am (thus rendering the scream heard by the constable irrelevant) was undoubtedly persuasive for some.

The other factor that was held against Gardner (and apparently strongly so) was the sudden appearance of mysterious bloodstains at various places around his house a few days after the murder. The prosecution theory appears to have been that he planted these stains in order to incriminate Humbler, although where the blood came from for him to do this wasn't stated. If this seems hard to understand, the theory appears to be that the stain on the shutter was planted there because Humbler was said by Gardner to have closed one of the shutters, although there wasn't any hard evidence of this, so that, if she had simply denied ever touching the shutters, or even just not admitted it, the so-called 'planted evidence' would have been useless against her. In any case, this could only have been on the Monday, because Humbler didn't go into the house after that day, so that it would have been an odd plan by Gardner to plant blood supposed to incriminate her some days later, after he knew that the house had been searched by the police. Nevertheless, although Gardner offered up the theory that the blood might have been spread when the body of his wife was being washed (something that Sergeant Mobbs, without explanation, during the first inquest hearing, said would have been impossible in respect of the blood on the cornice), he remained silent at another time when he was told by a police officer that some of the blood hadn't been there when the house was searched previously. Although his silence shouldn't have been held against him, it would appear that it was, so that he was seriously prejudiced by this part of the police evidence.

What about Gardner's whereabouts during the morning of his wife's death? While four witnesses had contradicted his account, Gardner was able to produce five solid and respectable witnesses who corroborated his evidence that he was out cleaning chimneys in the City between four o'clock and eight o'clock that morning. While it's fair to say that Gardner's defence team was unable to shake the evidence of the prosecution witnesses, it's equally the case that the prosecution wasn't able to shake the evidence of the defence witnesses. Assuming that those defence witnesses were truthful, as they appear to have been, one can only conclude that the prosecution witnesses had either estimated the times incorrectly, or confused the day of the week that they recalled seeing Gardner. In this respect, Mr Ribton informed the judge that he had additional witnesses ready to be called who could prove that Gardner was in Aldgate at seven o'clock on the *Saturday* morning, subsequently in Fenchurch Street and outside the King's Head public house, not the Monday morning as the prosecution witnesses had claimed, but the judge said that those witnesses weren't material to the inquiry so they weren't called. In private correspondence to the Home Secretary after the trial, the judge made it clear that he believed the defence witnesses were telling the truth and that Gardner's alibi between four and eight that morning was, indeed, solid. Hence, he wrote that Gardner 'was clearly away from the house from 4 o'clock to 8 o'clock and could not have caused the death [between those times]'. Given that conclusion, it is somewhat surprising that Gardner's barrister told the jury that, in respect of the witnesses who were called to prove that Gardner was working that morning, 'I, myself, do not see the importance of this evidence, and, if the matter rested with myself, I should probably not have called those witnesses, but the prisoner insisted upon my doing so, and I had, of course, no alternative but to comply'. This attitude seems a bit strange because if the jury concluded that the death had occurred at 6am - when Constable Blanchard heard screaming - those very same witnesses would have provided Gardner with an alibi which would have cleared him of the murder.[51]

Ultimately, it seems to have been the case that Gardner's alibi of working in the City was unshakable but, if the murder had occurred between 3.15am and 4am, as the medical 'evidence' suggested, his alibi didn't help him at all. It only helped him if the scream heard by the

---

[51] There is a slightly odd coincidence in that, of the first place Gardner went to that morning, Baker's Coffee House (referred to as Baker's Chop House during the trial), the licensee of that establishment is listed in the 1862 Post Office directory as one Mary Ann *Gardner,* the wife of the recently deceased William Gardner who had run it during the previous decade, while the manager of Reeves' Chop House, the fourth establishment visited, appears to have been one George Reeves, and 'Reeves' was the surname of Gardner's brother-in-law. There is no apparent family connection between Samuel Gardner and those two individuals but it wouldn't be so surprising if there was one as it might explain why Gardner had the contract to sweep their chimneys in the first place. In any case, at the time the prosecution witnesses came forward to say that Gardner had been spotted around the area of Northumberland Avenue that morning, Gardner was in prison so he couldn't have influenced any of the witnesses to give false testimony in response.

constable at 6am was the sound of Mrs Gardner being murdered, or committing suicide, about which there was no certainty.

Under the rules then in place, Samuel Gardner wasn't allowed to give evidence in his own defence and, having called witnesses for the defence, Mr Ribton was obliged to deliver his closing speech before the prosecution's closing speech. His main problem was that he wanted to keep the option open as to whether Mrs Gardner had committed suicide or had been murdered by Elizabeth Humbler. That being so, as he couldn't choose between the two, it might have seemed to the jury that the case for either possibility was weak. In respect of the medical evidence that it was 'improbable' that Mrs Gardner had taken her own life, Ripton said that, 'What are considered improbabilities come to pass every day'. He suggested that Mrs Gardner was 'miserable, wretched and unhappy to the last degree' and that it was probable that she had 'been guilty of the desperate act of self-destruction'. He argued that, 'The fact of the wedding ring, the letters and the likeness of the prisoner being placed on the chair appeared to him to afford a strong corroboration of the suggestion that the deceased committed suicide'. If, however, the jury was against him on this and believed that the case was one of murder, not suicide, then 'it was as probable, if not more probable, that the girl had committed the murder as that it had been committed by the prisoner'. In this regard, his best point was that the murder had obviously been carefully made to look like suicide by the placing of the personal objects on the chair, yet Gardner never made any suggestion of it being a suicide at the time he discovered his wife's death, accusing Humbler of the murder immediately. By contrast, Ribton continued, 'What was the conduct of the girl Humbler? Why directly she saw the dead body, she exclaimed that the deceased had cut her own throat, and it was evident that she was most anxious to make it appear that this was the case'. This was a reference to the fact that Humbler had told Dr Sequeira to come to her house quickly because 'Mrs Gardner has cut her throat'. As to the time of death, Mr Ribton submitted to the jury that, 'there is nothing upon which they could rely to show that four hours had elapsed, and that it is just as probable that only two hours was the period.' He suggested that the evidence was consistent with Humbler having murdered Mrs Gardner at 6am, thus explaining the scream heard by the constable at that time. He said there was no motive for Gardner to murder his wife and no sounds of a quarrel or a struggle had been heard at the time Gardner had been in the house, least of all by Humbler who had been sleeping in the room above. On the other hand, he said that Humbler had a motive because she had been told to leave the house that day. He said that on the night before the murder, 'She went to bed two hours before her usual time, and, according to her own statement, she sat for one whole hour brooding over what had occurred, and, as she said, thinking of the sufferings that the prisoner had occasioned her.'

One of the strongest points in favour of Humbler's innocence was the absence of blood on her hands on the Monday morning and the fact that she couldn't have washed her hands after killing Mrs Gardner because they were found to be so dirty. Mr Ribton, however, attempted to turn this into a point against her, asking, 'How could the extraordinary condition of the girl Humbler's hands, appearing not to have been washed for several days, be accounted for?' He continued, 'There could be very little doubt that she had washed her hands on the Sunday and if she committed the murder and had left the room of the murdered woman with her hands all covered in blood, what was easier than to cover them with ashes and dust which would have had the effect of obliterating all traces of that blood?' Ribton also drew the jury's attention to the fact that the murder weapon wasn't known to any member of the family and that, 'the woman Humbler was the only person who accounted for it by saying that it had been brought there by some stranger on the Sunday before the murder.' He stressed, however, that he wasn't asking the jury to conclude that Humbler *had* committed the murder, only that there was sufficient doubt in the matter to cause them to acquit Gardner.

In concluding what was a three hour speech, Mr Ribton told the jury that the life of Samuel Gardner was in their hands and that, 'they ought not to return a verdict that would have the effect of consigning a fellow creature to an ignominious and dreadful death, except on the most conclusive and irresistible evidence'.

Mr Poland, for the prosecution, told the jury in his own closing speech, that the medical testimony 'entirely disproved the supposition that the death arose from an act of suicide'. In particular, he drew attention to the fact that 'one of the fingers of the deceased was actually cut to the bone, evidently in the act of grasping the blade of the knife to defend herself from the attack that was being made upon her' which, he said, was 'quite conclusive upon this point.' Interestingly, according to the press reports of his speech (which may not be exhaustive), he didn't expressly mention Dr Sequeira's claim that Mrs Gardner couldn't have cut her own throat, which is perhaps not surprising as it appeared to have been admitted that she could have done so with her left hand, albeit that the evidence of Gardner was that she was right handed. As to the possibility of Humbler being the murderer, Mr Poland said that it was 'monstrous to suppose that a young girl nineteen years of age should have lifted the unhappy deceased out of bed and placed her on the floor and committed this dreadful crime'. He said that the only conclusion was that Gardner had murdered his wife and he asked the jury to find accordingly.

Finally the judge summed up the evidence in the case. His first comment was that, 'it was certainly a remarkable circumstance, if it were a case of suicide, that no blood should have spurted about the room and that there should be none on the lower part of the person of the deceased'. This was an unfair comment because no medical evidence was directed to this point and it's difficult to see why the absence of blood around the room, or on the lower part of Mrs Gardner's body, should have been any different in a case of murder as in a case of suicide. The judge was obviously also influenced by the sudden appearance of blood in parts of the house during the days following the murder. Thus, after reminding the jury of the evidence of Sergeant Mobbs 'as to the prisoner having pointed out to him certain marks of blood on the wall, the shutters, and the window blind, which marks he was certain were not there two or three days before, and the prisoner having stated that the girl Humbler had opened the shutter where the bloody mark was on the Monday morning', the judge wondered, 'whether the inference that must naturally be drawn from this conduct was not that the prisoner was attempting to fix the crime of murder upon this girl.' As reported in the newspapers, those were the only two points which the judge felt the need to stress to the jury. He didn't apparently focus on any parts of the evidence which suggested that Gardner was innocent or, if he did, this wasn't reported. A letter writer to the *London Daily News* a few days later would ask rhetorically, 'is it not a fact that, in his charge to the jury, not one circumstance favourable to the prisoner was pointed out to them by the judge?' Baron Pollock concluded his summing up by informing the jury that, 'if positive evidence were required in cases of this description a conviction would rarely or never take place'. He told them that their duty was 'to look calmly and dispassionately at the evidence, and if that evidence left no fair and reasonable doubt upon their minds, and that the whole of it tended to but one result, this was all that was necessary, and no more could be expected'. He did tell them that they owed a duty to the accused but, equally, 'they should not at the same time forget their duty to the public.' It was obvious to everyone that the judge wanted a guilty verdict from his jury.

After deliberating on their verdict for over ninety minutes, the foreman of the jury delivered a verdict of guilty but with a recommendation to mercy on the basis that that Gardner had probably argued with his wife on the subject of Humbler during the Sunday night and 'the act was committed in a fit of anger.' It later transpired that this recommendation was included as a compromise only agreed to by the jury members because one of their number was holding out against a guilty verdict and would only vote for such a verdict if a recommendation to mercy was made, thus saving Gardner's life. Nevertheless, on hearing the jury's verdict that he was guilty of murder, the deputy clerk of the arraigns, asked Gardner if he had anything to say as to why a sentence of death should not be passed on him. In response, Gardner delivered the speech of his life. One, indeed, on which it could be said his very life depended. In a firm, clear voice, he announced: 'I can safely declare upon my word and honour, that I am as innocent of my wife's death as an unborn babe, or of knowing anything about it. Any man who could destroy the life of his wife with his own flesh and blood in his body, hanging is too good for him. I swear before God that I am innocent of this crime – it is not in my instinct to do such a thing. I could not do it for the world.' Addressing the judge directly, Gardner continued, 'There is a greater judge than your Lordship who knows all. I fear him more than any earthly judge, and I thank God I have not got this crime to answer for.' It was impressive stuff and was widely reported in the national newspapers. He had even managed to add a further point in his defence, not apparently mentioned by his Counsel, as to why he was unlikely to have murdered his wife: because it would have meant murdering his unborn child too. It had no effect on the judge. Although he said he would forward the jury's recommendation to mercy to the proper authorities, he made clear that, 'taking into consideration the nature of the crime I do not feel myself justified in holding out any expectation that it would have any effect' and, donning his black cap, he passed a sentence of death upon Samuel Gardner. 'Prisoner at the bar', he said sternly, 'You will be taken from whence you came; a day will be fixed when a scaffold will be erected without the prison walls; you will be led to it and hanged by the neck until you are dead.'

Gardner had one more thing to say in response which was, perhaps, even more powerful than the speech he had already delivered. 'My Lord,' he said, 'I should say that any man who was guilty of such a crime as this ought to have no mercy.' It was a point against himself which one would only expect an innocent man to make. While he might have been a nasty brute of a man who beat his wife and threatened his mistress, he didn't sound like a murderer.

CHAPTER FOUR

Uproar

The date of Gardner's execution was set for 17 November 1862 but the result of the trial had caused uproar throughout the nation. For many observers, the evidence against the prisoner seemed terribly weak, yet he was going to be put to death on the strength, or rather the weakness, of that evidence. With no right of appeal, only public pressure on the Home Secretary could lead to a reversal of the sentence of death. Gardner's legal team and the British public had seventeen days to save him. Although the jury's recommendation of mercy was passed on by the judge to the Home Secretary, Sir George Grey, as he said it would be, he negated it at the same time by informing the Home Secretary that there was no evidence of any kind of quarrel between Gardner and his wife so that the jury members had been speculating about the murder having been committed in a fit of rage, which they weren't entitled to do. He didn't see the irony in the fact that there was no real evidence of Gardner having murdered his wife either, and the jury had been rather speculating about that too. Baron Pollock also held Gardner's own fine words against him, writing to the Home Secretary that he agreed with his sentiment that any man guilty of the crime ought not to have any mercy. Accordingly, Gardner wasn't shown any by the judge.

The Home Secretary, did, however, ask Baron Pollock to provide his written observations about the trial, and the Lord Chief Baron complied with this request on 6 November. He told the Home Secretary plainly that, 'I entirely concurred with the jury in the verdict they returned – I think it would have been a lamentable failure of justice had they returned any other verdict.' He explained that a murder *must* have occurred because one of Mrs Gardner's fingers was cut to the bone which, according to the doctors, she couldn't have done herself in the circumstances. Given that it was definitely a murder, there were only two suspects, and the judge noted that all of the girl's clothes were examined on the Monday but no speck of blood was found on them whereas, 'the sooty marks on the left wrist and elbow and the broad mark on the right thigh pointed to the prisoner'. This wasn't an entirely fair comparison because no blood was found on Gardner's clothes either but it was, nevertheless, reasonable to say that the blood mark on the right thigh did point to a man as the murderer, if Dr Sequeira's evidence was to be trusted, because it was apparently the mark of a large (and therefore male) hand.

How did that mark get there? Could anyone else have touched Mrs Gardner's body? Well Sergeant Mobbs obviously did. We know this because he had informed the Lord Mayor during the committal proceedings that the body was cold when he arrived but he said that he only touched her face and didn't attempt to move any of the limbs. But there might have been others. Dr Sequeira didn't say precisely when he first noticed the blood mark on the thigh but it evidently wasn't on his initial visual examination because he said he noticed it only when he 'minutely examined' the body. When was that? He doesn't appear to have carried out such an examination during the Monday morning because he informed the police during the morning that it was a case of suicide, not murder. He would surely not have done this had he spotted a large (male) bloody palm print on Mrs Gardner's thigh. It is quite possible that Gardner's account that he was twice asked to move the body (once on the Monday, and again on the Tuesday morning) is true so that he could have accidentally got blood on his hand which he placed on the body. We should note that Dr Sequeira said that he had an assistant who initially helped him to move the body and the presence of this (unnamed) assistant was confirmed by the Ward Beadle who said this man was in the bedroom when he arrived at 8.30 on the Monday morning. Gardner didn't mention the presence of this assistant in his later account of moving the body but, even if Gardner's memory was faulty, this means that the assistant, who was never questioned, might have been the person who accidentally put the bloody palm mark on the thigh. The murder scene was far from forensically secure. It doesn't seem to have been beyond the bounds of possibility that the bloody mark was accidentally put onto the body by one of the people in the house after the discovery of Mrs Gardner's death. There certainly appears to have been plenty of blood in the room. Whether it had dried or not by 8am is something that was never quite established. Dr Sequeira spoke of there being 'a pool of blood' under both sides of the throat of the body and this was corroborated by Sergeant Mobbs who spoke of 'a large pool of blood' which had soaked into the carpet. He also said that when you stepped on it, 'it spurted from the carpet into the passage'. Humbler, of course, spoke of stepping in some blood which was wet and damp immediately before she ran to fetch the doctor. Gardner recalled that there was plenty of blood in his wife's hair at the time the body was moved. In any case, it's difficult to see why, if the murderer would have needed to have placed his hand on Mrs Gardner's thigh during the process of cutting her throat, there would have been any blood on his hands at this stage, with the throat yet to be cut. It might have happened if the murderer moved the body after killing her but there's no obvious reason why a bloody hand needed to be placed on the thigh in order to cut the throat. For these reasons, we should be cautious about concluding that the blood on the thigh was placed there by the murderer.

As to the time of death, Pollock referred to the evidence of the doctors that Mrs Gardner must have been dead at least four hours when examined at 8am and told the Home Secretary that, 'I believe this opinion would be confirmed by the highest authority'. This was an odd statement for him to have made. The 'highest authority' at that time, in the world of medical jurisprudence, was Professor Alfred Swaine Taylor who had not given evidence at the trial. How could the judge possibly have known what Professor Taylor would or would not have thought about the time of Mrs Gardner's death? Well, it's by no means impossible that the two men had privately discussed the case because, as it happens, they were both fellows of the Royal Society. For the judge, a time of death of 4am, or earlier, furnished 'conclusive proof that the prisoner and no other was the murderer' thus demonstrating how important the medical opinion as to time of death was in this case.

An equally important consideration in the mind of the judge, which seemed to him to point towards the guilt of Gardner, was that, 'there was strong evidence that someone had made marks of blood on the walls, on a curtain and on a shutter to which marks the prisoner called the attention of the police, obviously in order to prove her [Humbler's] guilt'. He said that, 'if the jury believed the evidence and drew the reasonable conclusion from it – it might well be clear to them that the attempt to fix the crime upon the girl by fabricated and false evidence was strong proof of his own guilt'. It was, of course, always possible that Gardner, certain that Humbler was guilty of the murder, but feeling that she was going to get away with it, planted evidence against her, even though he was innocent of murdering his wife himself. At the same time, however, it wouldn't be an unreasonable conclusion that if Gardner *had* planted evidence against Humbler he was likely to have committed the murder.

The police evidence as to the discovery of the blood marks in the house was inconsistent to say the least (and is discussed further in Appendix A) but, as there was no significant challenge made to the police evidence on this issue by the defence, the essence of the story, that Gardner drew the attention of the police to some blood marks in (at least) the parlour, must be considered to have been true. However, if Gardner had planted all the blood in the house that was seen by the police it would have been very odd behaviour. One could almost understand that he might have planted some blood on the shutter and curtain of the window in the parlour on the basis that Humbler had opened the window in that room on the morning of the murder and he wanted the police to think that she had transferred the blood after having murdered his wife. It wouldn't have been the best plan in the world because Humbler could innocently have transferred blood when opening a window after discovering the body (as to which there was no evidence about what time of the morning the window was opened and only Gardner's word, apparently, that she *did* open the window) but it made no sense whatsoever for Gardner to have planted the splashes of blood in the bedroom because there was no reason to think that those splashes had been made by Humbler in particular and Gardner never even suggested that Humber could have been responsible for them, theorizing that they had occurred when the body was being washed. As to that, Eleanor Buckstone, who was one of three women who washed the body, denied in her evidence at the trial that she could a have caused the splashes but the other two ladies didn't give evidence so it is not known what they would have said about it.

Despite the judge's confidence in the correctness of the verdict, public opinion was widespread that there might well have been a miscarriage of justice in the case. An editorial in the *Star* on the day following the conviction said that, 'Circumstantial evidence, by no means of the most cogent character, has secured another capital conviction', adding that, 'The proofs on which this verdict was based were wholly inferential.' A key factor in the case identified by the newspaper was that, 'the body was so clearly adjusted after death as to suggest the idea that Mrs Gardner had put an end to her own existence' yet Gardner had repudiated this idea while only Humbler of the two suspects had suggested that it was a case of suicide. Something just seemed wrong.

Three days later, the same newspaper published a letter from a correspondent signing as 'Curious' in which a number of questions about the case were asked including, 'How could the jury have found a verdict of guilty upon such evidence as was adduced at the trial?' A second letter to the *Star*, published on 6 November, came from 'A Constant Reader' in Farnham who wrote, 'There are in this case several circumstances which, in my opinion, go far towards clearing the man, and point to the woman Humbler as the guilty person.' The suggestion was that the murder had been committed at 6am, at which time Gardner was proved to have been at work in the City. 'Had I been on the jury', the author of the letter concluded, 'my first exclamation would have been on retiring to consider the verdict, "We have been trying the wrong person; the evidence against the man is feeble and weak, and…points in the clearest possible manner, to the woman Humbler as the guilty person".'

The next day, a very long letter was published in both the *Star* and the *Daily News* from 'J.W.S.' of Elm Court Chambers in the Temple, undoubtedly James Walter Smith, a barrister, who, coming from the same chambers as defence barrister William Ribton, evidently had a detailed knowledge of the case. Rejecting the medical opinion from the trial, and suggesting that the murder occurred at six o'clock, he said, 'From six to eight one would think was time enough for a dead body to become cold, especially on a cold morning, and naked on the floor'. He addressed the point about the supposedly fabricated bloodstains and accepted it would certainly have been a wicked thing for Gardner to have planted those stains but suggested that the police might simply have not searched the premises with sufficient care in the first instance (and had then been unwilling to admit it). This was a theory that had already been expressed in public by the press: the *Star* for example, commenting on 7 November that, 'Policeman are not more infallible than other men, and it is possible that certain marks may have in the first instance escaped the notice of Sergeant Mobbs, diligent as may have been his search – not to suggest the by no means wholly incredible supposition that his first perquisition may not have been quite so complete as he wishes us to suppose.' Ultimately, Mr Smith said that the same evidence in the case could just as easily have convicted Humbler as Gardner and he was critical of a system which didn't allow an accused person to give evidence on their own behalf.

On 8 November, the *Star* said, 'We have received innumerable letters on the subject of this man's conviction for murder. We never remember a case in which the opinion was so general – indeed we may say it is universal – against the carrying into effect the extreme penalty of the law. We believe without exception every one of our correspondents expresses the strongest doubts of Gardner's guilt, and many are confident of his innocence.' It noted that, 'The press, too, appears for once to be unanimous in its dissatisfaction with the verdict.' The following day, Sunday, 9 November, *Reynolds's Newspaper* joined in with a long editorial criticizing the verdict. It said that it wasn't even certain that there had been a murder in this case for, 'The proofs that the poor woman did not commit suicide are far from convincing'. It noted that 'doctors are not infallible' and that, 'medical men of the highest standing in their profession have been proved wrong'. Altogether, it said, 'the conviction of Gardner is most unsatisfactory, and if he should be executed, it is difficult to see how Sir George Grey can escape being a party to judicial murder; for to hang a person who may be possibly not guilty upon insufficient proof, is to be guilty of legalized assassination'. This was strong stuff but, even more radically, the newspaper suggested that, if Gardner was hanged, 'even-handed justice requires that some of the Home Secretary's noble friends should be hanged in his company, or as soon after as may be convenient'. This was almost revolutionary talk.

Gardner presented a petition to the Home Office on 11 November via his solicitors, Lewis & Lewis, who requested a personal interview with the Home Secretary. This was rejected the same day. Sir George Grey said that he had read the judge's notes of the evidence at the trial which had convinced him that 'the guilt of the prisoner was clearly proved'. He agreed with the trial judge that the jury's recommendation to mercy was 'founded only on a possible hypothesis resting on no valid foundation and unsupported by any evidence'. As a result, he didn't see any advantage in agreeing to a personal interview with Gardner's solicitors.

Gardner's petition contained a couple of new pieces of information which hadn't emerged during any of the legal proceedings. Gardner stated in the petition that his wife had frequently told him that she thought that Humbler 'would not mind doing her some mischief' and that she had been 'alarmed' to have heard Humbler going up and down the stairs during the greater part of the night prior to her death. He also stated that Humbler had been jealous of the fact that his wife was pregnant and had frequently said to him that she wished it was her and not Mrs Gardner who was in the family way. The petition, however, had no effect.

On the next day, Samuel's brother, Henry, who lived in Plaistow, presented a petition to the Home Secretary signed by some residents of West Ham, which referred to 'the repeated acts of kindness shown by the convict to his own family, and particularly to his widowed mother whom he supported for many years' which suggested to Henry that 'the convict could not be guilty of so great a crime', and he asked for mercy to be shown. It met with the same response from the Home Secretary. Nothing, it seemed, was going to prevent Gardner's execution which was now less than a week away.

However, there were a number of members of the medical profession who were far from happy with what they had read about the case in their newspapers. Prominent amongst them was Dr Benjamin Ward Richardson, the Senior Physician to the Royal Infirmary for Diseases of the Chest, and author of various papers relating to forensic medicine, who wrote to the Home Secretary on 9 November. Pointing out that the body of Mrs Gardner was not universally cold, because the abdomen was warm, he referred to some experiments and observations of his own (mainly involving animals in a slaughter house) and said that, 'where the blood is let out of the body and death occurs from the loss of blood there is the most rapid cooling'. He concluded that, 'dying as she (Mrs Gardner) did solely from loss of blood is quite conclusive evidence that she died within two hours'. Mrs Gardner had not, however, died from loss of blood but from suffocation. This was a mistake that also was being made in some of the newspapers. The *Morning Post*, for example, claiming that 'Mrs Gardner bled to death', said that 'every physician and surgeon knows, or ought to know, that under such circumstances the body loses its warmth with much greater rapidity than in cases of death from natural causes'. It was an unfortunate error by Dr Richardson but, nevertheless, being a respected medical practitioner, his opinion on the matter could not simply be discarded.

The very next day, on 10 November, Thomas Herbert Barker, a Doctor in Medicine of the University of London and a fellow of the Royal College of Surgeons, wrote a memorial to the Home Secretary in which he stated that, having carefully considered the evidence regarding the condition of the body of the deceased, and the length of time which would be required for it to become cold after death, he saw 'nothing incompatible with the supposition that death may have taken place at a later period than stated in the evidence.' He explained that a number of factors could affect the time of cooling of the body, namely the manner in which the death had been caused, the mode of clothing, the position of the body with reference to the currents of cold air and the temperature in the room. Having taken into account all the circumstances, he said that he could come to no other conclusion than that 'death might have been caused considerably later than was supposed by the medical witnesses.' He asked that, 'in a case surrounded with so much doubt' the sentence of death passed on Gardner be commuted.

The third medical man to write to the Home Office with objections was Dr Edward Ballard who was no lightweight, being the medical officer of Islington and author of a number of papers on medical matters. In his letter, he criticised Dr Sequeira for not using more 'scientific and conclusive' means of judging how long the body had been dead, expressing the view that he was guilty of 'unpardonable neglect'. He concluded that the length of time since she had been killed of three or four hours wasn't conclusively or scientifically proved during the trial. While agreeing that it wasn't a case of suicide, he didn't think the rest of the evidence against Gardner was sufficient to prove he had murdered his wife. He considered it was neglectful for the bloody mark on Mrs Gardner's thigh not to have been examined under a microscope to discover whether sooty particles could be found amongst the blood. Bearing in mind that the sooty marks on the body were also attributed to Gardner, this was a good point. The sooty marks, themselves, he believed, could have been caused by Gardner sleeping with his wife. He thought that the bloody marks might well have been caused by Sequeira himself after 'manipulating the wound'. Had Gardner planted the other bloody marks around the house, Ballard considered that 'it was quite consistent with his own innocence that he should be capable of manufacturing false evidence to aid in fixing the guilt upon the party whom he truly believed to be the criminal'. Ballard also suggested that, 'if Gardner had placed the letters on the chair they would have retained marks of his bloody or of his sooty hands' and the absence of such marks tended towards his innocence. Finally he argued that Gardner wouldn't have repudiated suicide in favour of murder if he had gone to the trouble of making it look like suicide.

The correspondence from Richardson and Ballard was forwarded to the Lord Chief Baron for his urgent comments. Pollock was dismissive. He felt that Richardson's mistake as to the cause of death – that it was due to loss of blood instead of suffocation – undermined his claim that Mrs Gardner could have died within two hours of her discovery. As for Ballard's criticisms of the medical examination, the judge defended Sequeira on the basis that he was called into a case of what he thought was suicide and, thus, did not obtain as much conclusive and scientific evidence as he might have done. That, however, wasn't much of a justification in a capital case. The judge didn't think there was any warrant for the notion that Sequeira could have had blood on his hands when he touched the body due to the 'manipulation' of the wound not having occurred until the post-mortem examination (and here the judge seems to have assumed that the bloody mark was seen before, not during, the post-mortem examination). Nor was he impressed by the idea that Gardner could have planted the bloody marks around the house yet still be innocent. He pointed out to the Home Secretary that, 'In administering justice, falsehood and deceit have always been considered as evidence of guilt'. The idea that the sooty marks could have got onto Mrs Gardner's body during the night was, said the judge, a matter for the jury and not for a medical expert to opine on. According to the judge, the fact that there was no blood on the bed or on Mrs Gardner's clothes, or on her body anywhere below the collar bone, meant that the wound to the neck must have been inflicted while she was lying in the position in which she was found, which in turn meant that her murderer must have forced her to floor, something which, he felt, pointed rather more towards her physically strong husband than the nineteen-year-old servant girl.

The weakest response by the judge to Ballard's letter was in respect of Ballard's claim that, if Gardner had been guilty of the crime, he wouldn't have repudiated suicide in favour of murder. To this, Baron Pollock said that Gardner, 'did not repudiate suicide – for after 10 o'clock he spoke to Meagher about it and even now in his position, he does not give up suicide'. This rather missed that point that Gardner's *initial reaction* to his wife's death was to accuse Humbler of murdering her, the very opposite of what would have been expected if he had taken the trouble to make it look like a suicide. By 10am, when Gardner spoke to Constable Meagher, Dr Sequeira had announced that it was a case of suicide, not murder, which Gardner was entitled to rely on. In any case, what Constable Meagher testified that Gardner told him at 10am was that he did *not* think his wife would have been guilty of committing suicide because they were on good terms. He also mentioned that whenever his wife read an account of suicide in a newspaper she said that anyone who did so couldn't be in a proper state of mind. In other words, if anything, he was suggesting that suicide was unlikely. And this was a full two hours after the discovery of the death when he had already spoken to the investigating officers in the case, and to the doctor. As for the judge holding it against Gardner that his defence at trial was that Mrs Gardner either committed suicide or was murdered by Humbler, it is somewhat absurd for the judge to suggest that Gardner should not have run such a defence – and that he incriminated himself in doing so – when Gardner's position was that he couldn't possibly have known whether it was suicide or murder.

Meanwhile the pressure on the Home Secretary was building. On 13 November, William Ribton wrote to him to set out his reasons why he thought the trial had been unfair due to Humbler having been acquitted at the direction of the judge, despite both a coroner's jury and the grand jury having decided that Humber and Gardner should be tried together for the crime. While the judge did have some good reasons for acquitting Humbler – he pointed out that, had she not been acquitted, she wouldn't have been able to be cross-examined – Ribton made the reasonable point that he hadn't had sufficient time to prepare for her cross-examination bearing in mind that she gave her evidence on the very same day that she was formally acquitted of the murder. Not surprisingly, Mr Ribton also claimed that the murder must have occurred at 6am and that the medical evidence relating to the estimated time of death was inadequate.

The *Star* also kept the pressure on the authorities with another editorial on the subject, on 13 November, which stated that Gardner was tried and found guilty 'upon what evidence, however, it is difficult to discern'. It noted that, 'No one saw Gardner commit the murder – no one seems to have imagined it probable that he would do violence to his wife – there was no object in perpetrating the crime – his whole conduct before and after it was much more consistent with his innocence rather than his guilt'. The finger of the newspaper was pointed very firmly at Humbler, and the *Star* called for the establishment of a Criminal Court of Appeal for cases such as this.

Other newspapers had been commenting on the case. The *Morning Post* said that the circumstantial evidence against Gardner was 'of the weakest kind' and that 'the verdict of the trial was not satisfactory'. The London *Evening Standard* offered the view that Gardner was convicted on 'slight evidence', with there being 'nothing to justify carrying out the sentence'. The *Daily News*, noting that 'the doctors examined were not positive as to how long Mrs. Gardner had been dead' thought that the facts 'tended strongly in Gardner's favour' and believed that the evidence against him was 'difficult to discern'. The *Morning Herald* felt that, 'there is an almost total absence of anything beyond suspicion to imply that he (Gardner) is the murderer' while the *Daily Telegraph*, although admitting that Gardner was 'a low ill-conditioned reprobate at best', and being of the view that the balance of probabilities did somewhat incline towards him being guilty, nevertheless felt that the evidence against him wasn't sufficient to convict and that, 'It is quite possible that Humbler committed the murder'. The *Sun* said that, 'Sir George Grey would do well, we feel persuaded, while there is yet time, to issue orders for a reprieve being despatched to Newgate.' The *Shoreditch Observer*, which didn't normally comment on such matters, expressed the view, similar to *Reynolds*, that, 'the sentence, if carried into execution, will be nothing less than a judicial murder, and a crime upon the country', and stated that, 'The duty of the public, therefore, is clear', exhorting its readers to exert their influence on the Crown to 'speedily restore the condemned to the liberty to which an innocent man is entitled.'

In one of its long editorials, the *Star* thundered that, 'If Samuel Gardner is hanged, it will be upon the faith of the speculative opinion of two medical witnesses'. It certainly didn't rate those witnesses very highly, saying of Dr Sequeira that he was not, 'as far as we are aware, a gentleman whose scientific repute is so high as to compel us to bow in deference to his dictum…but it is obvious that he has no lack of confidence in his own judgment.' As for that judgment regarding the time of death, the newspaper stated that, 'the circumstances in the case were by no means ordinary. It was a cool morning, the thermometer being 59 deg. in the shade at eight o'clock, the body was lying all but naked on the floor, and the wound in the throat which caused death had necessarily drained away a considerable portion of that vital fluid upon which the maintenance the warmth of the body depends.' As a result, it asked, 'Does it not seem possible, not to say probable, that under such conditions two hours might have sufficed to bring it to a state which Mr. Sequeira describes?' If Mrs Gardner had been dead for less than four hours, the newspaper argued, then 'Gardner was guiltless'. The editorial concluded by saying, 'To hang a man merely because two medical practitioners unknown to fame see fit to dogmatise on a point which the most scientific writers have not presumed to grapple with, is a monstrosity not to be endured these days, when the quirks of chemists and physicians send so many victims to the gallows.'

Newspaper opinion wasn't, however, unanimously in favour of Gardner. The editor of the *Illustrated Times* thought that, 'it is difficult to find in the evidence any defect upon which the hypothesis of the convict's innocence can be supported.' Nevertheless, he said that it was 'unpleasant to hang any man who protests his innocence of which there may be the slightest chance' and admitted that the fact Gardner had accused Humbler of killing his wife, despite the murderer having carefully made the crime look like suicide, was 'a strong fact in Gardner's favour'. More adverse to Gardner, the editor of the *Cambridge Chronicle* was convinced of his guilt. In an opinion piece, he commented sarcastically that the *Star* thought it would be a pity to kill 'so useful a member of society'. He also said that, 'a sweep, by name Samuel Gardner, has a wife and concubine; and wishing to rid himself of one, he cuts his wife's throat; attempts to cast blame on his paramour, and finally places the body of the murdered woman in such a position as, he thinks, will lead to the supposition that she committed suicide'. This person didn't seem to notice the contradiction between Gardner casting blame on Humbler while, at the same time, placing the body to make it look like suicide. Nor did he consider a point made by the editor of the *Morning Post* that, with Gardner's marriage being bigamous, due to his wife already being married to his brother, he would have had no problem obtaining a decree of nullity or could equally just have walked out on her without any legal consequence. The editor of the *Cambridge Chronicle* continued, saying that, 'This man's trial lasted two days; upon the clearest evidence he was convicted and sentenced to death.' Such views were, however, very much in the minority.

While most newspaper editors clearly thought that suicide or a murder by Humbler was at least as likely the solution to the mystery, if not far more so, than a murder by Gardner, the editor of the *Evening Standard* appears to have been alone in thinking that an unknown intruder might have been responsible, saying that, 'there is certainly no proof that some third party – through motives nobody can comprehend – may not have been concerned in it as the sole murderer, or at all events as one of the murderers'. While one can't entirely rule out either Humbler or Gardner having had an accomplice, although it seems unlikely, it was all but certain that if a murder did occur in the house that morning one of the two of them must have been responsible. The front door was locked after Gardner left and there was no sign of a break-in or forced entry. The murderer must have had intimate knowledge of the household in order to locate both the portrait of Gardner and the hateful valentines, the latter of which were, according to Gardner, locked in a drawer for which only he had the key – a key which was in one of his trouser pockets (presumably one that he wasn't wearing on the day but to which Humbler had access). For an intruder to have known that the valentines even existed would have shown a high degree of inside knowledge but for that intruder to also know that it would make sense to have them carefully arranged on a chair with Mrs Gardner's precious possessions to indicate a suicide suggests a level of knowledge that surely no one who wasn't living in the house could have possessed. In reality, if a murder had been committed, as the medical witnesses said must have been the case, it could only have been by either Humbler or Gardner.

On 14 November, Sir George Grey held a lengthy meeting with the Lord Chief Baron about Gardner's case. On the same day, a hairdresser called James Broad wrote to the Home Secretary to inform him that he had been one of the 'jurymen in waiting' who had heard the entirety of the evidence at the trial of Gardner and didn't agree with the verdict. Noting that the strongest part of the evidence against Gardner related to the length of time it would take for the extremities to become cold, he commented, 'It appeared to me that depends in a great measure upon the state and condition of the person killed. A stout fleshy person would retain warmth much longer than a spare, thin person as Mrs Gardner was proved to be. In the absence of any medical prudence upon that point I think it worthy of consideration.' For a layman, it was a surprisingly bold point on a medical matter outside of his expertise but one that was well made. He added that there was 'great public doubt' about the verdict and he said that he firmly believed that, if Gardner had been tried by himself and the other jurymen in waiting, he would not have been convicted. On the same day, Lewis & Lewis wrote again to the Home Secretary enclosing a letter from the jury member who had insisted on the jury recommending Gardner to mercy before he would agree to a guilty verdict. He was a fishmonger called Raphael Benjamin who said that he had 'a doubt at the time to the presence of guilt' but nevertheless agreed to the majority verdict on the basis that Gardner would not be executed due to the jury's recommendation. The solicitors also enclosed two other letters, one being from a Dr John Henry Dook of Berkshire who claimed that Mrs Gardner had frequently visited him and had threatened to commit suicide on a number of occasions (something that is impossible now to verify[52]) as well as one from a surgeon from Plymouth, William Pearse, who stated that, in his experience, a body could be cold at the extremities within two hours of death.

---

[52] There is, however, no Dr Dook in the *Medical Directory* for 1862 so it's entirely possible that the letter was a hoax.

During the morning of Saturday, 15 November, Gardner was visited in his cell by the chaplain of Newgate Prison at the same time as the stones were being brought in to fix the outer barriers for the gallows on which he was to be hung. The Reverend Davis asked him if he was afraid to die and Gardner calmly replied that he wasn't and, indeed, was prepared and ready for the end. He had maintained this stance since the verdict was announced and the newspapers had reported that he was showing 'extraordinary fortitude' while waiting for his death, enhancing his popularity amongst ordinary people. At shortly after noon, the chaplain returned with the prison governor, Mr Jonas, holding a piece of paper, and read out words to the following effect: 'The prisoner Gardner, now lying under sentence of death, is hereby informed that the sentence passed upon him will be carried into execution on the date before mentioned, and we have to express our regret that the jury recommended him to mercy.' Gardner bravely told the governor that if he had been the Secretary of State he would have written exactly the same thing because, as he had told the judge, if he was guilty, he couldn't rightfully be recommended to mercy. During the weekend, Gardner had a final visit from his children and friends during which he said goodbye to them and prepared to die.

In the meantime, the Home Secretary wasn't impressed by the letter from Mr Benjamin which had been forwarded to him by Lewis & Lewis. He said in a reply letter to Gardner's solicitors dated 15 November that he was unable to attach any weight to the declaration of a jury member who had disregarded his oath to find a true verdict by concurring in a guilty verdict despite holding doubts as to that guilt. Nevertheless, with two days to go before the scheduled execution, he informed Lewis & Lewis that he had recently received 'several communications from medical gentlemen' which appeared to him to have 'a material bearing on the very important point of the evidence of the time during which the murdered woman had been dead before the discovery of the murder at 8am.' Having had several personal interviews with the Lord Chief Baron, the Home Secretary now said that he had 'arrived at the conclusion that on this very material point there is not that absolute certainty which is desirable and that it is possible that the medical opinion submitted to the jury may have been in some degree erroneous.' The press confirmed that the material point in question concerned, 'the evidence as to the time which elapsed between commission and discovery of the murder.' Although, according to one newspaper report, 'Judge Pollock was all for hanging', the pressure from all sides on the Home Secretary had clearly forced him to relent. Consequently, the execution of Gardner was cancelled. The governor of Newgate prison was informed at about midday on Saturday, 15 November, that the penalty was to be respited.

According to Gardner, writing much later, he wasn't immediately informed of the Home Secretary's decision or, indeed, told anything. Without access to newspapers or to his legal advisers, all he knew on Monday, 17 November, was that his execution did not take place. He was moved from his cell for condemned prisoners to an ordinary cell but it wasn't until Sunday, 30 November, that he was given any information as to why he was still alive or what was going to happen to him. He said that the chaplain and the governor approached him on that day, with the chaplain holding a folded piece of paper in his hand. The chaplain said: 'Gardner, I have just received the paper from the Secretary of State; I need not open it to read it to you. I can tell you its contents. The Secretary of State has looked very carefully into your case, and finding several parts which leave him in doubt, he has been kind enough to give it in your favour, and your future prospects will be that you be kept in penal servitude for the remainder of your life.' Gardner's response was that this was cruel treatment but the chaplain told him that both he and the governor considered him to be guilty. According to Gardner, the chaplain, who had made enquiries as to his moral character, accused him of the 'vile crime of dishonour of my wife' and 'the moral ruin of one Catherine Smith'. It isn't known who Catherine Smith was but Gardner said it was a 'base and untrue allegation'.

The immediate public response to Gardner's reprieve was that it seemed to lack logic for there to be sufficient doubt for the execution to be abandoned yet for him to still be kept in prison for the rest of his life. As an editorial in *Reynolds's Newspaper* of Sunday, 23 November, stated: 'Sir George Grey is now placed in this unpleasant dilemma. His reprieve of Gardner is tantamount to admitting that a doubt exists as to his having committed the murder of which he was found guilty. Unless the doubt is satisfactorily and completely dispelled, and his criminality placed beyond the regions of uncertainty, the man must be pardoned and released.' A reader's letter published in the *Weekly Dispatch* on the same day made the same point, saying that, 'It will be too sorry a confession of the law's inefficiency and the incompetency of those who administer it, up to those who finally review its sentences, that another convict should be half punished because a crime is half proved.' Even the legal journal, *The Law Times*, was of the same mind, saying in its 22 November 1862 edition that, Gardner 'is either wholly guilty, or wholly innocent; he ought to be hung or he ought to be set free.' This type of argument received short shrift from Baron Pollock who, in an angry letter to the Home Secretary, wrote that, 'Some of the newspapers say – The man must be guilty or innocent – if guilty he ought to be hanged – if innocent to be pardoned and set at liberty – this is specious but shallow and false.' He explained that, 'If a prisoner has been found guilty on satisfactory evidence – but some fact or some scientific opinion appears <u>after the verdict</u> which throws some doubt on the conviction – it may be very right not to execute the criminal – but before he be pardoned and set at liberty his innocence ought clearly to appear.' While this might have been how things were viewed by the judiciary at the time, it would be very different today when, at the very least, Gardner should have had a retrial due the admitted unsatisfactory nature of the medical evidence against him. Baron Pollock continued his letter by stating that, while some people had doubts about the verdict, 'when studied and examined for the purpose of doing public justice all doubt disappears'. However, he continued, 'the certainty cannot be made apparent except by those who will take the trouble to become accurately acquainted with the facts – and will reason accurately from them.' It was an attitude which basically said that the critics of the decision were either not sufficiently acquainted with the facts of the case or not clever enough to draw the appropriate conclusions from them.

The Law Times, however, didn't agree with the judge, saying that, 'The evidence against Gardner did not justify the conviction', and it claimed that this was a universal belief amongst the profession and that, 'On this we have heard no difference of opinion from any lawyer'. The journal's editor stated that, while Gardner *may* have done it, 'there was no *sufficient* proof either that the woman was murdered at all, or that, if she died by the hand of another the wound was inflicted by him.'

With Gardner's life having been saved, there wasn't much further public appetite for a campaign to have him released from prison or for a retrial, albeit that calls remained for the establishment of a criminal court of appeal. Most people forgot about the Gardner case and got on with their lives. Not for one of his sisters, though, who became mentally deranged and, 'caring neither for her children or husband and coming lately dangerous and violent' was removed to the Shoreditch Union. Her family blamed her sudden change of personality on the 'agonizing mental sufferings' caused by her brother's death sentence.

Elizabeth Humbler, on the other hand, was doing rather better. If she did murder Elizabeth Gardner she showed enormous nerve by commencing legal proceedings in the City of London Sheriffs' Court during December 1862 to recover her possessions from Gardner's house, including, apparently, the very bed Elizabeth Gardner had died beside. After Gardner had been sentenced to death, his possessions had been put up for sale. One of the offspring of Gardner's first wife (from her marriage to Thomas Dewis), purchased about thirty pounds worth of items from his house. Humbler went to court claiming that some of the goods acquired by Dewis belonged to her, including a bed, bolster, pillow, washstand, two-flounced silk dress, plates, a dish and a mug. She said that she had earned them all by shoe-binding, and Sergeant Mobbs supported her. Dewis said in his evidence that he gave Gardner thirty pounds for his possessions, 'because I respected the man, and I believe he was innocent'. In finding for Humbler, with costs, the judge said, 'It is somewhat curious to find defendant expressing respect for a man who has been indicted for murder.' The judiciary obviously couldn't compute that there might have been a miscarriage of justice.

CHAPTER FIVE

Experiments

The unsatisfactory outcome of the Gardner case had an immediate impact upon the medical profession. There was a realisation from the testimony in the trial of a huge gap in the scientific knowledge of how long it took for a dead body to become cold. The *Lancet* of 6 December 1862 stated that the estimate that the body of Mrs Gardner had been dead for four hours was, 'little more than a guess, as there is no exact data on which to found such an opinion.' It continued:

> In the first place all we know is that the cooling of a body depends on the circumstances under which it is placed. The limbs of a corpse may become cold in a few hours, or not for a couple of days, according to the temperature to which they are exposed. Secondly, the extremities in certain cases may become cold even before death. We know that even in diseases such as cholera, or in death from poisoning by hydrocyanic acid when given in small doses not only the extremities but even the trunk of the body feels cold almost as soon as life is extinct. Thirdly and lastly, we know that in death from haemorrhage the cooling of the body is greatly accelerated. If we turn now to the case under consideration, we shall find that there are many circumstances connected with it which lead to the conclusion that two hours would have been ample time to allow of its becoming cooled down to the state described by the surgeon. 1st we have death by haemorrhage, 2nd the corpse is but slightly

covered, 3rd, it is found lying on the cold floor near to a door under which no doubt a tolerably strong current of air entered; and 4th all this occurs not only in early morning, but during a cold season of the year.

The notion of a 'death from haemorrhage' in the Gardner case would have irritated Baron Pollock when it was, of course, a death by suffocation, but the *Lancet's* other points were sound. The article concluded by wondering why no expert in the subject had been consulted in the matter, saying that, 'if the medical evidence was, as one of the daily papers stated, "the back-bone of the case", the surgeon ought to have consulted some medical jurist before imperilling the life of a human being, on the imperfect data he had at his disposal.'

The first such jurist to attempt to fill the gap in the knowledge of body cooling was Dr Benjamin Ward Richardson, one of the medical men who had written to the Home Secretary about the case. He wrote a paper entitled, 'On Cooling of the Body After Death' which was published in *The Medical Critic and Psychological Journal* in January 1863. He noted in the introduction that he had been asked to write the paper due to the importance of the trial of Samuel Gardner in which, 'His fate turned exclusively on the vague question whether a dead body could become cold on the external surfaces of the head, chest, and upper and lower limbs, within three or from that to four hours' yet, as Richardson pointed out, the question of the cooling of the body was 'one on which but little has been said'.

Richardson hadn't had time to perform any experiments (other than on sheep) so most of what he said was anecdotal. He gave an example from his own experience of a thin, pale anaemic girl who had died of effusion of blood into the lungs while working in a laundry. He said he arrived at the laundry within half an hour of her death, at which time, 'She was cold universally, and white as the sheet on which she lay'. He noted that, while he was present, rigidity commenced in the limbs. 'Had the fact not been indisputable that this girl was working at the iron within the hour', he said, 'I should, at that time, have guessed that she had been dead three or even four hours.' Another example from his experience, germane to the Gardner case, was one in which he was on the spot within an hour and a half of the death of a woman in her eighth month of pregnancy who had died suddenly but he found the deceased woman was 'as marble, and the fingers were rigid; her body universally cold'. A third example was given of a man who had died from rupture of an aneurism in his water-closet and, although he had certainly been dead less than an hour (because his family had seen him healthy at the breakfast table before he entered the water-closet) his body was, nevertheless, 'cold, and partly rigid'. He made the point that no two bodies are alike so that, 'the rate of cooling of any dead body is subject to great variations', and that, for example, 'Persons who are naturally very thin, cool after death with great rapidity, whatever may be the form of death'. Mrs Gardner had been a very thin woman.

Richardson also made the point that his patients were frequently cold on the surface of the body while they were alive which he thought would confuse anyone attempting to assess time of death after such people had died. Thus, for example, 'I have seen patients with phthisis [i.e. tuberculosis] pass before me in the heat of summer, and as pulse after pulse was taken, I have felt the antecedent coldness of death in the most chilly hand', but, 'have known no difference between the temperature of the external surface of the body before and after the fatal event'. From experiments with sheep and observations of humans, he said he had come to the conclusion in respect of the human subject that, 'for the first two hours the body covered with bedclothes would retain its warmth in parts such as the abdomen and flexures of the limbs, but that beyond that time the loss of external temperature is so decided and universal as to render any opinion mere vague conjecture altogether inadequate in the way of evidence.' He had noticed, however, that 'the question of the last meal makes a difference in the cooling process'. If someone hasn't eaten, 'the cooling is much quicker than during the assimilation of a hearty meal'.

Controversially, Richardson claimed that in cases of massive blood loss, such as haemorrhage, 'where the blood is suddenly removed from the circulating channels, the decrease of temperature is immediate.' As a result, he said, 'In cases of sudden death from effusion of blood, where even the blood is not lost from the body, the cooling process may be perfected so quickly that the suspicion of death having taken place some hours might occur to one who is not familiar with the facts.' Conversely, he also warned that he had experience of cases where the body temperature increased after death so that a body still warm many hours after death did not necessarily mean that death had occurred recently.

Perhaps most important of all, Richardson gave a warning to the medical profession about assessing body temperature with the hand. Thus, he said, 'In taking observations for medico-legal purposes, in any suspected case, the mere test of the hand is altogether unreliable: for as the terms heat and cold are relative only, and as between the hands of different observers the greatest difference may prevail, – that which to one hand would signify warmth, to another would signify cold.' He stated unequivocally that, 'If any observation in respect to temperature be made…it should be carried out with the thermometer, the points at which the temperature is taken being the flexures of the joints, the mouth or the nostril.' He also cautioned that the temperature of the surrounding air should be taken and a comparison instituted between the body and the air.

The message that Richardson wanted to send to his colleagues was very clear. Although he believed he had looked into the matter, 'as carefully as any other physician or physiologist of my day', he would 'sooner cut off my own right hand than send any human being to the scaffold on a dogmatic statement based upon the hypothesis that the period of death can be determined by the temperature of the dead'. His two targets here were not difficult to spot: Dr Henry Sequeira and Dr John Comley. Richardson expressed the hope that, 'never again will the life of a human being be allowed to rest on the question of the time required for the body of a dead person to become what is called "*cold*"' and that it would be 'impossible that any man will ever again be tossed over to the executioner on the speculation that a body must have been dead *so long* because it was *so cold*.' He described the Gardner case as, 'a blot on our national character for knowledge, and on our humanity, that such a hazard has ever been played.' It was a scathing attack on the medical profession: one which other senior members of that profession could not allow to go unchallenged.

Professor Alfred Swaine Taylor was particularly concerned about the effects of the Gardner case on public confidence in medico-legal matters. He would have noticed that the question had been raised by Gardner's barrister that no assistance to medical practitioners on the subject of time of death was provided in his own standard textbook. It was something he wanted to rectify as soon as possible. As there hadn't been any accurate scientific experiments on the subject, Professor Taylor, along with a colleague from Guy's Hospital, Dr Samuel Wilks, conducted tests on one hundred corpses of patients who had died at the hospital between January and May 1863 in order to record the body temperatures of those corpses after death, noting various factors, including age at time of death, cause of death, the temperature of the air and, crucially, the temperature of the body at one or more intervals after death. As the aim was to assess the temperature at the surface of the body, a naked bulb of a thermometer was placed on the skin of the abdomen, a location chosen because it retained heat longer than the limbs.

There were some problems with the tests, though. The corpses were all those which had been taken from the hospital wards to the morgue (then known as the 'dead house'), some considerable time after death. If a patient had died late in the evening, the body would lie in the ward all night, for ten or twelve hours. If death occurred during the day, the body would still lie in the ward for somewhere between two and four hours before being taken to the morgue. Even worse, the first temperature readings were never taken less than an hour after the body was brought to the morgue but in most cases, two, three or even four hours afterwards, which could, therefore, be six, seven or eight hours after death if that death had occurred during the day or up to sixteen hours if it had occurred during the night. The temperature at time of death, either internally or on the surface of the body, wasn't taken, so could only be *assumed* to have been about 98 degrees even though there is natural variation in the temperature of living human beings around that temperature; and the temperature of the surface of the skin (save for the region of the armpit) can be expected to be a few degrees lower than the internal, or core, temperature. Indeed, in 1885, Frederick Womack, a lecturer in chemical physics at St Bartholomew's Hospital, revealed in a paper read to the hospital's Abernethian Society that his experiments had shown that the average surface temperature of living persons at the abdomen was 93.1 degrees.

The results of Taylor and Wilks' experiment were published in *Guy's Hospital Reports* for October 1863, in a paper entitled 'On the Cooling of the Human Body After Death'. Their summary table showed that two or three hours after the bodies had been received in the morgue, seventy-six observations had been carried out showing an average temperature for that period of 77 degrees Fahrenheit. From four to six hours after receipt, the average temperature was 74 degrees Fahrenheit, then 70 degrees in the period of six to eight hours following receipt of the body and, finally, 69 degrees in the fourth period of twelve hours after receipt. According to the authors, writing their conclusions below the summary table, 'As the above periods date from the time at which the bodies were received at the dead house, it is obvious that the temperatures above given are under rather than over stated.' They explained that, 'in order to determine how long a period had elapsed since death, the time which the body remained in the ward must be added to the time at which the observations were made'. There was an obvious problem here, though, which Taylor and Wilks themselves noted by saying, 'As the time [in which the body remained in the ward] varied greatly we have found it impossible to include it in the calculations above given'. Nevertheless, they went on: 'but the facts show that a dead body cools slowly and progressively, and that, as a rule, the abdomen retains considerable warmth for upwards of twelve hours after death'.

That conclusion seems suspiciously like an attempt to justify the opinion of the doctors in the Gardner case that a body should not be found cold after just two hours, albeit that, in the Gardner case, the abdomen was found to still be warm, so that no conclusion as to time of death could possibly be drawn from that. According to Taylor and Wilks, however, it was only 'the lower part of the abdomen' in which any warmth was found about the body in the Gardner case. This was a serious mistake, albeit one made by a number of newspapers reporting and commenting on the case. Dr Sequeira had, in fact, testified at the Old Bailey that the part of the body that was warm was 'the lower part of the trunk' whereas, by contrast, 'the upper part, the shoulders, was quite cold'. He never said anything about the lower part of the abdomen. This is confirmed beyond any doubt by Judge Baron Pollock's notes of the trial evidence which record Sequeira as saying, 'I had my hand on the thigh – it was quite cold – part of body warm – lower part of trunk. Shoulders quite cold.' The reporter for the *Daily Telegraph* reflected this correctly in his report of the proceedings, quoting Sequeira as saying, 'The lower part of the trunk was warm'. For the avoidance of any doubt as to what this means, according to a nineteenth century work on medical jurisprudence, 'The lower part of the trunk is divided into the Abdomen (vulgarly termed belly) and the Pelvis.'[53] It was the *Times* reporter who caused the confusion because his report of the trial evidence, which was syndicated to a number of other newspapers, had stated that, 'the lower part of the abdomen was warm'. This was the error which evidently confused Taylor and Wilks and meant that they proceeded on an entirely false basis, thinking that at least part of the area of Mrs Gardner's abdomen was cold. If that was the reason they chose the abdomen to take the temperature of the bodies in their experiment, it was a critical failure of their methodology, to the extent that they wanted to use their findings to justify the time-of-death estimate of the medical witnesses in the Gardner case which, as we will see, they did.

The main failure of the experiment performed by Taylor and Wilks, however, was that it wasn't possible from their data to say whether a body could be cold (or, more to the point, *feel* cold) within one to three hours after death, which the medical witnesses in the Gardner case had said wasn't possible. Taylor and Wilks didn't take the temperatures of *any* bodies within that period so that they couldn't draw any conclusions about how rapidly bodies cooled within the first hour or two but even that wouldn't have resolved the issue because they also didn't define what temperature would be considered to be cold to the human hand. In this respect, however, they did caution that temperatures were best taken with a thermometer. Thus, they said:

> It is customary to judge the degree of coldness by the sense of touch; but it must be remembered that the dead human skin is a good conductor of heat, and thus the surface may appear icy cold to a moderately warm hand. The condition of the hand itself may lead to an erroneous impression. If the two hands are of different temperatures, a recently dead body may appear cold to one and warm to the other. Another fact should also be borne in mind, that in the chest and abdomen the viscera may retain a well-marked warmth when the surface of the skin is actually cool or cold.

Perhaps for this reason there was no indication in the paper of whether the dead bodies used in their experiment felt cold or warm to the touch

---

[53] *A Practical Treatise on Medical Jurisprudence* by Joseph Chitty (1834), p.35.

except, oddly, in a single case where, fifteen hours after the body had been brought into the morgue, the room temperature of which was 38 degrees Fahrenheit, the body temperature at the abdomen of one of the corpses showed a reading of 64 degrees Fahrenheit (and then two hours later a thermometer was placed *inside the body* - which one would expect to be warmer - to produce a reading of 76 degrees Fahrenheit). In the column for the final observation, which was presumably at least seventeen hours after the body had been brought into the ward, the authors noted that, 'Body felt warm outside and inside. Extremities rigid.'

Writing more than ten years later, in another context, Professor Taylor referred to another one of the cases in which the body temperature had actually risen after death from 72 degrees after two hours in the morgue to 75 degrees after four hours although the room temperature of the morgue remained at a steady 42 degrees throughout, and the body, like all the corpses in the morgue, was only covered with a single sheet or shirt. Of this corpse, Taylor wrote, 'It was sensibly warm to the hand'. At the same time, he referred to five other cases, saying that their temperatures ranged from between 70 and 84 degrees within two to four hours 'after death'. In doing so, he had rather confused himself writing all these years later because none of the temperatures in his study were taken within two to four hours after death, rather two to four hours *after the bodies had been brought into the morgue*, but the important point here is that he said: 'It will be seen that, in these cases, the skin maintained a temperature which would be very sensibly warm to the hand'. This hadn't, however, been claimed to be the case in the 1863 paper, and Taylor seems to have forgotten the caveat in that paper which had noted that 'a recently dead body may appear cold to one [hand] and warm to the other'. As it is known that some living bodies can feel cold to the touch, and that a person with a core temperature – taken in one of the cavities or under the armpit – of 95 degrees will probably be suffering from hypothermia, it seems likely that a surface temperature in the eighties must be *capable* of feeling cold even if it is, objectively and relatively speaking, a high temperature. Taylor and Wilks advised in their paper that, 'The retention of heat may be better determined by applying a thermometer to the skin of the abdomen or of the flexures of the joints (as in the axillae), or in the mouth, throat or rectum'. They were not, however, critical in any way of the doctors in the Gardner case for not doing this.

An example of a living body being cold to the touch can be found in the evidence at a trial at the Old Bailey a couple of years after the Gardner case. In December 1864, William Gee and James Smith were tried for the manslaughter of John Smith who was knocked unconscious in an unofficial boxing match on 22 November 1864 and died shortly thereafter. When he was examined by surgeon James Connor, however, he was still alive. Dr Conner said in evidence at the trial that when he saw John Smith, 'he was in a complete state of insensibility – the surface of his body was cold – his pupils were widely dilated, and blood was oozing from his nostrils and mouth – he died afterwards from the compression of the brain; that was the result of fall.' In this case, the surface of the man's body was cold while he was still alive so that his core body temperature can be assumed to have been in the nineties Fahrenheit at the time.

While the 1863 paper was a joint one in the names of both Taylor and Wilks, the reality is that Wilks only assisted with that part of the paper dealing with the experiment. The rest of it was authored by Professor Taylor, as demonstrated by the fact that it was reproduced almost in its entirety in Taylor's later books which were in his own name. Some of it is also written in the first person with Taylor setting out his own experiences. That being so, we can rightly proceed by naming Taylor as the sole author when discussing the rest of the paper's comments and conclusions.

Professor Taylor took issue with the claim of Dr Richardson that a loss of blood, as in cases of death from haemorrhage, is a cause of rapid cooling of the body. 'The sudden cold of collapse observed on the surface of a living body', he said, 'is here confounded with the slow and progressive cooling of a dead body', and he suggested that, 'the cases which have been adduced in support of this view are exceptional instances of disease, and have no practical bearing on the question at issue, namely, the cooling of the body after the sudden death of healthy persons from wounds.' He was, as a consequence, critical of Richardson's conclusion that, in cases of absolute loss of blood, cooling to the temperature of the surrounding medium could be completed in regard to the external surface within two hours, saying that this 'may lead to a serious error, and implicate an innocent person in a charge of murder.'

Taylor dealt at some length with the Gardner case, and his conclusions were the very opposite of those put forward by Dr Richardson. Having set out his view that the nature and direction of the wounds on Mrs Gardner, the position of her body and of the weapon, 'as well as of other circumstances' proved that she had been murdered, he noted that there was 'no evidence' against Humbler so that Samuel Gardner was the obvious suspect. Taylor accepted that it was proved that Gardner had been absent from his house between four and eight o'clock that morning, carrying out his work as a chimney sweep, but believed that the murder had been carried out at some point *before* four o'clock. Despite the fact that Dr Sequeira had failed to use a thermometer to take Mrs Gardner's temperature but had only used his hand, and despite the fact that there was still warmth in the region of the abdomen, Taylor nevertheless believed that, 'The opinions given by the medical witnesses at the trial, regarding the inference derivable from the state of the dead body, were reasonable, and in accordance with scientific observations'. By assigning four hours for the 'almost cooling and commencement of rigidity in the dead body of a woman suddenly dying in the prime of life, the body not being exposed to any specially cooling influences', Taylor concluded that, 'it is obvious that they could not be charged with overstating, but rather with understating, the period of time required.'

So the 'highest authority', Professor Taylor, had ridden to the defence of doctors Sequeira and Comley. They had been 'right' after all!

It will be noticed, though, that Taylor speaks here of the 'rigidity' of Mrs Gardner's body. Elsewhere in the paper he says that when her body was found, her 'upper limbs were cold and rigid' although he claims there was 'no rigidity' in the thighs and legs. He even goes into some detail about the rigidity in saying that, 'the neck was so rigidly fixed with the trunk, that the entire body was lifted with it when the head and neck were raised'. This is interesting because there was no evidence whatsoever adduced during the trial as to any rigidity or stiffness in the body. It formed no part of the prosecution case and was not a factor in Gardner's conviction. There was only one mention of it in the entire proceedings – at least as reported in the newspapers – which was at the inquest hearing on 24 September when Dr Sequeira, as we have seen, said that, when he and his unnamed assistant lifted the body, 'it was quite stiff'. That was it. Nothing was said about the neck being rigidly fixed with the truck when the body was lifted or about the absence of rigidity in any parts of the body so that, if he was correct, Taylor must have been provided with the medical depositions from the inquest which contained more information than was reported. Even if that is so, the evidence of the body being 'quite stiff' was only noticed by Dr Sequeira when he lifted the body, which must have been at around 9am, because the body was only lifted after the police left the house that morning. In other words, if death had occurred at 6am, the stiffness was noted *three* hours later, not two. Lifting a body, though, is not the correct procedure for testing for rigor mortis in a corpse and, if Dr Sequeira only noticed it when the body was lifted, as the evidence of the inquest tells us was the case, he obviously hadn't done any tests for it prior to the lifting. Furthermore, if rigidity, or rigor mortis, was a factor in this case, it is surprising, to say that least, that it wasn't mentioned at all by either doctor during the trial.

In his paper, Taylor relied on observations from fifty years earlier by the French physiologist Pierre-Hubert Nysten to the effect that, in cases of sudden death in healthy persons, 'cadaveric rigidity did not commonly appear until sixteen or eighteen hours after death'. More recently, he noted, Charles Edouard Brown-Séquard, a physiologist from Mauritius, had claimed in an 1861 lecture for the Royal Society that such rigidity did not appear sooner than ten or twelve hours after death in healthy persons (although he didn't go on to mention that, in cases of poor health, Brown-Séquard had said that he was aware that cadaveric rigidity could become evident within three minutes of death[54]). Not only were these estimates inconsistent with each other but it's hard to square them with a time of death suggested by Taylor himself of between midnight and 2am which was six to eight hours before the body of Mrs Gardner, supposedly found rigid in the upper body, was first examined. Taylor, though, bafflingly stated that in the circumstances under which the body of Mrs Gardner was found, 'the assignment of a period of six or eight hours would have been quite within the limits of experience and observation'. If both sixteen to eighteen hours and ten to twelve hours for the appearance of rigor mortis were wrong, it's a little difficult to see why six or eight hours (or seven to

---

[54] 'On the relations between Muscular Irritability, Cadaveric Rigidity, and Putrefaction' by C.E. Brown-Séquard, *Proceedings of the Royal Society*, 16 May 1861.

nine hours if one factors in the correct time that the stiffness was noted) should be correct. In any case, Taylor was ignoring the experience and observation of Dr Richardson who had reported that he had personally seen rigidity develop within an hour of death.

Taylor also noted, as did Baron Pollock, that the death of Elizabeth Gardner had occurred by suffocation, which it was believed would lengthen the amount of time required for the body to cool, especially in comparison to cases of hemorrhage. He said that, if the doctors in the Gardner case had assigned six or eight hours as the time which had lapsed since death, 'it would have been consistent with ordinary experience'. Indeed, he went further by saying that, 'It is indeed more probable that this time had actually elapsed, and that the woman had died in from two to four hours before the male prisoner left the house, than that her body, under the circumstances proved, had become cold and partially rigid in less than four hours.' This was some statement, placing the time of death of Mrs Gardner at between midnight and 2am on 15 September, some six to eight hours before the body had been seen by Dr Sequeira.

Taylor took aim again at Dr Richardson and his experiments on sheep by saying, 'Irrelevant experiments on animals and theoretical speculations of an *ex post facto* kind, advanced for a particular object after a conviction for murder, should not be allowed to weigh against opinions deliberately formed and expressed by professional eye-witnesses, who, by their evidence on oath, could have had no intention to exculpate one person, or to inculpate another'. The medical establishment appeared to be fighting back, perhaps with the assistance, in the background, of one of Taylor's fellow members of the Royal Society, Baron Pollock.

We have seen that Pollock was greatly annoyed by the fact that Dr Richardson had written to the Home Office in the belief that Mrs Gardner had died of loss of blood, as opposed to asphyxiation, although Richardson hadn't made such a claim in his published paper. Sure enough, in his assessment of the evidence in the Gardner case, Taylor wrote that there was nothing against Humbler, 'but an extemporised medical speculation, that a body dead from asphyxia, not, as it was erroneously assumed, from loss of blood, might become cold and rigid in less than four hours.' This really was a remarkable statement because it suggested that anyone who thought that Mrs Gardner's body could become cold in less than four of hours must have misunderstood the cause of death, thinking it to have been the result of loss of blood instead of suffocation. While this had certainly been the understanding of the *Lancet*, that editorial wasn't mentioned by Taylor, and it's hard to avoid seeing the hand of Baron Pollock behind this kind of statement by Taylor; one can imagine him still fuming at the fact that Dr Richardson's letter to the Home Secretary appears to have persuaded Sir George to save a convicted murderer (convicted in his own court!) from the gallows, thus he quite conceivably passed on depositions and other documents relating to the case to Taylor to enable him to write his paper.

It's also remarkable because the evidence of rigidity wasn't produced during the trial and, in any case, the paper of Taylor and Wilks had simply failed to demonstrate that an almost naked body in an unheated room in the early hours of a cool September morning could not become cold and rigid in less than four hours, whatever the cause of death. Yet, Taylor and Wilks attempted to justify their conclusion in respect of coldness by reference to their own table in which it was stated that 'the average temperature of the dead body four to five hours after reception into the dead house, as observed in forty-nine cases, was 74 degrees'. But, as Dr Sequeira hadn't taken the temperature of Mrs Gardner with a thermometer, what use was that information? Would 74 degrees feel warm or cold to a warm human hand? Taylor and Wilks didn't even say. What use is the average in any case? One surely needs to look at the lower temperatures bearing in mind they were obviously *possible*. In this respect, their table showed that the minimum temperature of the body four to five hours after reception into the morgue, as observed in those same forty-nine cases, was 62 degrees[55] (with the maximum temperature being 86 degrees). Of course, that three or four hours could have been fifteen or sixteen hours after death if the patient had died in the evening, or five to eight hours after death if the patient had died during the day. But without knowing what temperature at the body surface a dead body will *feel* cold in the region of the abdomen, the figures provided by Taylor and Wilks were useless.

Furthermore, and crucially, Taylor and Wilks concentrated solely on the body surface temperature in the region of the abdomen, which was, ironically, found to have been *warm* in the Gardner case, although Taylor and Wilks don't seem to have been fully aware of this due to the aforementioned

---

[55] This was in respect of a woman aged 74 who had died of an ovarian tumour.

reporting error by the *Times*. If one assumes a temperature of 74 degrees at the abdomen, what one really needed to know the temperature of in the period between two and four hours after death was that temperature at the surface of the limbs and upper body where Elizabeth Gardner was positively found to have been cold, albeit only by touch.

Nevertheless, despite these omissions, Taylor was quick to say that if the 'medical speculation' – by which he presumably meant the speculation of Dr Richardson in his private letter to the Home Office – had been adopted as true, and had been acted upon in the Gardner case, 'it would have exculpated the man, and have led to the conviction and execution of the woman'. This wasn't in any way correct and was a pure failure of logic, because the notion that the body of Mrs Gardner *could* have cooled within two hours would not have meant that it definitely *had* cooled within two hours. While it might have caused sufficient doubt as to the guilt of Samuel Gardner, it would not on its own have been sufficient to convict Humbler of the crime. The entire point of Richardson's paper was that *no one* should be convicted on the basis of medical opinion as to time of death based on body cooling because of the many uncertainties involved. This is something that Taylor completely ignored.

Taylor and Wilks' paper was undoubtedly, to some extent, a work of propaganda aimed both at justifying the verdict against Gardner and in reassuring the medical profession that they *could* reasonably continue to use body temperature (and the onset of rigor mortis) to estimate the time of death in capital cases. This is particularly obvious by the inclusion of a statement in the paper that 'The commutation of the sentence to penal servitude for life is a clear proof that the authorities did not believe that this man was innocent'.[56] While this might well have been true, it was also clear proof that the authorities had some doubt in the matter, and the inclusion of advocacy of this nature was surely inappropriate in a scientific medical paper.

We have already seen that Taylor used the questionable example of the Mundo murder case in the 1848 edition of his book on medical

---

[56] Two years later, Taylor would amend that sentence in his book *The Practice and Principles of Medical Jurisprudence* to read: 'The subsequent commutation of the sentence to penal servitude for life is a proof that the authorities considered that he was the principal if not the sole perpetrator of this crime'.

jurisprudence. Two brand new but equally historic examples were offered up by Taylor in the 1863 paper to demonstrate the success of medical examiners in assisting the police with their investigations. One was a French case from August 1830 when the Duke of Bourbon had been found hanging dead in his bed chamber at eight o'clock in the morning, with his body cold and lower extremities rigid. Using a very complicated train of reasoning, it was apparently concluded by the French medical examiners that this meant that the Duke had committed suicide. The thinking was that in cases of asphyxia the body takes longer to cool than normal so that the Duke must have died very shortly after he retired that evening at 10pm, fourteen hours before his cold dead body had been discovered. This was also considered a sufficiently short period of time that rigidity would not have been expected to have set in throughout the entire body. As it was considered that the Duke's attendants would have heard any sounds of a struggle at 10pm, if the Duke had been murdered at that time (whereas presumably they would have heard nothing in the middle of the night), the verdict was that the Duke had hanged himself. It's probably not the best example that Taylor could have provided and his other case study wasn't much better.

This was a case from March 1836 in which an unnamed couple were found dead with their throats cut, the man's body being warm but the woman's cold and rigid, suggesting that the man had murdered his wife then cut his own throat. From modern electronic searches, we can establish that this was the case of Francis Frith who was found to have murdered his wife, then committed suicide, in Eyam, Derbyshire. The report of the inquest stated that, 'it appeared that after he committed suicide he had thrown the instrument of death (a razor) from him, as it was found on the bed a short distance from him, the arm remaining outstretched, as though he had not had the power to withdraw it.'[57] That was regarded as a good indication that the man had cut his own throat even though his hand wasn't firmly grasping or clenching the knife. The newspaper report continued to say that, 'The bodies were both attired in their night clothes; that of the unfortunate woman was quite cold when found but some warmth remained in that of her murderer'. None of the reports state that woman's body was rigid when found. It's possible that Taylor had

---

[57] *Morning Post*, 17 March 1836.

access to the case documents, although the fact that he was referring to an incident twenty-seven years in the past, and one which he hadn't referred to in his 1848 book, suggests that what he knew of the case was based on second-hand information.

If the theory was that Frith murdered his wife, one has to wonder why he would have cut his wife's throat then waited a significant amount of time in his night clothes to take his own life. It seems unlikely that he went to sleep after murdering his wife then woke up and cut his throat. One would naturally assume that the suicide followed quite closely after the murder. That being so, perhaps the explanation for his body being warm and his wife's being cold was simply due to a different rate of cooling in their respective bodies. It's impossible to say for sure but Taylor didn't consider the point. One can't help wondering if he would have concluded that the wife was the murderer if *her* body had been warm but her husband's cold, with his arm still being outstretched in the way that he was found as if he had thrown the razor from him.

It's difficult to avoid the conclusion that Taylor added these two old cases, about which he probably had no first-hand information, into the paper in order to demonstrate how medical science was able to accurately identify time of death from an examination of a body at a crime scene, particularly in respect of body temperature and rigidity.

In addition, to these historic cases, three more recent cases were included in the paper. The first was a repeat of the 1860 case of Hopley, which Taylor had already included in the 1861 edition of his book. The second example provided by Taylor to show how medical investigators could solve crimes was one in which Taylor had given evidence as an expert witness. This was the case of John Doidge who had been convicted at the Bodmin Assizes in August 1862, and hanged, for the murder of Roger Drewe, a shopkeeper living in Langore, Cornwall, who had been killed by repeated blows to the head and then robbed. There was witness evidence that Drewe was alive up to midnight on 7 June 1862 and, according to Taylor, 'He was found the next morning, about 9.30am, dead in his house…The body when found was quite cold, and the members were rigid.' Taylor then wrote, 'It was considered by Mr Thompson, who saw the body and myself, that deceased under these circumstances had been dead from eight to ten hours.' The time of death was, therefore, being placed at between 11.30pm and 1.30am. This fits perfectly with the fact that a neighbour had heard Doidge and Drewe talking in Drewe's house at about midnight and then being awakened shortly afterwards by the sound of a heavy fall coming from Drewe's kitchen. Thus, says Taylor, 'The coldness and rigidity of the body...when discovered at 9.30am, considering the season of the year, and the circumstance that the deceased was in his clothes, were facts in themselves quite consistent with the occurrence of death soon after twelve o'clock at night, or about the time when a heavy fall was heard by the neighbour.'

The problem with this account is that, while it is true that the body was discovered at 9.30am, the evidence at the inquest (which wasn't attended by Professor Taylor) was that it wasn't until about 11am that the local medical practitioner, Dr David Thompson, the first person to examine Drewe's body, was able to reach the scene of the crime from his surgery at Launceston, having been sent for at 10.30am. In thinking that Dr Thompson had examined the body at 9.30am, Professor Taylor was an hour and a half out in his calculation. When he gave evidence at the inquest, Dr Thompson merely said that the body 'was cold, and had been dead some hours.'[58] From the newspaper accounts, nothing at all seems to have been said about the body being rigid.

Given that Professor Taylor was wrong about the time that the body was found cold, we need to recalibrate the estimated time of death on the basis of the first examination of the body being 11am. If we apply Taylor's estimate that Drew had been dead for some eight to ten hours, this would mean that death occurred between 1am and 3am. The problem here is that Doidge was seen by two Longore residents, John and Elizabeth Hunkin, at 1am. He was said to have been looking 'stupid and agitated' but, if Taylor's estimate is taken literally, he must have had an alibi at the time of the murder!

There was, in fact, no doubt that Doidge had committed the murder. He had been in Drewe's house shortly before midnight, his clothes were covered with spots of blood and Professor Taylor's contribution to the prosecution case was that he had found microscopic spots of blood on a billhook that he owned and which had obviously been used as the murder weapon. Yet, it is difficult to avoid the conclusion that the time of death

---

[58] *Tavistock Gazette*, 13 June 1862.

in this case, and in the other cases referred to by Taylor, was being subtly and perhaps unconsciously manipulated to fit into the witness evidence rather than standing alone and apart from that evidence. We can see that in the Doidge case, the normal time of six to eight hours for a body to become cold and rigid, which was usually adopted by Professor Taylor in such cases, was extended to eight to ten hours on the basis of the warm time of year and the fact that Drewe was wearing clothes. Yet, there doesn't seem to have been any *scientific basis* for Taylor to have added on an extra two hours to the estimate, as opposed to, say, four hours or six hours or just thirty minutes.

The final example in the 1863 paper was the case of Jessie Macpherson, a maidservant who had been missing for three days in Glasgow when her dead body was discovered on Monday, 7 July 1862. Dr George Macleod, who saw the body on the evening of that day, found that rigor mortis was present, but departing, while the body was perfectly cold throughout, with no signs of decomposition. In his report, prepared with the police surgeon, but not cited by Taylor, Macleod had stated that, 'her death had taken place within three days.' According to Taylor, Dr Macleod considered that rigor mortis commonly appears in ten hours to three days after death and that, because it is only slowly developed in cases of sudden death, he 'thought it probable that forty-eight hours after death (at the longest) would represent the time when rigidity would appear.' Thus, said Taylor, 'the conclusion was arrived at that about three days had probably intervened since death; and it will be remembered that this was, as nearly as could be, the time which had passed between death and the examination of the body.' There are a couple of problems with this. In the first place, Macleod's conclusion had actually been no more than that death had been *within* three days, which could equally have meant that death had taken place the previous day, or two days earlier. Also, in referring to the supposedly known time which had passed 'between death and the examination of the body', Taylor appears to have got himself confused here because the time of death was precisely what Macleod was supposed to have been attempting to establish.

There were two prime suspects in the case, both of whom accused each other of having committed the murder. The first was an elderly man called John Fleming, the father of Macpherson's employer, who was the only person other than Macpherson living in the house at the time. He behaved suspiciously because, despite becoming aware on the Saturday that Macpherson had gone missing, he didn't mention this to anyone, or inform the police, claiming he thought she had just decided to visit friends over the weekend without saying anything. However, it wasn't Fleming who was charged with the crime but Macpherson's friend, Jessie McLachlan, who was arrested after she was found to have pawned articles which had been stolen from Macpherson. Following her conviction for the murder, for which she was sentenced to death, she told a story (which her solicitors hadn't allowed her to present at the trial) in which she claimed that Fleming had murdered her friend, after having sexually assaulted her, and he had allowed her to take Macpherson's possessions to ensure her silence, because Macpherson had confided the details of the assault to her before she passed away. She said that Macpherson died in the early hours of Saturday morning following the original assault on her which had occurred on the Friday evening. Unlike in the Gardner case, an official Home Office enquiry into the case followed and, just like the Gardner case, which was then going on at the same time, due to certain doubts as to her guilt in the matter, Macpherson's death sentence was commuted to life imprisonment.

Consequently, when Taylor said that Macleod's estimate of three days was the time that had passed between death and examination of the body, he was presumably thinking of Macpherson's claim that her friend died in the early hours of Saturday morning. Certainly, when Professor Taylor wrote further about the case two years later, he said, 'The medical opinion formed from the state of the body, tended to confirm that part of the prisoner's story which related to time of death.' Considering that Macpherson hadn't been seen by anyone since Friday evening, and had then been found dead on the Monday, it would have been a reasonable assumption by *anyone*, medically qualified or not, that her murder had occurred within that period, which is all that Macleod's report had actually said.

Two years after his paper on the cooling of the human body, Professor Taylor published *The Principles and Practice of Medical Jurisprudence* which was, to all effects and purposes, a new edition of his standard work, *Medical Jurisprudence*, although it was labelled as a first edition of a new work. The first chapter of the book dealt with questions connected with a dead body, including body cooling, and included much of his (and Wilks')

1863 paper, although he also included, in a separate chapter, issues relating to the inferences to be drawn about the time of death from the state of a body, mentioning all the examples from his previous works, namely the historic cases of the Duke of Bourbon (1830), Frith (1836) and Mundo (1847), albeit with the parties not named in the latter two cases, and the more recent cases of Hopley, Doidge, Gardner and Macpherson that we have already discussed.

In outlining the case of Gardner, in which he said that it was unlikely that her body had become cold and partially rigid in less than four hours, Taylor added something not mentioned in his 1863 paper, namely that, 'In the hundred cases observed by Dr Wilks and myself, there was not an instance in which such rapid cooling and access of rigidity occurred.' Given that, out of the one hundred cases, only one of them had been manually assessed by hand to establish whether it 'felt' cold, this was a highly misleading statement on its own but, as we have seen, Taylor, perhaps confused by the mis-reporting of the evidence in the *Times*, appears to have been unaware that Dr Sequeira had said that the entire area of Elizabeth Gardner's abdomen, i.e. 'her lower trunk', was 'warm' when he had felt it, so that if she had been one of the hundred patients in the study, of which body temperatures were only taken at the abdomen, she too would presumably have been classified as 'warm' by Taylor and Wilks.

Even taken on its own terms, though, many of the corpses in the Taylor/Wilks study didn't have their temperatures taken within four hours of death (or were not examined for rigidity within that time) but, in any case, there was no information in the paper as to what temperature should be regarded as 'cold'. Taylor seems to have assumed that any temperature equal to or above 60 degrees falls into the category of 'warm' despite the fact that such temperature might well feel cold to the human hand. Furthermore, none of the bodies he examined had been lying on a cold floor in a state of undress for the entire period. While the bodies he examined were covered only with a sheet or a shirt in the morgue, they had been in warm beds, covered with bedclothes, before being moved from the ward. One might also note that none of the cases examined by Taylor had been involved in a life or death struggle with a murderer and none had died of suffocation following a cut throat.

None of them were pregnant either. Elizabeth Gardner was, and it's not impossible that this was why Taylor and Wilks discarded the evidence about the warmth in what they believed was the lower part of the abdomen, perhaps thinking that it was emanating from the unborn child in the womb, and thus not a true indicator of the temperature of her corpse. As we've seen, it was certainly the evidence of Dr Comley at trial that the fact of 'the woman being with child' was something 'which would keep up partial heat'. It will also be recalled that Taylor himself had testified in 1850, with reference to Jael Denny, that pregnancy would 'tend to prolong the warmth of her remains after death'. If the foetus in the womb *was* responsible for Mrs Gardner's abdomen still being warm, either in whole or in part when being examined by Dr Sequeira, it's not inconceivable that, just prior to her death, much of her body surface, such as the areas of her thighs and shoulders, was colder than it would otherwise have been if she hadn't been pregnant because, due to the body's thermoregulatory mechanism, internal heat on a cold September morning was being drawn to the womb from those areas in order to keep it warm, in the same way as the fingers and toes of Arctic explorers become cold quicker than the rest of the body in order to retain as much heat as possible in the vital organs. This might have led to her thighs and shoulders feeling colder at a point in time much sooner after her death than a medical practitioner would have expected. In any event, as there weren't any deceased pregnant women in Taylor and Wilks' experiment, any consideration of the effects of her pregnancy on her body temperature can only have been speculation. Indeed, in an article published in the *Lancet* of 3 January 1863 entitled 'Temperature of the Human Body After Death', after noting that a medical witness in the Gardner case had 'explained' the high temperature of the abdomen by stating that the woman was pregnant, the author, W.C. Maclean, a professor of Military Medicine, said that, 'it was a very general impression that no facts exist on which so confident an opinion could be grounded'.

Another addition by Taylor in his 1865 book was some form of explanation for the otherwise inexplicable (to the uninformed) statement that it had been erroneously assumed that Mrs Gardner had died from loss of blood. He now stated that, 'In Mrs Gardner's case, it was supposed that the loss of blood would account for this state of the body at so early a period of death; but, in the first place, the deceased did not die from haemorrhage but suffocation; and secondly a well marked case elsewhere related, shows that the loss of twice as much blood in haemorrhage proving suddenly fatal, led to no acceleration of cooling or rigidity in the dead body.' In doing so, however, he still hadn't explained *who* had supposed that the loss of blood would account for a faster blood cooling in the Gardner case (although he was obviously directing his fire at Richardson). The 'well marked case' he was referring to was one which occurred in Guy's Hospital in February 1863 when a healthy man, aged 43, died suddenly from hemorrhage, losing four pounds of blood, and was seen by Professor Taylor four hours after his death when he recorded the skin of the abdomen as having a temperature of 84 degrees Fahrenheit (dropping to 80 degrees after eight hours) despite the temperature of the morgue being only 38 degrees and the body being covered loosely with a shirt. According to Taylor, 'The alleged effect of loss of blood in accelerating the cooling of the human body when death has occurred suddenly from haemorrhage, has, therefore, no foundation in fact'. While he might have been correct (the subject remains somewhat controversial today[59]) drawing such a firm conclusion from a single case is not normally best practice and, in any case, he has still only established the surface temperature when taken by a thermometer, not whether the body would have felt 'warm' or 'cold' to the touch.

One further addition by Professor Taylor in his 1865 book was to describe three periods through which a dead body passes prior to putrefaction. The first, he said, is where the heat of the body is more or less preserved, from which 'an inference may be drawn that death has taken place from a *few minutes to twenty hours*' although it was said that it was rare that heat would be preserved for as long as twenty hours, with ten or twelve hours being a more normal extreme. Interestingly, he didn't identify a period in which the body was 'so warm' that it could only have died within the last hour, thus negating the entire point of his story about the

---

[59] Although most modern authorities say that loss of blood will not have any impact on the rate of cooling of a body, this conclusion is questioned by Jessica Snyder Sachs, the author of *Time of Death: The True Story of the Search for Death's Stopwatch* 2003, Arrow Books (p.37) on the basis that the loss of a significant amount of warm blood from a corpse must surely have an effect on the temperature of that corpse. It may also be noted that Charles Meymott Tidy and William Bathurst Woodman, the authors of *A Handy-Book of Forensic Medicine and Toxicology*, published in 1877, stated that they agreed with Richardson that 'large losses of blood can cause rapid cooling'.

1847 murder of Josefa Martínez Mundo. In the second period, according to Dr Taylor, the body is perfectly cold throughout and the cadaveric rigidity is well marked. In such a period, 'death may have occurred from ten hours to three days' but, said Taylor, 'It is impossible to give a more definite opinion than this, since there are conditions which may develop rigidity, and under which a body may become cold in ten hours or even in a shorter period.' Taylor cautioned that, 'in forming an opinion we are bound to regard the age, the mode of death, and the circumstances under which the body of the deceased may have been exposed' but didn't give any specifics about exactly how a medical practitioner was supposed to do this. The third period is where the body is perfectly cold but is free from cadaveric rigidity in which, 'it may be assumed that the person has been dead from three to eight days.' Taylor was obviously aware that these three periods contained rather wide ranges of time, saying, 'Notwithstanding the apparent want of precision which medical evidence necessarily presents in investigations relative to the period at which a person died, yet the cases already related show that the approximate results are often of great value'. As we've seen, however, this statement is questionable and it may be noted that Taylor went on to say that, 'When founded on a correct knowledge of the state of the body, and when they are corroborated by other circumstances, they are received in law with the greatest benefit to the administration of justice.' To the extent that the medical opinion needed to be 'corroborated by other circumstances', this seems to go back to Dr Male's advice to check when witnesses last saw the deceased alive. It's not entirely clear that the medical profession had moved much further forward in fifty years because that – and a knowledge of any witness evidence as to when death had likely occurred (such as hearing sounds of violence) – still seemed to be the best way of estimating a time of death while giving the impression that there was also a scientific way of doing it based on body temperature and rigidity.

Despite its faults, the paper by Taylor and Wilks was very influential and formed the basis of much of a revised section in an updated third edition of Professor Guy's *Principles of Forensic Medicine* published in 1868. In this book, Guy stated that, 'Some important medico-legal cases which have lately occurred (Cases of Hopley 1860, Doidge, Gardner the Sweep and Jesse M'Pherson 1862) have shown the necessity of examining the subject more closely, with a view if possible, of determining the rate of cooling of the dead body, and the time at which death took place.' Guy then noted the observations of Taylor and Wilks in their 1863 paper which, he said, 'are found to yield some instructive results'. Unfortunately, he completely misunderstood the paper, evidently not having read it with sufficient care, for he thought that the reference in the paper to body temperatures taken after 'a period of two hours' was two hours after death when it was, in fact, two hours after the body had been brought into the hospital morgue. This led him to some strange conclusions. Having noted that Taylor and Wilks had recorded eighteen cases of body temperatures after two hours with a maximum of 88 degrees Fahrenheit, a minimum of 76 degrees and an average of 83 degrees, and also that they had found the average rate of cooling to be one degree an hour, he therefore assumed that the temperature of the abdomen at death must have been 90 degrees Fahrenheit so that, with the temperature of the air being 60 degrees, 'it would not be reasonable to expect the temperature of the abdomen to have fallen to that of the air till the lapse of at least 30 hours.' There were two fundamental flaws in this analysis. The first being that Taylor and Wilks hadn't stated that the average rate of cooling was one degree an hour. The second was that the cases with a maximum temperature of 88 degrees Fahrenheit reflected the temperature two hours after the bodies had been brought into the morgue, not two hours after death. Therefore, Guy seems to have led himself into error in assuming that the temperature of the abdomen at death in those cases would have been 90 degrees Fahrenheit. Also, if the average rate of cooling was more than one degree an hour this would result in a faster time before the body temperature fell to the temperature of the surrounding air. He did nevertheless acknowledge that the rate of cooling of a dead body could sometimes be as high as three or even four degrees an hour.

We may note that in Guy's fourth edition, published some twenty years later, his error was posthumously corrected (by Dr David Ferrier, Guy having died in 1885) and it was now said that, 'The observations of Taylor and Wilks have the disadvantage of not having been commenced for some hours after death, and the method of taking the temperature is not such as usually followed during life'. The latter criticism showed that the author hadn't understood the point of the experiment which was, in the context of the Gardner case, specifically to assess the temperature of the surface of the body in order to establish when it can be said to become 'cold'. But with the passing of the years, that aim had obviously been forgotten and it seemed to be more important to establish the internal temperature, which is what the medical profession should have been taking at the scene of a death but were repeatedly failing to do.

Back in 1868, in his third edition, Professor Guy, like Richardson and Taylor before him, adopted a strict view as to the use of the hands to assess body temperature. 'The use of a thermometer may be very properly insisted on in every case, as far more satisfactory than the sensations of the observer', he warned, 'and it is not to be doubted that very incorrect inferences may be drawn from the sensation of cold as imparted to the hand of an observer on touching the hands or feet, or nose or ears, of a corpse recently dead'. He added that, 'A man may have little experience of living bodies who does not know what a sensation of icy coldness may be imparted to the warm hand by contact with the hands or feet of another.' This was a familiar refrain from those with experience of feeling dead bodies which demonstrates that such bodies with internal and surface temperatures undoubtedly in the ninety degrees Fahrenheit can nevertheless feel cold to the touch.

CHAPTER SIX

Australia

On 14 January 1864, one hundred and thirty-three convicted prisoners from Chatham Prison boarded the convict-ship Clara destined for Western Australia. Amongst them was Samuel Gardner whose sentence had, by virtue of the Home Secretary, become one of transportation for life. After proceeding slowly along the south coast of England, collecting further prisoners along the way, on 30 January the Clara set sail from Portland Harbour. The journey to Australia took some seventy-five days, anchoring near Freemantle on 13 April.

Gardner was sent to the Toodyay district of Western Australia and put to work. Despite his life sentence, he became eligible for a 'ticket-of-leave' after just four years and was discharged under licence on 1 April 1868. He was free to leave for Perth and was there engaged for a few months working as a bootmaker. After that, he was entitled to set himself up in his own profession as a chimney sweep which he did, announcing in the *Perth Inquirer* that he had been established in the City of London for twenty years and that he was 'perfectly qualified in effectually cleaning all kinds of chimneys and flues to the greatest satisfaction'. His rate was 'one shilling and upwards, as the job may deserve', and he was also selling soot, which could be used as a fertilizer by farmers, for six pounds per ton. His business appears to have been successful and, eventually, he became the sweep to the Governor of Perth. He was even allowed to form relationships. In 1873, he married an Australian woman called Mary Ann Stotter. Incredibly, though, he still hadn't learnt his lesson as to how to treat members of the opposite sex. On 27 April 1875, as he would later recount, 'my present wife and I had angry words, and sorry I am to say that blows were exchanged on both sides'. He was, in other words, once more guilty of having beaten his wife. She lodged a complaint, and he was arrested and charged with 'brutally assaulting and ill-using' her. During the hearing against him, it was stated by the police that Mary Ann Gardner was suffering from internal injuries. Gardner was fined and bound over to keep the peace for twelve months. His goods and chattels were liable to seizure in order to pay for the fine so that, as he complained, 'the very bed I worked hard and honestly to get was to be taken from me'. He protested that he had worked diligently as a sweep in Perth and said, 'I defy any person in any part of the world to prove anything against me more than sometimes getting a little too drunk'. He included the charge of murder of his second English wife in this, claiming, of course, to be innocent of that crime.

On 5 May 1880, Gardner applied for a conditional release from his licence but this was refused because his conduct had 'not been uniformly good' due to his conviction for wife beating. It seems to have been this refusal which reignited Gardner's sense of injustice at his murder conviction some eighteen years earlier and which drove him not only to petition Her Majesty's Government for a retrial but also to wage a massive publicity campaign in Perth to protest his innocence. He had, no doubt, recovered from the 1875 fine, and business as a chimney sweep must have been good over the subsequent five years to enable him to fund the campaign, which involved a large advertisement placed in numerous issues of the *Perth Inquirer* over a four-year period commencing on 26 May 1880. 'If the Crown is honest', he pleaded in the advertisement, 'let me have a fresh trial; and if I do not prove my innocence without the slightest doubt I am willing to suffer death, without one murmur.'

In this advertisement, Gardner also set out in some great detail the faults in the case against him for murdering his wife and the reasons why he was innocent of that crime. Amazingly, however, he didn't once mention Elizabeth Humbler in his account. He no longer accused her of having (possibly) murdered his wife. Instead, his entire defence was that his wife had committed suicide. His main line of attack in his demand for a fresh trial was that the medical witnesses had only been able to say that suicide was 'improbable', not that it was impossible, and on that basis, he complained, he had been convicted and sentenced to death.

What should we make of Gardner's change of tack? Did he now genuinely believe that Humbler was innocent? Or did he make a tactical decision to focus on suicide as the cause of his wife's death because he had come to the conclusion that no one would believe that a nineteen-year-old girl could have been responsible for it? Or perhaps he simply wanted to remove his own adultery from the story to make him a more sympathetic character. If that *was* the case he was seriously weakening his argument because the obvious reason for Elizabeth Gardner to have taken her own life was because of that adultery and, more particularly, the fact that she was being humiliated by the presence in the house of Humbler. By whitewashing the girl out of the account, and not mentioning that she had been his mistress, the motive given to the readers of his story was unfathomable. Indeed, in his account from Australia, Gardner didn't provide any explanation at all for why his wife would have wanted to take her own life.

Given that we know about her unhappiness with her domestic situation and the fact that there is some evidence showing that she had been thinking about ending her life, did she commit suicide after all? It seems strange for her to have done so if Humbler was meant to be leaving the house that day because that would have removed her main obstacle to happiness and left her alone with her husband, which is what she appears to have wanted. Despite Humbler's own denials, there can't be any real doubt that Mrs Gardner had told her that she had to leave the house on Monday 15 September. Where there is some doubt is in whether Samuel supported her in making this a firm deadline. It may be that he equivocated when he later spoke in private to his wife in their bedroom on Sunday night and merely said he would talk to Humbler the next day, when he returned from work, making his wife think that he had backtracked and wasn't going to insist on her leaving. Perhaps they did quarrel about it in the morning and Gardner didn't want to admit to the police that his own behaviour might have led his wife to commit suicide.

If that was the case, Elizabeth might well have gathered some possessions around her, like her wedding ring, a portrait of her husband and the wicked valentines, before cutting her throat and then, while dying an agonizing death through suffocation, cutting her own fingers while grasping the blade of the knife, causing her to scream loudly. The medical evidence was that she would have been able to scream after cutting her throat and, while one might have thought such a scream would have woken up Humbler in the room above, one can't entirely rule out the possibility that she slept through it. In support of the suicide theory is the evidence of Samuel's sister, Sarah, who said that, at the inquest on 24 September, her brother had told her that he had 'heard the dresser drawer open on the Sunday night by his wife' and that he had gone on to say that, if she had taken the knife, he didn't think she would have done anything to herself. If Gardner really did hear his wife opening the drawer containing the knife on Sunday evening it might go some way towards the idea that she had decided to end it all.

Against the idea of suicide is that it would have meant Elizabeth taking her own life while her two- year-old daughter lay in bed without having made any provision for her welfare. Perhaps she thought she would have been found by her husband when he returned from work at 8am, or earlier by Humbler, but one would have thought she might have asked a neighbour to look after Eliza before taking such a drastic step. There is, of course, also the matter of the very deep cut to one of her fingers which the doctors said she couldn't have done to herself but it seemed that the evidence on this ended up as it being possible that she could have done this after all.

If Samuel Gardner was the murderer then not only did he behave very strangely in accusing Humbler of committing the crime, after having carefully arranged the personal items on the chair to make it look like suicide, but he showed remarkable stubbornness in continuing to plead his innocence over a twenty-year period and conducting a campaign at some considerable expense when he could simply have let it go and got on with his life in Australia. It doesn't seem likely that he did it, nor does it seem likely that he would have wanted to have murdered his unborn child. While we can't know for sure if he regarded another baby as a financial burden on him, he'd had two daughters and no son which makes it a little hard to believe he'd have murdered his wife in a late stage of pregnancy when there was the prospect of him having his first son in just a couple of months' time.

There doesn't seem to have been any motive for him to have murdered his wife. He was very quick to accuse Humbler of the crime which would have led to her being executed if she was found guilty and there isn't evidence of any other woman in his life for whom he might have wanted to clear the way to marry. Gardner seems to have been the type of man who would have hit his wife in temper but not one to cut her throat.

There's no doubt that Gardner did one or two suspicious things. Removing the knife from his dead wife's hand was certainly an odd thing to do, despite his explanation that he thought she was still alive and might harm herself, although it's hard to see what advantage it brought him, or could have brought him, if he was the murderer. Sure, if his hands had been bloody, it might have explained where the blood had come from but no one pointed out any blood on his hands that morning. It's conceivable that in removing the knife he wanted to cover up the fact that it was only loose in his wife's hand but that would have required a level of understanding and appreciation of cadaveric spasm unlikely in a chimney sweep. Another suspicious thing is that he told two of his sisters, Sarah and Amelia, that he thought his wife had killed herself until he examined her hands and saw the deep cut to one of the fingers. Given that he had, in fact, immediately accused Humbler of murder in front of both the doctor and the police, this obviously wasn't true but perhaps he hadn't wanted to admit to his sisters that he had accused a young woman of such a heinous crime without even knowing if there actually had been a murder in the first place.

In view of the medical evidence about an apparently large male palm print on Elizabeth Gardner's thigh, and the police evidence that blood marks had suddenly appeared in the house on a window which Gardner claimed Humbler had touched on the day of the murder, one can understand to a certain extent why the jury decided to convict him. They obviously weren't swayed by his Counsel's argument that it didn't make sense for him to take the trouble to stage a suicide yet accuse Humbler of murder almost as soon as he walked into the room, but, in the cold light of day, this must surely go a long way to acquit him of the crime.

If it wasn't suicide, and Gardner didn't murder his wife, then that only leaves Humbler. One can see that, if she had been given a deadline of Monday to leave the house, but didn't want to go, staging a fake suicide of Mrs Gardner would have solved all her problems perfectly. With her lover's wife out of the way she would, in her own mind, surely have taken her place as the next Mrs Gardner, which seems to have been her main ambition. It's certainly hard to understand why her hands were caked in such dirt on the Monday morning. Gardner's barrister said they would have been cleaned on the Sunday evening (although it's unclear if there was any evidence to support this) and it would have been a neat trick to hide any blood by covering it in dirt or soot. Gardner dealt in soot while living in Aldgate as well as sweeping chimneys so there would, presumably, have been plenty around the house.

We have seen that Humbler's original story was that she went into Elizabeth Gardner's room for a lucifer match but stepped in some blood, which is what drew her attention to the dead body, but, when she told the story during the trial, she omitted the part about stepping in the blood. Did that show she was lying? The absence of any blood being spread around the house by her stockinged foot seems suspicious. When she arrived at Dr Sequeira's surgery she told him to come quickly because Mrs Gardner had cut her throat and unless they moved fast he 'should not find her alive'. While it's true that Samuel Gardner said he thought his wife was alive when he first saw her, which is why he removed the knife from her hand, it seems strange that Humbler had not checked closer on Mrs Gardner's condition which would have made clear that she was dead. It's also instructive to consider the way that Dr Sequeira first told the story of his arrival at Gardner's house that morning, which he did at the Mansion House Police Court on 7 October. Then he said that Humbler, 'who preceded me by a minute or two, pushed the door open, and we went into the ground floor room first, but found no one there.' Although the two of them would have had to go through the ground floor room to reach the upstairs bedroom, this reads like Humbler was looking around the room on the ground floor to give the impression that a wounded Mrs Gardner might have walked around the house while she had been out. Even if this was only Dr Sequeira's wrong impression of what was happening, it is still the case that Humbler had told the doctor it was a suicide, or attempted suicide, which is exactly what one would have expected the murderer to say, having deliberately staged such a suicide.

There is, however, one thing that seems strange about Gardner's change of heart in 1880. Assuming that what he told the police in 1862 was true, he must have sat through Humbler's cross-examination watching her lying repeatedly under oath. She denied that she had been told to leave on the Monday (which Gardner said had been made clear to her) and she also denied what Gardner claimed she had said to him about the knives and that she was prepared to take his life and her own. One would have thought that this would have convinced him of Humbler's guilt and left him determined to have his revenge on her and ensure that she was rightly convicted of his wife's murder but, when he told his story in the *Perth Inquirer* in 1880, his venom was reserved for Baron Pollock (who was then dead), Dr Sequeira, Sir George Grey and the governor and chaplain of Newgate Prison. He might, of course, have believed that Humbler murdered his wife yet felt it wise to keep that opinion to himself but, still, if his aim was for a retrial, he would almost inevitably have found himself in serious difficulty once again in arguing that it was a case of suicide if it was really one of murder.

Gardner attracted some support from thirteen citizens of Perth who signed a petition addressed to the Imperial authorities in 1883 supporting his claim that his case should be reopened for further inquiry. They were particularly impressed by the amount of money and effort Gardner had expended on his campaign and said: 'We have each of us frequently read with feelings of pain the sad and grievous statement this man has, during the last three years, so frequently courageously published in a portion of the local Press. The truth of these statements has never yet to our knowledge been even impugned, much less contradicted; and when we remember that the very great expense Gardner has necessarily incurred in publishing a history of his sad case has been defrayed by him out of the proceeds of his laborious and honest industry, we feel that the action he has so boldly taken in this matter proves him to be a person possessed of upright and honourable principles, and to be a man of the most praiseworthy independence of character. Further, judging from the uncontradicted statements we have read, and also from his uniformly good behaviour while he has been living in this City, we think that Gardner is innocent of that crime for which he has been so severely punished.'

In the event, Gardner's petition to the British government was ignored, almost certainly due to the fact that Baron Pollock's comments on the case were still on the Home Office file, and Gardner's argument that the medical witnesses couldn't conclusively rule out suicide was never going to override the judge's strong views about his guilt. Having apparently reconciled with his wife, before falling out with her again, Gardner died in Western Australia in September 1898 at the age of 74, still a convicted murderer.

Resolving whether it was suicide or murder is, thankfully, not the main purpose of this book. What does seem overwhelmingly likely is that Mrs Gardner's death occurred at 6am and that it was her screaming that was heard by Constable Blanchard, forcing him to stop and walk back towards the Gardner house at number one Northumberland Alley. This means that she had only been dead about two hours whereas doctors Sequeira and Comley had estimated a minimum time of death as being four hours. Given that Gardner had a solid alibi at 6am, it's hard to avoid the conclusion that failings of the medical profession had caused an innocent man to be sentenced to death and, in fact, to suffer a term of imprisonment and transportation for life to Australia.

CHAPTER SEVEN

1864-1873

In the decade following the Gardner trial there were a number of cases of interest which involved estimation of time of death, although they didn't all seem to adopt the principles advocated by Professor Taylor.

On 18 August 1864, Elizabeth Fisher, a young woman from the small fishing village of Appledore, Devon, was found dead in her room with her throat cut after neighbours heard loud screams at half-past seven in the morning. Her mother was by her side when one of the neighbours rushed in and was told that she had suffered an epileptic fit, of which she was known to be prone, and had fallen on the chamber utensil, cutting her own throat. This seemingly unlikely scenario turned out to have been what almost certainly did happen (although the inquest jury delivered an open verdict). Half an hour later, at eight o'clock, a message reached the local surgeon, Edward Pratt, who 'immediately went to her house'. At the inquest, he said that, when he arrived at the scene, 'The body was cold', and he estimated that 'she had been dead two or three hours.'[60] This is an interesting case because the time of death is known to have been at about 7.30am, when the screams were heard, and Pratt, who was based in Appledore, would have been in Fisher's room by 8.30am. She must, therefore, have died within the hour when he examined her, yet her body was cold when he did so. Not only does this seem to demonstrate that a dead body can easily become cold to the touch within an hour, it also

---

[60] *Standard*, 25 August 1864; *North Devon Journal*, 25 August 1864.

seems to show a reluctance on the part of the surgeon to give such a low estimate of time of death when feeling a cold body, perhaps based on what the experts, such as Professor Taylor and Dr Wilks, were saying about the amount of time it should take for a body to cool, assuming he was aware of their opinion. Equally, in light of the well-publicised Gardner case in which it was stated that a body did not become cold until four hours after death, one has to ask whether he should even have been giving an estimate of time of death as recently as two or three hours where a body had been found cold. Perhaps he was one of those medical men who believed Gardner to have been innocent!

When reporting a case of suicide by poison in Italy of two British citizens in November 1864, the *Sun* newspaper of 7 December 1864 noted that, 'The unfortunate couple had been dead at least six or seven hours, for their bodies were cold.' So on the one hand, in August 1864, we have a cold body indicating death had occurred two or three hours earlier yet, four months later, a cold body apparently indicated death as having taken place at least six or seven hours earlier. There doesn't seem to have been any consistency in the matter.

Similarly, when a body was found to be warm, the estimate given could be anything from one or two hours up to as much as twelve hours. Thus, in the case of a murder by hanging of a young boy by his father, the medical evidence given by a Dr Alfred Harvey during a magistrate's hearing at Bow Street Police Court in September 1866 to commit for trial the accused murderer, John Richard Jeffery, was, according to the *Sun*, that, 'When I first saw the body of the boy he had been dead about one or two hours. The body was warm but the limbs were stiff.' The *Times* reported the same evidence a little differently, recording that the doctor said that, 'from the stiffness of the limbs he should judge that the child had certainly been dead from one to two hours; it might be three or four. He could not tell within a few hours. The body was warm, but that might continue as much as 12 hours.' Either way, it's interesting that here we have a warm but stiff body about which there was very little in the literature to assist in timing of death. At Jeffery's trial, Dr Harvey confirmed that, 'His limbs were rigid, and he was quite warm.' Interestingly, Harvey testified during the trial that, when he examined the body at the morgue (which appears to have been very shortly after his initial examination), 'The limbs were rigid. The stomach and chest were slightly warm. I should imagine the child was then dead about four hours.'[61] This was, of course, precisely the period since death that the medical witnesses during the Gardner trial had estimated when dealing with a body which was mainly cold, but warm at the abdomen.

Frequently the approach adopted by medical witnesses was to keep it vague. Dead bodies, either cold or cold and stiff, were often referred to during the rest of the 1860s as having been dead 'for some hours' or 'for several hours'. One 1869 case in which a specific estimate of time of death was given involved the death of a two-week-old baby called James Nevill, the illegitimate son of Susannah Nevill, who had been abducted and murdered by being suffocated. At an inquest into the child's death, Dr Francis Buckle, the divisional surgeon, who examined the dead baby at Islington Police Station, found that, 'The body was cold in most parts, except the back of the head which was warm'. From this, 'he believed the child to have been dead about two or three hours.'[62] The baby had gone missing shortly after 9am on 5 July and had been discovered at quarter to ten. Dr Buckle had examined the dead body at shortly after 11am. From that information alone, it wasn't possible for the child to have been murdered more than two hours prior to Dr Buckle's examination so his estimate of two hours must have been correct yet it's hard to believe that he did it from body temperature alone. At about the same time that Dr Buckle was giving his opinion at the inquest into the death of baby Nevill, Dr Frederick Wilson was telling an inquest into the death by prussic acid of Emma Duggan that 'her body was quite warm, and there was no rigidity' which indicated to him that, 'She had been dead about two or three hours, as far as I can judge.'[63] It would seem, therefore, that a predominantly cold body as well as an entirely warm one indicated to different medical examiners that death had occurred two or three hours earlier, which seems confusing.

Did a mainly cold body after death indicate death having taken place two or three hours earlier, four hours earlier or six or seven hours earlier?

---

[61] *Times*, 21 September 1866.
[62] *Islington Gazette*, 9 July 1869.
[63] *Times*, 1 July 1869. There was no indication given by the doctor in this case that he thought that the prussic acid had affected the post-mortem warmth of the body.

No one seemed to know. And still no one was taking the body temperature with a thermometer as advised by multiple experts. In fact, Professor Taylor had reproduced this advice in his 1865 book, *The Principles and Practice of Medical Jurisprudence*, slightly amended from the wording of his 1863 paper in that whereas he had said in 1863 that the surface of a dead body may appear 'icy cold' to a human hand he now said, 'the dead human skin is a good conductor of heat, and thus the surface may appear cold to a moderately warm hand'. He also now said that, 'In all observations on the temperature of the dead body, a thermometer should, if possible, be employed'. As in the 1863 paper, albeit slightly modified, he said that, 'This may be applied for the exterior, either to the skin of the abdomen or to the armpits; and for determining the temperature of the interior, the bulb may be introduced into the mouth, throat or rectum.'

Still medical examiners did not use thermometers at crime scenes. One can only speculate as to why not. Presumably, being fragile instruments, they didn't want to carry them around if they could avoid doing so, assuming they owned one, nor stick them in the rectum of dead bodies when they might have needed them for their living patients. In 1866 the *Times* newspaper carried an advertisement for a clinical thermometer at a price of 25 shillings which was not outrageously expensive but perhaps sufficiently so for most doctors to have only owned one which they liked to keep in their surgeries. An 1874 lecture on the use of clinical thermometers (for living patients) published in the *British Medical Journal* said that, 'the cost and fragile nature of the instruments now in use constitute still a serious drawback to their employment.' It may also be because any temperature reading medical examiners took of a dead body at the scene of the crime would have got them no further in their attempts to estimate time of death. The experts simply hadn't been able to work out any kind of formula for calculating a time of death based on a body temperature (either internal or on the surface) of, say, eighty-five degrees. It would have taken the investigation no further than touching to feel 'cold' or 'warm'. It will be recalled that Dr Leeson in 1832 had speculated that a body might take about two hours to lose 18 degrees – so that he must have thought that a body lost 9 degrees of heat an hour on the surface – but this hadn't been confirmed or approved in any medical text book and was no more than guesswork, not based on any scientific testing.

In an attempt to rectify this absence of a formula to calculate time of death, Dr Harry Rainy, Professor of Medical Jurisprudence at the University of Glasgow, published in the *Glasgow Medical Journal* during 1869 a paper entitled 'On the Cooling of Dead Bodies as Indicating the Length of Time that has Elapsed since Death'. Rainy opened the paper by noting that, 'When dead bodies are found in suspicious circumstances, it is often important to ascertain as nearly as possible the length of time that has elapsed since death'. The reason for this, he said, was because, 'In various cases this inquiry is found to throw light on the probable guilt or innocence of individuals who are suspected of murder'. A person who had an alibi for the time of the murder could be cleared but someone who was 'close to the place where the body was found' would be considered a suspect. Other than the presence and progress of chemical composition, the two chief factors in ascertaining the length of time that had elapsed since death were, Rainy noted, body temperature and cadaveric rigidity. His sole focus in the paper was on body temperature and the circumstances which influenced the rate of cooling of a dead body in still air of uniform temperature.

Rainy relied on observations made by Dr Joseph Coats of the Glasgow Royal Infirmary involving 46 dead patients whose rectal temperatures were taken at varying intervals after death over a twenty-four hour period. Unlike in the experiment conducted by Dr Wilks and Professor Taylor, Coats claimed to know the precise time of death in each case, although it isn't stated in Rainy's paper how he knew this. One imagines that the 'Hours after death' recorded in the table in Rainy's paper are those since the death was noted by either Dr Coats or the staff in the infirmary. Yet that creates somewhat of a puzzle. In none of the 46 cases was the temperature taken at the assumed time of death. The earliest it was taken was 30 minutes after death (in one case) but most were much later than this; in some cases no temperature was recorded until fifteen or sixteen hours after death. Nine cases in total involved no temperature being recorded until more than ten hours after death. No explanation is provided as to how Coats could possibly have known the precise time of death in these cases yet failed to take the body temperature for such a long period. In one case, where the temperature wasn't taken until fifteen-and-a-half hours after death, it is stated that the cause of death was haemorrhage from a railway accident which, if death had been instant, would have allowed the precise time of death to be established but other cases in which the first temperature reading was taken more than ten hours after death involved cases of typhus, bronchitis, cancer and compression of the brain. A couple of other cases, such as death from 'smashed foot' and 'Rupture of arteries of mesentery from a blow on abdomen', might have enabled the time of death to be precisely ascertained but those are the exceptions and most deaths were of disease, making it inexplicable as to why the medical staff participating in the experiment failed to record the temperature for so many hours after life had ceased. Only eight of the cases involved a temperature being taken within, or exactly, one hour after death.

In only one case did the temperature of the corpse increase after death, rising from 96 degrees, ninety minutes after the supposed death, to 98 degrees two-and-a-half hours later. In twenty-three cases the rate of cooling per hour increased steadily while, in eleven further cases, the rate of cooling per hour increased steadily at first, only to slow down, something Rainy was unable to fully explain. According to Rainy, 'the cooling may be retarded in the earlier stages by continuance of obscure vital processes, and at a later stage by the heat arising from incipient decomposition and other unknown causes'. This meant that human bodies did not always cool in conformity with Newton's law of cooling which said that rate of cooling of a body (not necessarily a human body and usually a liquid), was proportional to the difference of temperature between the hot body and the surrounding cool medium. Rainy stated that this law of cooling was not absolutely correct when applied to a human body where the body was warm and the surrounding temperature cold. Bodies recently discovered dead were also found not to cool in conformity with the law. Nevertheless, Rainy concluded that if one took the temperature of the corpse at least twice, at intervals of one hour, 'though we cannot calculate exactly the period which has elapsed since death, we can almost always determine a maximum and a minimum time within which that period will be included, sufficiently close for all practical purposes…'

Somewhat problematically, Rainy stated that, in performing such a calculation, 'we may assume the temperature at the instant of death to be 100° F.' Given that the average body temperature is usually said to be 98.6 degrees, that assumption may not be correct in all cases. However, taking body temperature at hourly intervals (or intervals of two or three hours) would certainly establish the rate of cooling. Rainy then provided a formula by which, as long as the temperature of the rectum was found to be below 85 degrees, it should be possible to fix the minimum and maximum periods since death. It was a complicated formula which supposed a knowledge of logarithms on the part of the person carrying out the calculation. Rainy advised that, 'Persons unacquainted with logarithms may make the necessary observations when the body is found, and the proper inferences may be deduced by competent parties afterwards.'

A few things are immediately obvious about Rainy's method. Firstly, it provided no assistance in estimating time of death from simply feeling whether a dead body was cold or warm and it required the use of a thermometer to establish the rectal temperature, with more than one reading required to be taken at intervals. Secondly, as Rainy himself said, it didn't work in circumstances where the rectal temperature was 'near the normal temperature of life' so that, where a dead body was very warm, his formula was effectively useless. Thirdly, it could only provide a maximum and minimum range within which death could occur (but without any mathematical confirmation from Rainy as to the likely accuracy of this range). Fourthly, it assumed a body temperature at death of 100 degrees, which was rarely likely to be correct. Fifthly, it required the air temperature to be constant. Sixthly, it required familiarity with logarithms. As most medical examiners were probably unfamiliar with them, it's not difficult to see why Rainy's method wasn't universally popular. Indeed, there is no evidence that Rainy's formula was ever used in a criminal case. Medical examiners seemed to continue to prefer to feel a body at the scene death rather than use a thermometer and, while it wouldn't have been too difficult to take temperature readings during a post-mortem, the whole process, including making the calculation, was quite fiddly and complicated and unlikely to produce a reliable estimate that could be used in court.

Interestingly, an article by Dr Francis Goodheart in *Guy's Hospital Reports* in 1870 entitled 'Thermometric Observations in Clinical Medicine' commented in respect of living patients that, 'It is often urged against the thermometer that the hand is quite as good an indicator as is needed, and that the question of degree is a matter of no importance; or, again, that the true use of a thermometer is to educate the hand'. However, he gave an example of one of his patients whose skin felt 'cool and moist to the hand' but whose temperature, when taken with a thermometer, turned out to be 104 degrees. He said that this was no isolated example. Dr Goodheart also considered the issue of temperature after death from a medico-legal perspective noting that, 'Medical evidence is most often required on this point in cases in which the question of homicide or suicide turns on the length of time a body has been dead.' He asked the question, 'How far would disease be likely to act upon the normal temperature and thus lead to the giving of an erroneous opinion?' As for the 'normal temperature', he noted that a person's body temperature at time of death was not always within the 'normal' range of between 96 and 98.6 degrees especially in cases of long-standing disease with emancipation when temperature just prior to death was often found to be below 96 degrees, something which could affect a calculation of time of death if one was assuming a 'normal' temperature at time of death.

We find in Goodheart's data one patient suffering from heart disease ('mitral') whose temperature taken under the armpit was 97 degrees yet of whom it was noted 'Surface feels cold'. The same comment of 'Surface cold' was repeated for another patient with the same disease with a temperature of 94.6 degrees. Similarly, another patient suffering from a form of cardiac disease had temperature under the armpit recorded as 'Feels cold to the hand' while one patient with a temperature as high as 98 degrees attracted the comment, 'Feels cold'. Another with a temperature even higher than normal, of 98.7 degrees, suffering from phthisis (tuberculosis) and heart disease, was in a state whereby it was recorded 'Surface always cold during life'. So, clearly, there isn't always a connection between (a warm) internal body temperature and (a cold) skin temperature as felt by the hand. Whether medical examiners of dead bodies always appreciated this fact is another matter.

Some more cases of note occurred in the early 1870s, the first being what was known as 'The Finsbury Murder' in which Jacob Spinasa was charged and convicted of the murder of Cecelia Aldridge, a prostitute residing at 56 Flower and Dean Street although he had murdered her in a hotel in Finsbury Square where he was the night porter. The murder had been discovered at 5.30am on 15 January 1870 when, after some crashing sounds disturbed people in the hotel, Spinasa had been heard by the wife of the hotel's owner, Sarah Buecker, 'raving in the most frantic manner' while saying that the devil was down in the basement room in which he lived.[64] A junior porter then noticed Aldridge's dead body lying in a pool of blood in Spinasa's room. She had died from a fractured skull, having been beaten by Spinasa with a candlestick. The porter then called the police. A local doctor, Augustus Hess, was one of the first on the scene, arriving at about 5.45. At the trial of Spinasa, he said that 'the body was warm all over' and that, 'my impression was that she had not long been dead; I mean to say an hour or somewhat less, or perhaps much less.' About an hour later, Dr George Yarrow, the police divisional surgeon, arrived at the hotel. He said at the inquest that he should 'imagine' that the woman had been dead about two hours but didn't explain his reasoning.

Dr Hess was reported as saying at the trial that 'the limbs were perfectly flexible'. When giving evidence at Worship Street Police Court, however, Yarrow said that, when he examined the body (an hour later), 'Rigor mortis had set in'. After noting that the stomach contained about three-quarters of a pint of undigested food, mainly potatoes, and also some wine, he stated that Ms Aldridge had 'then been dead two hours', but added, 'It might have been from three to four hours.'[65]

While it was perfectly clear that Spinasa had committed the murder so that very little turned on the time of death, his Counsel, Mr Sleigh, argued in his closing speech that, 'Dr Hess has stated that the body was warm, but nothing was said with reference to its becoming rigid or stiff; and I venture to say, therefore, that the deceased had died but after a short time previous to Mrs Buecker coming down into the passage. It is perfectly clear that death must have ensued within a short time after the noise was first heard by Mrs Buecker, and not at the time suggested by the counsel for the prosecution'.[66] Presumably the prosecution were following the opinion of their divisional surgeon that death had occurred prior to 5am. It didn't change anything and, after a failed argument by Mr Sleigh that his client might have murdered the woman in a hallucinatory state, Spinasa was found guilty and sentenced to death but this was controversially commuted

---

[64] *Daily Telegraph*, 17 January 1870.
[65] *Standard*, 27 January 1870.
[66] *Daily Telegraph*, 4 March 1870.

to life imprisonment by the Home Secretary on the basis that Spinasa was suffering from 'homicidal mania'.

In a case of sudden death in Clerkenwell on 6 March 1871, Harriet Trotter had seen one of her fellow lodgers, Mrs Sarah Dawson, at an attic window of their shared house at 10.45am and then heard a fall. On rushing up to the attic she found Mrs Dawson, who was aged 52, dead on the floor. At the inquest, Dr Edward Dyer told the coroner that he arrived in the house within half an hour of the time Mrs Dawson had been heard to fall. He said that 'The body was warm' and, hey presto, he thought that 'she had expired about half an hour previously'.[67] If he managed to do this simply from the fact that the body felt warm it was quite an achievement bearing in mind that other doctors who gave an estimate based on this fact invariably concluded no more than that death had taken place within one or two (or even three or four) hours.

In December 1872 the body of a woman was found in a tunnel at Charing Cross Railway Station. It looked to the divisional police surgeon, Dr Samuel Mills, that she had been murdered. When he saw the body of the deceased woman in the tunnel, he said, 'The lower extremities were cold, but a part of the body was warm. The deceased when he saw her had been dead two or three hours.'[68] Again, a cold but partially warm body is said to have been dead for two or three hours.

In Paddock, Huddersfield, on 29 June 1873, Joseph Wilson, the local surgeon, was visited by the daughter of Sarah Stansfield at shortly before 5am who told him that her mother was very ill and she would like him to visit her. He did so but by the time he arrived she was dead. He said that, 'The body was cold' but despite this, and perhaps influenced by the fact that the woman's daughter had given the impression that she was recently alive, and believing that the woman had died from apoplexy, he said 'she had been dead about two hours'.[69] This was rather lucky for John Stansfield, Sarah's husband, who claimed that at half past four that morning he had heard his wife give 'a kind of scream' and say 'Oh my head, what shall I do?' before collapsing on the floor. He then walked to the daughter's house in Brierley Wood which was, apparently, three-quarters of

---

[67] *Clerkenwell News*, 11 March 1871.
[68] *Morning Advertiser*, 7 December 1872.
[69] *Huddersfield Daily Chronicle*, 3 July 1873.

a mile away (something he would be criticised for doing by the inquest jury) rather than contacting neighbours who were nearer. When his daughter returned with him to his house, she saw that her mother's hands were 'quite cold' and her lips were blue, although she must have thought her still alive, and she then went straight to Dr Wilson. Despite there being some bruises on Mrs Stansfield's body, Dr Wilson was satisfied it was a natural death but, if he had given the usual estimate of time of death for a cold body, he would surely have estimated death as having occurred at about 1am, which would have placed John Stansfield in some difficulty, having to explain why he was saying she was still alive more than three hours later. In the event, the inquest jury returned a verdict of 'sudden death from natural causes, probably due to apoplexy'.

In a case of double murder in Wapping in November 1873, the examining surgeon, Hardwick Braye, informed a magistrate at Thames Police court that he saw two children lying side by side with their throats cut from ear to ear. He said, 'The bodies were warm, and I should think they had been dead about half an hour'.[70] Braye had arrived at the scene of the murder at 1pm on 23 November after their father (their murderer) had handed himself in at King David Lane Police Station at 12.15pm on the same day. The children had been seen alive at midday so they couldn't have been dead more than about one hour when Braye saw them but it must have been more than half an hour.

With no consistency as to what time-of-death estimate could be drawn from warm or cold bodies it really is hard to avoid the conclusion that medical examiners were making up time-of-death estimates as they went along, perhaps based on their personal experiences but with no real scientific basis for them and usually driven by other non-medical evidence as to the likely time of death.

---

[70] *Morning Post*, 25 November 1873.

CHAPTER EIGHT

The West Haddon Controversy

It was in the small village of West Haddon in Northamptonshire in November 1873 that the next controversy relating to body temperature began with the death of an old lady. It was an unusual case because body temperature wasn't used by the medical men involved to estimate the time of death, rather the very *cause* of death was deduced from a body being warmer than expected after death.

Mrs Alice Gulliver was 72 years old when she became ill on the morning of Saturday, 22 November 1873, with what she attributed to a 'bilious attack'. She died the next day. The doctor attending her certified her death as due to heart disease.

An old lady had, therefore, died unremarkably of heart disease, and that would have been the end of the matter had it not been for rumours circulating around the village which reached the coroner for Northampton who ordered that Mrs Gulliver's body be exhumed and a post-mortem examination conducted. As a consequence of the post-mortem and further examination of the stomach contents, the doctor demurred from his previous opinion and felt that he could not now say that the death was due to heart disease. It might, he implied, have been due to poison. Suspicion fell on Mrs Gulliver's niece by marriage, Mrs Mary Ann Waters, the subject of the rumours, who had attended her during her illness. Mrs Waters stood to benefit from Alice Gulliver's death as she and her husband,

Mrs Gulliver's nephew, a surgeon from Worcester, were mentioned in her will. But did she kill her?

We need to understand the circumstances surrounding Mrs Gulliver's death before we can appreciate why Mrs Waters was suspected of murder.

Mrs Gulliver awoke two hours later than normal on the Saturday morning. Normally she would be up at 8am but, on that particular morning, she didn't rise until ten. Her maid, Jane Middleton, found her with her head over the side of her bed trying unsuccessfully to vomit into a basin. The only other person in the house was Mrs Waters. She had been visiting for the past couple of days, since Thursday, and put her aunt's sickness down to some stale pork pie she had eaten on the day of her arrival, which tasted sour and which was, according to Mrs Waters, 'scarcely fit for consumption'. Mrs Waters noticed during the evening that her aunt's head had fallen back and the old lady explained that she had suffered from a fluttering of the heart which often made her feel faint. After a little brandy and water, she retired to bed. The next morning Mrs Gulliver seemed to have recovered but was troubled by a cough. She was well enough, however, to enjoy some boiled fowl which Mrs Waters had brought with her as a gift, along with some ham and pudding. During the evening, according to Mrs Waters, Mrs Gulliver ate two large apples and some more of the stale pork pie.

On the Saturday morning, Mrs Gulliver did eventually vomit and the maid suggested calling over one of Mrs Gulliver's friends from the village for assistance but Mrs Waters rebuffed her, saying, 'I can do very well on my own.' Nevertheless, Mrs Waters went to fetch the local surgeon, Thomas Osborne Walker, who was, as it happened, also related to Mrs Gulliver. She arrived at his surgery at 11am and told him that Mrs Gulliver had vomited up 'two pieces of apple as large as walnuts'. Dr Walker was about to go on his rounds, which would take him some hours to complete, but he proposed postponing them in order to go and see Mrs Gulliver at once. Mrs Waters, however, told him not to do this because Mrs Gulliver was in 'a nice sleep'. Dr Walker pressed the point but Mrs Waters repeatedly told him not to interrupt his rounds. Coming any time in the day would be satisfactory, she told him. As a result, he didn't arrive at Mrs Gulliver's house until 5pm when he was somewhat perturbed to find that she was so ill that she was upstairs in her bedroom. When he went upstairs to examine her, he was 'really astonished' to find that she was very ill, being much worse that he had expected. Although she had been poorly in the summer, he had only checked up on her the previous day when she had been 'unusually well' and, indeed, he had then complimented her on how good she looked. Taking Mrs Gulliver's pulse now, he found it flagging and weak. Upon examining her chest with his stethoscope, he detected a sound indicative of heart disease. At the same time, he thought she was drowsier than she should be from heart disease alone. She was in a state of 'profound stupor' and appeared 'overpowered with sleep', answering several of the doctor's questions with her eyes closed.

Believing that Mrs Gulliver was dangerously ill, the doctor informed Mrs Waters of the situation and instructed her that she should inform Mrs Gulliver's sister, Miss Ann Watts, who lived in the village, how ill she was. He also instructed her to call him up any time during the night if the patient took a turn for the worse and directed that she was to have beef tea, wine and water with occasional brandy to try and perk her up. Once he returned to his surgery that evening, he sent over a two ounce bottle of 'medicine' comprised of camphor water, spirits of ether and a compound tincture of lavender. Miss Watts came over a little later, during which time Mrs Gulliver was sick again, but she left at 9pm, by which time another niece of Mrs Gulliver's, rather confusingly called Mrs Elizabeth Watts, had come to the house and she, along with the maid and Mrs Waters, sat up with Mrs Gulliver for the greater part of the night. Both Mrs Watts and Mrs Waters gave her some biscuits and sherry, and the patient seemed a little better at 4am saying that the biscuits and sherry had done her good. At 7am, however, she complained of having wind on the stomach and thought she would be sick. Mrs Watts brought her some tea and she also had some toast.

Mrs Gulliver complained that the tea was bitter. Unknown to her, Mrs Waters had surreptitiously put something into it, explaining afterwards to Mrs Watts that it was Dr Walker's medicine which she didn't think Mrs Gulliver would take otherwise. She seemed to recover her health for, when Dr Walker arrived at 9am to check up on her, he found her much better. He happily expressed the view that she would make a full recovery in a few days. By this time, Mrs Watts had already gone back to her own home so that when the doctor left there was only Mrs Gulliver, Mrs Waters and the maid in the house.

At 11.30 am, Mrs Waters, who was sitting in with Mrs Gulliver, came down for a clean top sheet and then returned to Mrs Gulliver's bedroom. A few minutes later, the maid, having heard Mrs Waters shut the bedroom doors and open all the bedroom windows, went upstairs, curious to see how Mrs Gulliver was. Mrs Waters prevented her from entering the room for a minute or two and then, when she was eventually allowed in, she found her mistress dead in her bed. 'Why, missus is dead!' she exclaimed. 'Oh, I think not', replied Mrs Waters. The astonished maid also smelt some kind of weak scent. Convinced that Mrs Gulliver had indeed died, she rushed off to fetch the doctor who was somewhat astonished at hearing the news, having certified the old woman as perfectly healthy only about two hours earlier.

Even when the doctor arrived about thirty minutes later, Mrs Waters continued to assert that Mrs Gulliver wasn't dead. Critically in this case, as it would turn out, Dr Walker felt the body and thought it was 'quite warm, unusually warm for a corpse'. To ensure that she really had died, he poured a teaspoon of brandy down her throat and, on there being no response, was satisfied that she had passed away. 'She is dead' he told Mrs Waters who responded by saying, 'She's not dead. Oh she's not dead.' He confirmed again that she was indeed deceased and waited until the return of the maid who had run off to fetch Mrs Watts. Mrs Waters then said, 'Oh I am so sorry now that I was here.' Dr Walker asked her why that was, to which she replied, 'Oh, Mrs Gulliver made a will in favour of my husband and the other members of the family know nothing about it, and there will be a rumpus when they find out.' As they conversed, Dr Walker noticed that the windows of the room were open and he felt so cold that he went downstairs into the living room. Mrs Waters explained that Mrs Gulliver had asked her to open the windows because she felt faint. She said she had then applied eau de Cologne to the face of Mrs Gulliver who, somewhat bizarrely, had supposedly liked the sensation so much she had asked for it to be poured into her mouth. Mrs Waters said that she had done so. 'That would not hurt her, doctor, would it?' she asked. The doctor reassured her that the eau de Cologne would not have caused Mrs Gulliver any harm.

Before he left the house, Mrs Waters said she was expecting her husband to join her that evening and invited him (Dr Gulliver) to come over and smoke a pipe with him. The doctor had no intention of doing so and started to make his excuses when Mrs Waters said, 'Oh, do come, we will have a fire lighted in this room. My husband will be delighted, for there will be no one for him to speak to but the ignorant old woman in the other room', meaning herself. She then pressed the doctor to accept a guinea 'for his kindness' but he declined, saying that he hadn't shown any kindness, only his duty to his patient. She then asked him to take it as a present for his wife, which he also refused. In the end she sent the money in the post to his sons who had taken a couple of telegrams to the Post Office for her.

Aside from apparently attempting to force money onto the doctor, it can be seen that, when viewed in a certain light, Mrs Waters had done a number of suspicious or questionable things. Firstly, she had told Dr Walker not to interrupt his rounds to see Mrs Gulliver, on the basis that Mrs Gulliver was asleep. This might have been true when Mrs Waters left the house but, as a matter of fact, the maid was with her mistress while Mrs Waters was visiting the doctor and was talking to her while she was awake in bed, although at this point she was in such a stupor that she didn't recognize her, asking her who she was. Nevertheless she was awake and, there was, consequently, no reason why Dr Walker shouldn't have come immediately. Secondly, she had slipped something into Mrs Gulliver's tea after which Mrs Gulliver had complained it was bitter. It was supposedly Dr Walker's medicine but the doctor said that this wouldn't have made the tea taste bitter. Thirdly, at the very time of Mrs Gulliver's death, she had opened the bedroom windows, possibly to remove a scent that the maid had detected, and closed the doors. Fourthly, when the maid tried to come into the room she prevented her from doing so without explanation (and no explanation was ever provided). Fifthly, she denied that Mrs Gulliver was dead whereas the maid had noticed it immediately. Sixthly, she had volunteered the suggestion that she might be suspected by other family members of murdering Mrs Gulliver due to being a beneficiary in her will. All of these could have had perfectly innocent explanations but it was enough to spark suspicion in the village.

Although Dr Walker certified Mrs Gulliver's death as being caused by heart disease, and she was buried five days later on 28 November, the coroner subsequently ordered that the body should be exhumed and a post-mortem carried out, which was done immediately, on 23 December.

A Dr Buszard of Northampton was brought in to assist Dr Walker with it. The doctors found that the heart was in a fatty state of degeneration, although they couldn't detect any actual valvular disease. The brain and membranes appeared healthy. The contents of the stomach were sealed up in jars and sent to London for analysis. Later that same day, the coroner held an inquest into Mrs Gulliver's death. The facts weren't in dispute although the maid, troubled by a poor memory, couldn't quite remember the precise sequence of events as they occurred over the weekend, especially in respect of what food and drink Mrs Waters brought Mrs Gulliver, and at one point she burst into tears because she was so confused. In respect of the medical evidence about the cause of death, neither doctor wanted to commit himself at this stage until the stomach contents had been analysed. Dr Walker would only remark that he could not rule out the possibility that the appearance of heart disease he had noticed had caused the death of Mrs Gulliver. Dr Buszard, however, said that the symptoms mentioned by Dr Walker were not those he had met with in cases of heart disease which he had personally encountered.

At the conclusion of the inquest on 23 December, there was a discussion over whether to hear the evidence of Mrs Waters but it was decided against doing so at that stage and the inquest was adjourned until 8 January. It must have been an anxious wait for Mrs Waters who was aware that she was the subject of suspicion. In the meantime, the contents of Alice Gulliver's stomach were taken to London by Superintendent Bailie of the Northamptonshire Police for testing by an expert. Professor Alfred Swaine Taylor, the leading expert on poisons, was approached but he had recently retired and declined to take on the task. Instead, he recommended a colleague of his at the University of London who was a professor of Chemistry. However, when the officer visited the man, he found him absent and, due to the urgency of the case, instructed Professor Julian Edward Desborough Rodgers of the London Hospital College, an expert in toxicology, who was available.

At the adjourned inquest on 8 January, Professor Rodgers sensationally told the deputy coroner that there was 'not the slightest doubt' that he had discovered traces of morphia in the stomach, as well as in the oesophagus and the liver, although these traces were so small that they were not weighable. He then said that, based on what he had been told about

Mrs Gulliver's condition, especially regarding her stupor on Saturday afternoon, and based on the results of the post-mortem examination, her condition was 'consistent with the supposition that a narcotic poison, such as morphia, had been administered'. Further, he said, 'I cannot attribute the illness of the deceased on the Saturday to any other cause than having morphia administered'. Nevertheless, although he said that a dose of morphia which produced the effects observed, as described by witnesses, 'must necessarily tend to hasten death', the professor felt that he could not say what the cause of death was in this case, having only found *traces* of morphia in the stomach.

At the same time, Professor Rodgers stated in his evidence, 'I am positive that the death on Sunday was not occasioned by the narcotic administered on the prior Saturday, and I am equally positive that the death did not arise from the state of the heart'. This was a highly controversial statement. Having not even examined the heart, how could he possibly say that Mrs Gulliver had not died from heart disease? In answering this question, he stated that, 'The idea that the heart caused death was negatived by the high temperature of the body'. This was evidently a reference to Dr Walker's evidence at the previous hearing that Mrs Gulliver's dead body felt 'unusually warm' when he examined it within an hour of her death. Professor Rodgers seemed to be saying that it wasn't possible for the body of someone who died of heart disease to feel warm after death, although *why* he believed this wasn't stated.

Having ruled out heart disease, the professor allowed himself to go further in saying that he believed that Mrs Gulliver's death must have been accelerated by the administration of morphia but that the actual cause of death was the administration of some other noxious substance which he had been unable to detect from an examination so long after death. Asked whether a further dose of morphia had been administered on the Sunday morning but then ejected from her stomach causing her to die not from the morphia but from exhaustion caused by vomiting the professor said, 'I think not. The high temperature of the body negatives that supposition'. Again, the professor seemed to think that he could rule out any natural form of death due to the supposedly high temperature of the body after death. He added that, 'Had there been exhaustion it would have lowered the temperature immediately.'

In this book, we've been through all the leading textbooks on the subject of body temperature after death but have seen nothing to suggest that death from heart disease or exhaustion would invariably and immediately lower the post-mortem body temperature. On the contrary, the studies which had been carried out showed that in many cases of natural death the temperature of the body could increase after death. Professor Rodgers, however, seemed to be of the view that the body temperature would only increase after death in cases of poisoning.

At the inquest, Mrs Waters was represented by the coroner from her home town of Worcester, Ronald Tomkins Rea. He pressed Professor Rodgers as to whether Mrs Gulliver had not died of a fainting fit on the Sunday morning, as evidenced by her request for the windows to be opened showing that she was short of air. The professor said that he would not be surprised at her dying in a fainting fit in the circumstances were it not for the high temperature of the body which, he repeated, negatived that supposition. Mr Rea wasn't satisfied and asked the professor to give the ground on which he had come to the conclusion that death occurred from poison in this case. Professor Rodgers said, 'Having recovered from the morphia, death would otherwise be accounted for by the condition of the heart, which, if it were the cause of death, would have resulted in coldness, faintness, and a lowering of the temperature of the body considerably. As death could not have been caused by the condition of the heart I say there must have been some other cause.' Again, the professor was ruling out heart disease as the cause of death based purely on the fact that the body was warm after death.

Having heard the evidence of Professor Rodgers, Dr Buszard then testified that, while he would not like to say so with 'absolute certainty', he now believed it 'highly probable' that Mrs Gulliver's symptoms on the Saturday morning were caused by a dose of morphia. He also thought that such a dose of morphia, administered to someone with a heart condition, would 'undoubtedly' have accelerated her death. Nevertheless, like Professor Rodgers, he didn't think that Mrs Gulliver had died from the direct effects of morphia but it might have indirectly caused her death. Dr Walker then said exactly the same thing. But he also included some bombshell evidence. He said that, during the summer of 1873, on a previous visit to Mrs Gulliver, Mrs Waters had asked him for a solution of morphia on behalf of 'a poor suffering woman of West Haddon' who she said she had been in the habit of supplying. By way of explanation, she told him that she had forgotten to bring some from home and would be obliged if he would give her some as an act of charity. As he was aware that she was the wife of a medical man, he agreed to the request, and instructed his son to let her have nine grams of morphia after making sure that she understood what he was giving her. 'Are you aware this is a very powerful medicine?' he had asked her. She said 'Yes'.

Following the medical evidence, there was more harmful evidence against Mrs Waters. Jane Middleton, the maid, denied that the pork pie eaten by Mrs Gulliver on the Thursday was bad, or likely to have caused any ill-health, saying that she ate some of it herself without any issues. She didn't seem to be aware that more had been eaten on the Friday (if that was the case). Her mistress was, she said, very well on the Friday when she ate the boiled fowl. The maid also said she heard some rumpling on the Friday night in the room where Mrs Gulliver kept her papers. The only person who could have been making the rumpling sound was Mrs Waters.

Then it was revealed that the late Mr Gulliver had lent £385 to Mrs Waters' husband, Alfred, to enable him to pass through his college degrees and qualify to become a physician, having been a medical assistant at the time he had married Mary Ann in 1862. He was required to pay interest to the estate of Mr Gulliver but, at the time of Mrs Gulliver's death, was three years in arrears with the interest payments. It was also revealed that Mrs Gulliver wasn't particularly fond of Mrs Waters and had given her brother, Thomas Watts, the impression that she was 'very vexed, very cross' because Mrs Waters was coming to visit in November. He told the inquest that she had said that 'she did not care much about seeing her'. It's fair to say that there wasn't much good news for Mrs Waters in the emerging evidence but Thomas Watts did say of his sister that 'she would never take medicine if she would avoid it.' That could provide the explanation as to why Mrs Waters had felt the need to slip Dr Walker's medicine into Mrs Gulliver's tea without telling her.

While all this evidence was being given, Mrs Waters was sitting in a small room in the inn above the large room in which the inquest was being heard, expecting to be called as a witness. During a break in the proceedings, Mr Rea visited her and said: 'I think there is a communication which I ought to make to you. The index of the analysis points to morphia as having been administered by the deceased to someone. Mr Walker, the surgeon, has stated that you bought morphia off him about three months since, saying that you wanted it for an old woman at West Haddon, to whom you had been in the habit of giving it as an act of charity. What became of the morphia?' She replied, 'I took it myself, I cannot be without it, can I Alfred?' referring to her husband, and added, 'I have some with me now.' 'Well', said Mr Rea, it's very unfortunate for a person mixed up with an affair of this kind that there should be a constant possession of that class of poison'. To her husband, Mrs Waters said, 'You don't believe that I am guilty Alfred, do you?' In response, he burst into tears, kissed her and said, 'No dear, no dear. Calm yourself'. Her health at this stage visibly deteriorated and it was obvious that she would be unable to give any evidence to the inquest. At one point she said to one of the ladies attending her, 'They have persecuted me to death, and I have done nothing'. When another of the ladies confirmed that morphia had been found in Mrs Gulliver's stomach contents, she cried, 'I never gave it to her! I never gave it to her!' To her husband, she said, 'I shall have a fit, I know I shall. I can feel it coming.' She did indeed then have a paralytic fit and screamed loudly as she collapsed.

Her screams were heard by those attending the inquest in the room below and were soon followed by Alfred Waters interrupting the proceedings in an emotional state, crying out, 'I am sure my wife is dying, will any of the medical men go to her?' Professor Rodgers and Dr Buszard rushed out the room to provide assistance. However, the inquest continued normally, with everyone involved assuming that Mrs Waters was having nothing more than a hysterical fit. Some, no doubt, thought she was faking. Without having heard her evidence, the jury was asked to produce a verdict which they did, as follows: 'The jury are unanimously of opinion that the deceased, Alice Gulliver, did not die from natural causes. They also consider her death was caused by the administration of poison, but there is not sufficient evidence for them to express an opinion by whom the poison was administered.' Despite this apparent uncertainty as to who administered the poison, John Becke, representing the Gulliver family, immediately applied for a warrant for the apprehension of Mrs Waters on the charge of wilful murder of Alice Gulliver. Superintendent

Bailie of the Northampton police then stated that he had reason to believe that Mrs Waters *did* murder Mrs Gulliver; and, accordingly, the warrant was granted. It was never executed, however, for, shortly afterwards the news came through that Mrs Waters was dead in the above room. She had committed suicide by taking a dose of strychnine.

After her death, some new facts emerged. Her husband revealed that, since a libel action had been brought against her three years earlier, she had suffered from paralytic fits and had become suicidal to the extent that any little thing led her to think of taking her own life. She was also in the habit of taking morphia. He said that he wasn't aware that she had strychnine in her possession but that, as she assisted him with administering medicine, she would have been able to secretly take some. Shortly before she died, she had said to him, 'I have taken - ' but didn't manage to finish the sentence because she was overcome by paroxysm.

The events in West Haddon sparked off a major controversy in the medical community. There were many who felt that Mrs Waters was a harmless, if eccentric, woman who had, indeed, as she had said, been persecuted to death and had been forced to take her own life by the presentation of misleading medical evidence against her. In an editorial dated 17 January 1874, the *British Medical Journal* attacked the notion that it was possible to accurately assess body temperature after death, saying of Dr Walker's impression that Mrs Gulliver's corpse had a high temperature, 'it must be observed that this was not ascertained with any precision or exactness, nor was any means used to confirm what seems to have been a mere manual impression. It is unnecessary to observe how utterly unreliable, in such a case, is the impression of touch, not recorded at the time, but subsequently remembered; and how difficult it would be under any circumstances to base any conclusion on such an impression.' The suggestion of Professor Rodgers that poison causes a raise in temperature after death was said to be wrong, and his evidence on the subject was, accordingly, 'utterly worthless'. The verdict of the jury inquiring into the death of Mrs Gulliver was described as 'monstrous'.

The journal had also discovered something not mentioned in evidence at the inquest, namely that Mrs Gulliver had supposedly been freely using cough lozenges before her death which would, apparently, explain the minute traces of morphia discovered by Professor Rodgers. This came from a written account of events produced by Mrs Waters two days before her death. In that account she said that she had been invited to West Haddon by her aunt who 'expressed her delight to see me'. Regarding Mrs Gulliver's illness, she explained that, on the Saturday morning, Mrs Gulliver had positively instructed her not to call in the doctor but, as the old woman was obviously ill, she went out secretly to fetch him. The reason she didn't want him to come immediately was because she wanted it to look like it was an accidental call on his part. This was corroborated by a letter she wrote to her husband on the Saturday afternoon which the *BMJ* had also acquired. Mrs Waters also wrote in her account of events that, while Mrs Gulliver asked to drink the eau de cologne in the moments before she died, she only gave her sherry. She explained that she opened the windows in order to get some air into the room after Mrs Gulliver took a turn for the worse. For the *BMJ*, the story here was one of an old woman who had died of heart disease, and a nervous but entirely innocent middle aged lady persecuted by false medical evidence into taking her own life.

The *BMJ*'s account was reproduced in the *Times* which had been following events in West Haddon, and this prompted a letter in response from Professor Rodgers which was published on 21 January 1874. Claiming that the *BMJ*'s story contained inaccuracies, Rodgers claimed on the basis of the inquest evidence, and contrary to what Mrs Waters had said in her written account, that, 'The visit of Mrs Waters to Mrs Gulliver was both unexpected and unwelcome'. He pointed out that Mrs Gulliver was in good health two days before her death, said that the maid had testified that the pork pie was not stale and noted that Mrs Waters told the doctor not to come to the house immediately. He drew attention to Mrs Waters' opening of the windows of Mrs Gulliver's room which suggested she was trying to hide the scent of poison and to the fact that she had stopped the maid from entering the room in which Mrs Gulliver was lying dead. He claimed that the evidence of her relatives at the inquest was that Mrs Gulliver was not in the habit of taking lozenges containing morphia, or any other form of lozenge (although this evidence had not been reported) but he failed to address the issue of how the warm temperature of the body supposedly felt by Dr Walker could enable him to rule out heart disease as a cause of death, as he had claimed at the inquest. Instead, he focused on the fact that he had found morphia in the stomach and that, 'Although the history of the case did not show that morphia was the immediate cause of death, yet that same history would not permit me, after an experience of 30 years as a toxicological expert, to say that it arose from natural causes.'

A letter from Ernest Hart, the editor of the *BMJ*, responded to Professor Rodgers' letter in the *Times* of 23 January 1874 by pointing out that, while the professor had found unweighable traces of morphia in Mrs Gulliver's stomach, he had stated categorically that this morphia was not the cause of death, yet he had found no traces of any poison which *did* cause Mrs Gulliver's death so that it was no more than a theory that she had died of poison: a theory which was based entirely on Dr Walker's assessment that the temperature of the body was high after death. Of this, Mr Hart said that, 'The most eminent medical jurists in this country are not less ignorant than I of any justification for this reckless suggestion'. He asked the professor a number of questions about his conclusions but the professor declined to engage further in any correspondence.

Ernest Hart continued his response to Professor Rodgers' letter in the *BMJ* of 24 January 1874, claiming that Professor Rodgers had 'thought proper to answer our arraignment of his evidence, by drawing up afresh an indictment against the woman whom his evidence drove to suicide, and has framed it on the state of the doors and windows…and on the general basis of moral evidence, all of which are wide of the mark.' Going for the jugular, he said of Professor Rodgers' testimony that a high temperature after death was incompatible with heart disease as a cause of death, 'At this evidence we stand aghast, and we protest against it with stern indignation'. It was, he stated, 'without foundation in fact, and without justification even as a suggestion'. Further, a more general point about the problems with estimating time of death on the basis of body temperature was made:

> No statement whatever as to the temperature after death can have any real value, unless the circumstances under which the body was placed be carefully noted, such as the surrounding temperature, the amount of clothing, and the period which has elapsed since death; unless the thermometer be used; and unless the internal temperature of the body be noted as well as the surface temperature. The whole subject of temperature after death is one of much difficulty and uncertainty; and any conclusions drawn from it must, as competent men have

pointed out, be deduced with great caution, and must be regarded with doubt and suspicion.

The *BMJ* had, by now, been contacted by Professor Alfred Swaine Taylor who told them that his 1863 experiments with Dr Wilks had found that, 'sometimes the body cooled rapidly and sometimes slowly' and that, in cases of death of heart failure arising from sudden haemorrhage, 'we found the heat retained for some time after death, even where the conditions were favourable to rapid cooling.' The professor directly contradicted the evidence of Professor Rodgers by saying that, 'It is quite consistent with death from syncope, as a result of advanced fatty degeneration of the heart, that a high temperature of the body may be retained after death'. Professor Taylor's colleague, Dr Wilks, was also quoted as saying that he knew of no published opinions which supported Professor Rodgers' opinion. He said that the observations recorded by himself and Professor Taylor, 'clearly showed the error of the supposition that the body cooled more rapidly after sudden death – in fact, there were some reasons to suppose the contrary.' He added that, 'It is true that a great rise of temperature occurred in persons suffering from acute or active disease, and that the low temperature at the time of death was found in those who had long suffered from chronic disease: but in persons who had died from haemorrhage, syncope, or other similar cause, no rapid fall of temperature was found.'

Also contacted by the *BMJ* was Robert Christison, Professor of Medicine at Edinburgh University, who stated that, when he had performed pathological examinations in cases of deaths by natural disease, he was, 'much struck and not very seldom, by the maintenance after death, of a degree of heat most sensible to the hand of others, as well as to my own, both on the external surface and in the cavities of the human body.' He said he was never able to explain it but this heat, which he described as 'considerable', was present at least twenty-four hours after death, which was the earliest that such pathological examinations were carried out.

A letter from a Dr Moxon was also included in this issue of the *BMJ* in which Moxon supported the notion that heat can be retained in the body for some considerable time after death and that, 'after death from syncope the internal parts may be expected to show an increased amount of heat'. More generally, Moxon cautioned that, 'if we are called upon to pronounce upon the length of time which has elapsed since death in a given case, this is only to be done approximately and probably. It is necessary to take into consideration the cause and manner of death, the condition of the individual, the state of the atmosphere, the manner in which the body has been kept after death. And even after making these allowances, we can only say that probably a person has been dead for such and such a time.'

The debate continued into the following week as Dr Henry Gawain Sutton of 9 Finsbury Square wrote to the *BMJ* to say that, in his own experience of examining dead bodies at the London Hospital, those bodies with a thick layer of subcutaneous fat were so warm more than twelve hours after death that, 'it was very disagreeable making the examination'. With respect to Professor Rodgers' claim to be able to determine the cause of death due to the body being very warm after death, Sutton said: 'If a body cooled slowly, and it was in consequence unusually warm twelve hours, or even longer, after death, that circumstance would not enable me to give any opinion as to the cause of death.'

The controversy rumbled on into February and, at a general meeting of the Birmingham and Midland Counties branch of the British Medical Association on 12 February 1874, it was resolved that the best thanks of the meeting be given to the editor of the *BMJ* 'for his able and outspoken criticism of the evidence in the West Haddon case'. The editor commented in response in the *BMJ* of 28 February 1874 that the evidence of Professor Rodgers at the inquest into the death of Mrs Gulliver was so 'utterly without justification, and so much at variance with scientific facts, and with the duty of a medico-legal witness, as to constitute a grave scandal'. He suggested that the Council of the London Hospital should take some action against the professor for 'so flagrant breach of the rules which must guide a medical witness.'

In March 1874, evidently desiring to inform the medical profession further about body temperature after death, the *BMJ* published an article by Dr James Goodheart, the Assistant Demonstrator of Morbid Anatomy at Guy's Hospital, entitled, 'On Post Mortem Temperatures'. Although he didn't refer directly to the West Haddon case, Goodheart stated that he was aware of a number of cases where the temperature shortly before death was 102 degrees Fahrenheit. He revealed that in his experience the average hourly loss of heat during the first few hours after death was 3.37

degrees Fahrenheit but it was higher for emaciated subjects. According to Goodheart, 'most bodies decline in surface-temperature very rapidly during the first hour or so after death, compared with the loss afterwards.' He also said that it wasn't possible to predict with any certainty when a body would be perfectly cold. Goodheart's paper also touched on rigor mortis; he said that from his own observations, rigor would come on earlier than had usually been stated. He discovered that the average time for commencement of rigor mortis, as evidenced by stiffness of various parts of the body, was from three to four hours, with its complete development coming on average in five hours. 'It would not', he said, 'appear to be dependent on the temperature of the body' although, he suggested, 'It is possible that the early supervention of rigor mortis might have some influence in lowering quickly the surface-temperature of the body.'

In the same month, the *BMJ* published a short article by Dr J. Wilkie Burman, the resident medical officer and superintendent of the Wiltshire County Asylum, entitled 'The Cooling of the Body After Death'. He commented that the question of how long a patient has been dead, 'has generally been, and continues for the most part to be, based on the feeling or degree of warmth or coldness as experienced by the mere application of the living hand to the corpse – a process which, as compared with thermometric observation, I have found to be more or less fallacious and productive of uncertain results'. He stated his intention of conducting experiments using a thermometer under the armpit to take the temperature of moribund persons and then take temperature readings after death in order to produce a scientific basis on which to estimate time of death. While he felt that the research had not yet been done, and that he hadn't yet conducted a sufficient number of tests himself to allow him to speak authoritatively on the subject, he nevertheless said: 'I think I may safely venture to corroborate those who affirm that the cooling of the body after death, as indicated by a thermometer, is a much more gradual process than the experience of our unaided tactile senses has hitherto led us to suppose it might be'. Burman would go on to devote the best part of six years to trying to find a conclusive answer to the question.

The final word on the West Haddon scandal went to Professor Taylor who published an article in *Guy's Hospital Reports* of 1874 entitled 'Death From Disease or Poison: Does The Retention or Maintenance of Heat in a Dead Body Furnish Any Indication of the Cause of Death?'. After summarizing the facts pertaining to Mrs Gulliver's death, Taylor stated his conclusion that it was clearly a case of sudden death due to heart disease. As the leading expert of his day in poisons, he completely rejected the theory that Mrs Gulliver had died as a result of poison of any kind. He dismissed the idea that it would be possible to conclude that Mrs Gulliver had ingested any morphia based on the miniscule unweighable 'traces' of morphia that Professor Rodgers thought he had found. Nor did he think that Mrs Gulliver's symptoms were consistent with having been given any form of poison. 'The chemical hypothesis of poisoning constructed in this case' he said, 'is wholly untenable'.

Most of Professor Taylor's article concentrated on the issue of Mrs Gulliver's body supposedly being warm after death. He confirmed that, in his experiments on animals with prussic acid and other volatile poisons, he hadn't observed that the warmth of the bodies was retained beyond the usual period but, on the contrary, 'the rate of cooling took place as in death from natural causes'. Furthermore, in all his experience of cases of poisoning of human beings, 'in no instance has the unusual maintenance of heat been observed or described'. Referring to 'the works of the ablest writers on toxicology', Taylor stated that he was unaware of 'any case recorded in which the unusual retention of heat in the dead body has been described as a characteristic of poisoning by prussic acid or of volatile poisons generally.' That being so, Professor Rodgers' claim that unusual warmth of a dead body was an indicator of poisoning must have been unfounded. If Professor Taylor was unaware of such a phenomenon there can't have been any substance to it. Taylor also commented caustically that, 'It is a novelty in medical jurisprudence to find this maintenance of heat in a dead body positively set forth as furnishing any proof of death from poison.'

According to Taylor, it was perfectly possible that in a case of sudden death, including heart disease, the body could be slow in losing its temperature and he thought that would probably be sufficient to account for Dr Walker's observation as to the high temperature of Mrs Gulliver's body. Equally, however, he believed she could have been one of those exceptional cases which had been recorded where there was an unusually high temperature after death. He didn't find anything suspicious about Dr

Walker finding the body to be very warm within an hour or so of death and he also noted that 'the sole test of the alleged "high temperature" appears to have been the recollection of an impression conveyed to the hands a month before, and to which no importance was attached at the time.' Elsewhere in the article he referred to the term 'high temperature' as a vague one and he made sure to put it in quotation marks indicating that it lacked any real meaning. One can't help but contrast this with his acceptance in the Gardner case of the term 'cold temperature' by which he felt it *was* possible to accurately estimate the time of death.

Furthermore, Professor Taylor said that, 'In one case a body retains heat for an unusual length of time; in another, it loses it rapidly'. One body, he said, 'may be quite cold in nine hours, and another may retain its heat to such a degree as to be warm after ten hours!', and he admitted that, 'The causes of these variations are not apparent.' This too is in contrast to the way he dealt with the medical evidence in the Gardner case, assuming that it *was* possible to accurately calculate the earliest amount of time that Mrs Gardner's body could have taken to feel cold.

So what did happen in the case of Mrs Gulliver? Was Mary Ann Waters an innocent woman who tried to care for her aunt and was persecuted to death or was she a cunning poisoner? While there were a number of incriminating circumstances against her, there were some obvious innocent explanations for most of them. A big issue was made of her opening the windows shortly before Mrs Gulliver's death but that might have been no more than an attempt to ventilate the room, as she said. The fact that she secretly put Dr Walker's medicine into Mrs Gulliver's tea might well have been due to Mrs Gulliver's reluctance to take her medicine. Her desire to delay Dr Walker's visit on the Saturday could be explained by her desire to make it appear to Mrs Gulliver to be an accidental one. While Mrs Gulliver's family said that Mrs Gulliver did not welcome the visit from her niece, Mrs Waters claimed to have had a note from her aunt inviting her to stay with her. So there was another side to the story which wasn't heard at the inquest.

And yet. There can't be any doubt that Mrs Waters had lied to Dr Walker earlier in 1873 when she manipulated him into giving her some potentially deadly morphia. She told him that she wanted it for a local woman but privately admitted to her legal representative during the inquest proceedings that, having been taking it for some time to help her nerves, she had wanted it for herself. But was that even true? Was it possible that she thought it was a miracle cure that could help her aunt's health, so she surreptitiously slipped it into her drinks? It might have been done with the best of intentions but, after Mrs Gulliver's death, perhaps she thought she was responsible for it, which is why she took her own life. As to that moment of suicide, it must have been planned prior to the news which emerged from the inquest hearing. Times were certainly different in the 1870s but, still, not many women carried strychnine in their handbags. Mrs Waters did. She must have been preparing her final moments for some time. However, her husband says she often had suicidal thoughts so this might have been a continuation of those.

But there are still unanswered questions. Why did Mrs Waters prevent the maid from entering Mrs Gulliver's room without explanation for a couple of minutes at a time when she was already dead? Why did Mrs Waters claim that the pork pie was stale when the maid said that there was nothing wrong with it? Did Mrs Gulliver really ask to drink the eau de cologne a few minutes prior to her death? Why did Mrs Waters refuse to believe her aunt was dead? This might have been a genuine act of denial but she certainly took a long time to be convinced, not even accepting it after the doctor had arrived and pronounced death to have occurred.

The inquest jury was faced with an expert in toxicology telling them that traces of morphia had been discovered in Mrs Gulliver's stomach and Mrs Waters was known to have been in possession of morphia. They were also being told that the warmth of Mrs Gulliver's body after death was inconsistent with heart disease but consistent with poisoning. It's no wonder they came to the conclusion that there had been a murder. Mrs Waters had a financial interest in her aunt's death and thus a clear motive, so she had to be considered a prime suspect.

As to whether there were really any traces of morphia in Mrs Gulliver's stomach, we have to rely on the expertise of Professor Taylor who said that it was impossible to say so. There can be no doubt that Professor Rodgers was entirely wrong to draw any conclusions about the cause of death from the supposed warmth of Mrs Gulliver's body. It did not indicate that Mrs Gulliver had been poisoned and it did not negative that she might have died from heart disease.

CHAPTER NINE

1875-1887

While the year 1874 had seen renewed focus on body temperature after death, nothing changed in the following years when it came to the medical profession estimating the actual time of death.

At seven o'clock in the morning of 29 July 1875, Robert James Burton, a divisional police surgeon, was sent for by the police to go to the Red Lion Public House in Southwell. When he arrived, he found the dead body of a homeless woman, about 60 years of age, lying in the tap room, her temple bruised and bloody. As he informed a jury at the Old Bailey later in the year during the trial of the two men accused of her murder, on removing her clothes, 'I found the body still warm round the waist, where it had been covered by the clothes – the rest of the body was cold'. There were no other indications relating to time of death such as rigor mortis and, on the basis of the body being both warm and cold in different places, Dr Burton told the court that, 'I should say death had taken place from four to six hours when I saw the body.'

The body of the woman, whose identity was never established, had been discovered lying in the street at 4.45am that morning. A witness heard a quarrel involving the deceased woman outside the Black Horse Public House at 11pm the previous night, which was eight hours before Dr Burton examined the body at 7am, and, from information produced to the Home Office in a petition by Joseph Drinkwater, one of the two men convicted of the murder, it would appear that, shortly after 11pm, the homeless woman was the victim of a gang rape in a field by four men, including Drinkwater, and died as a result of her treatment by them.[71] Drinkwater said he fell asleep next to the woman, whom he said he thought was asleep, and then left the field at 3am. While there is no reliable evidence as to when the poor woman died, it really could have been at any time between eight and four hours prior Dr Burton's examination.

When, later that year, at 10am on 16 October 1875, Francis Smith (a surgeon) was called to examine the dead body of 30-year-old Mrs Naomi Youell, suspected of having been poisoned with prussic acid, he found 'the upper part of the body quite warm, but the hands and feet were cold'. From this, as he told the magistrate at Southwark Police Court, 'he judged that death had occurred shortly before.'[72] That wasn't terribly helpful but the time of death can easily be placed to between 8 and 9am that morning when a neighbour heard a quarrel between Mrs Youell and her husband followed by blows and groans. Interestingly, some years later, a 62-year-old woman, Mary Coughlan, who was a hawker of fish and fruit, was found dead in a room in her lodging house one morning in January 1879. When the surgeon, Dr Williams, arrived, he found the temperature of the body, as felt by his hand, to be similar to what Mrs Youell's had been, for he said, 'The face and hands were cold, but the body was warm'.[73] From the example of Mrs Youell it might be concluded that Mary Coughlan had died one or two hours earlier but Dr Williams said that he believed 'she had been dead three or four hours'. It was known that the woman had died sometime during the night, in her sleep, so, in truth, it was anyone's guess precisely what time that had been.

For some disarming honesty we find it in the evidence of Charles James Cullingworth, a divisional police surgeon, in a sensational case where a man had been arrested by police in October 1880 while transporting a corpse through the streets of Manchester in a hand cart. Dr Cullingworth examined the body of the dead woman, which was dressed in a chemise and covered with blood, as it lay on the hand cart. The body, he said, was cold, and 'death might have taken place one or two days previously, or only

---

[71] TNA: HO 144/19/47446.
[72] *Globe*, 19 October 1875.
[73] *Croydon Advertiser*, 18 January 1879.

some hours previously.'[74] This was quite a range but reflected the reality that in most cases it was all but impossible to say precisely when death had occurred simply from a body found to be 'cold' and that, if being honest, a medical examiner truly could not say whether death had occurred hours earlier or days earlier.

A finding of rigidity, in addition to coldness, however, seemed to give courage to medical examiners, and, in the following month, a Dr John Tanner, testifying at Southwark Police Court, where John Walker was charged with murdering his wife, said that, from the body of Mrs Walker being 'cold and rigid', he was able to conclude that, 'She had been dead eight or ten hours'.[75] At the Old Bailey, however, he modified this evidence slightly saying, 'she had, in my judgement, been dead from eight to ten hours perhaps more'. Tanner said he examined the body at 12.35pm on Sunday, 7 November 1880, which puts the time of death on this basis at between 2.35am and 4.35am, or perhaps earlier. A witness had heard Walker hitting his wife and knocking her down at between 6 and 7pm on the Saturday evening but she appeared to have been alive when another witness saw her sitting in her chair at shortly after 7pm. Between 8 and 9pm a fellow lodger heard Walker slap his wife and noises of quarrelling. At 10.15pm a young girl saw Mrs Walker lying on the floor in her back parlour when her husband kicked her hard and Mrs Walker said nothing. She appears to have been alive at this time for she was heard to be breathing heavily at about 10.30pm. About two hours later, at 12.45am, another witness heard Mr Walker say, 'Bleeding old cow' followed by a great fall. At some point during Saturday night yet another witness heard 'quarrelling and tumbling about and screaming' with Mrs Walker calling out, 'Don't John, you will kill me!' followed by silence then 'a great noise and quarrelling again'. When she was found dead by a neighbour at shortly after midday on Sunday her face was bruised and blood was still oozing from her nose and mouth, something the doctor said was still happening when he examined the body more than thirty minutes later. The blood oozing indicated a recent death, shortly before midday, but the witness evidence relating to the argument and fall suggested that Mrs Walker had died at about 1am, more than eleven hours before the discovery of

---

[74] *Bolton Evening News*, 30 October 1880.
[75] *Willesden Chronicle*, 19 November 1880.

the body, which might explain Dr Tanner adding 'perhaps earlier' to his evidence at trial compared to what he said at the Police Court.

By 1880, having retired from his position as medical superintendent at the Wiltshire County Lunatic Asylum, Dr J. Wilkie Burman felt it was time to publish the results of his observations on patients at the asylum. His article entitled 'On the Rate of Cooling of the Human Body after Death' was published in the *Edinburgh Medical Journal* in May 1880. Burman's stated aim was to enable the medical profession 'with tolerable precision (or at any rate with greater accuracy that at present) to estimate, by means of the thermometer, the probable time that has elapsed, since death, in a body found dead.'

The key difference between Burman's experiments and those of Taylor and Wilks, or so he claimed, was that 'in every case' his temperature readings 'were commenced *at the time of death* (and in some cases *before*)'. This wasn't actually quite true because, in one case, the first temperature reading wasn't taken until one hour and ten minutes after death. Also, unlike Taylor and Wilks, in most cases, he took hourly readings after death. He failed, however, to take any internal temperature readings which, he said, was 'an oversight' on his part that he regretted. All his patients after death were kept in bed, wearing their nightclothes and covered with ordinary bedding. The main weakness of his experiment was that it only involved seven cases. He did give the results of nine cases but excluded the last two because the observations in them were 'of a more incomplete nature' and were thus not factored into his conclusions. Considering that Burman had been working on the subject for six years, since his 1874 *BMJ* article, it is strange that his experiment involved so few cases but this might simply mean that there were very few deaths in the Wiltshire asylum during the period.

Burman found that in two cases where body temperature was, in his words, 'already unusually high at time of death' – being 109.4 and 108.2 degrees respectively – there was a rapid rate of cooling in the first hour, of an average of almost four and a half degrees, whereas in the other five cases it supposedly averaged 1.6 degrees (although, in fact, it appears that he only used the results of three cases to arrive at this figure, none of which individually involved a drop of 1.6 degrees during the first hour). When he collated his findings of all seven cases, he found that there was an average (mean) rate of cooling of 1.6 degrees an hour. This result, based on just those seven cases, led him confidently to put forward a mathematical formula by which he felt it would be possible for any medical practitioner to estimate the time of death based on the temperature under the armpit of the corpse. If, for example, a dead body was found with a temperature of 80 degrees, then, assuming the body was found in bed in a room with a normal room temperature, Burman's formula involved subtracting those 80 degrees from the estimated temperature at death, which he said was 98.4 degrees, to produce the number of degrees cooled as 18.4, which number was then divided by 1.6 which would give a total of 11.5, meaning that death must have occurred eleven hours and thirty minutes earlier.[76]

While this was a relatively simple formula, there were some serious problems with Burman's experiment and conclusion which don't appear to have been fully appreciated at the time. In only one of his seven cases would it have been possible to have used his own formula to estimate, with any degree of reliability, a time of death within four hours of death, had that time of death not been known. That's because, of the seven cases which did feature in the results, six of them involved (mainly sick) individuals with temperatures over 100 degrees at the time of their deaths, being above the average assumed by Burman of 98.4 degrees, and it took some hours for the temperature in those cases to drop down to that temperature. Burman's formula, of course, doesn't work for any temperature reading above 98.4 degrees.

Of the two cases with the 'abnormally high temperature' at the time of death, in the first case (for which Burman provided no cause of death), the temperature had fallen to 94 degrees five hours after death but, if a medical practitioner had taken that temperature, Burman's formula would have led to the conclusion that death had occurred within the past three hours. In the second case (involving death from acute bronchitis), the temperature didn't fall below 98 degrees until five hours after death. If a medical practitioner had taken the temperature of this corpse eleven hours after death, he would have found it to be 87 degrees which, according to

---

[76] In an age before calculators, for simplicity's sake Burman allowed an element of rounding whereby he felt that 'we might arrive at a sufficiently accurate conclusion' by assuming a temperature at time of death as a straight 98 degrees and a rate of cooling of 1.5 degrees per hour.

Burman's formula, should have led to a conclusion that death occurred seven hours earlier, an error of four hours. However, Burman felt such cases could be ignored from the medico-legal point of view because individuals with abnormally high temperatures at the time of death could reasonably be assumed to be under medical observation and treatment, 'and not likely, therefore, to be unexpectedly found dead'. While that was fair enough in most cases, it meant that his findings could only be properly applied to those in normal health, who could be assumed to have had an average body temperature of about 98.4 degrees, using Burman's number, at the time of their death.

Yet, in only one of the other five cases which shaped Burman's conclusion was it even *possible* that his patient had a temperature at time of death of 98.4 degrees. This was the case in which no temperature was taken until seventy minutes after death (from asthma, a weak heart and cyanosis) when it was 95 degrees which, if one assumes a temperature of 98.4 degrees at time of death, would have meant a fall of 3.4 degrees in the first hour after death. In this case, Burman then took temperature readings every hour for ten hours but only one of those readings produced a fall of 1.6 degrees. During some hours the temperature dropped by one degree or less and in one hour it dropped by two degrees. In this case, however, Burman's formula does work to a certain extent because after ten hours the body temperature was 82 degrees which is almost exactly where it should have been. It is, however, the only case out of his seven patients in which Burman's formula does work to any degree *at any time* after death. In respect of another of his cases, involving death by general paralysis, the body temperature didn't fall below 100.8 degrees when, after three hours, Burman stopped recording temperatures. In another, involving death after epileptic fits, it wasn't until three hours after death that the temperature had fallen (from 101.8 degrees) to 98.4 degrees and the temperature after four hours was 96.4 degrees which, if Burman's formula was applied, would have indicated a time of death less than one and a half hours earlier. In no single hour was there a fall by 1.6 degrees but, after ten hours it was closer, as Burman's formula would have given a time of death nine hours earlier. In another case of death arising from epileptic fits, after eleven hours the body temperature was 85.2 degrees which was five degrees higher than it should have been and would have led to an estimated time of death about eight hours earlier. In the final case, involving death from melancholia arising from refusal of food, the temperature four hours after death was 93.8 degrees, a temperature which would lead one to a conclusion that death had occurred within three hours, while, after eleven hours, it was 84 degrees, which would have given an estimated time of death nine hours earlier.

Considering that most of Burman's test patients were sick at the time of death, it's difficult to be certain if the rate of cooling he had supposedly discovered could be applied to healthy patients who had been murdered. It's also unlikely that a murdered person would have been murdered in their bed so Burman's formula couldn't be said to accurately apply to bodies found in the open. Burman did stress that, 'the circumstances under which the body is placed – such as the medium in which it is immersed (whether air or water), the surrounding temperature, the amount and nature of the clothing or bedding etc. – should all be carefully noted, as is generally the case, and due allowance made accordingly.' Yet he didn't explain what kind of allowance to his mathematical formula should be made depending on the surrounding temperature and the amount or nature of clothing. That was left open, perhaps for others to work out.

In assessing Burman's formula, it's also worth testing his results on those presented by Niderkorn in his 1872 paper on rigor mortis. In addition to conducting tests on 113 dead patients for rigor, Niderkorn took temperature readings on 136 dead bodies. After a period of two to four hours following death, he found the average temperature to be 96.9 degrees. Using Burman's formula this would indicate death had occurred within an hour, thus being all but useless from a medico-legal perspective. After four to six hours, the average temperature found by Niderkorn was 90.2 which, according to Burman's formula, means that death had occurred just over five hours earlier which is spot on. However, the average temperature in Niderkorn's data after six to eight hours was 81.7 degrees which Burman's formula tells us should be the temperature almost ten and a half hours after death. After eight to twelve hours, Niderkorn's average reading was 77.9 degrees which is close to where it should be, as Burman's formula would indicate death having occurred about twelve hours and fifty minutes earlier, which is only just outside the range.

As with Burman's own findings, there was quite a wide range of temperatures within Niderkorn's experiment. After two to four hours the maximum post-mortem temperature recorded by Niderkorn was 109.4 with the minimum being 89.6 degrees. With the former, it's impossible to use Burman's formula to calculate a time of death but the minimum time would suggest death had occurred five and a half hours earlier. After eight to ten hours, the former corpse still had a temperature as high as 100.2 degrees, while the latter corpse was down to 62.6 degrees in the same time period but Burman's formula would have told us that this death had occurred almost thirty-six hours earlier, creating a massive discrepancy. On the basis of the data that was available to Burman, one does have to question his certainty that a normal rate of cooling was 1.6 degrees Fahrenheit per hour.

There were three other interesting elements in Burman's paper. Firstly, he stated that, 'The retention of considerable heat in the *viscera* for a long period after death, and even after the surface of the body feels *cool*, is an occurrence that I have frequently noticed, and cannot fail to have been observed, from time to time, by all those who, like myself, have had much experience in post-mortem examinations.' This underscored the importance of taking the internal temperature of the body and, as mentioned, Burman regretted that he failed to do this in his experiments, relying on the armpit temperature, albeit that the armpit temperature is normally considered to be close to, but not the same as, the internal temperature. Secondly, Burman had an unusual theory that what he referred to as 'real and complete death' did not take place until the body commenced to cool down. Therefore, he would presumably not have regarded individuals as being dead whose bodies were warm 24 hours after death despite the fact that other doctors had conducted post-mortem examinations on those bodies which involved opening them up. Finally, in his total of nine cases studied, there was one case of a slight temperature increase after death which caused Burman to compare it to the West Haddon case, even though there was no evidence that the temperature of Mrs Gulliver actually increased after her death.

Despite the simplicity of Burman's formula, it doesn't appear to have been used in criminal cases during the 1880s or beyond. Medical practitioners continued to rely on touch to estimate body heat and then produce an estimate of time of death which appeared to be based largely on instinct. In June 1880, for example, William Hodgson Ryewell, a surgeon, gave evidence to an inquest concerning the death of Eliza Barlow, a young woman who had been murdered and decapitated by her deranged 56-year-old landlady, Anna Maria Martin, on 24 June 1880. Dr Ryewell told the coroner on 28 June that, when found (in a box) shortly after 7pm in the evening of 24 June, Barlow was, 'quite dead, her body not perfectly cold' and that, 'she could not have been dead more than 10 or 12 hours'.[77] He adjusted this estimate when giving evidence to the magistrate at Southwark Police Court on 9 July when he then said that, 'The body had been dead from 8 to 12 hours.' Yet, to the magistrate he said that the body was 'nearly cold, slightly warm' which, with no mention of rigor, makes his estimate a somewhat unusual one. Indeed, as he said there was 'blood coming from the nose' of the decapitated head (which had been wrapped in a piece of flannel), one would have thought that a later time-of-death estimate, or at least a wider range, might have been appropriate. The *Illustrated Police News* of 17 July 1880 reported his evidence at the police court as being that, 'The body was warm, and blood was still oozing from the neck' which makes his estimate even more surprising. Martin, who was regarded as unable to plead, was determined by an Old Bailey jury to be insane and detained at Her Majesty's pleasure.

In April 1881, John Smith, a surgeon, gave evidence at an inquest into the death of Mary Ann Murphy in Plumstead that, when he had examined her, 'She had been dead about half-an-hour, the body being warm.'[78] For a medical practitioner to arrive at the scene of a death within half an hour of that death was an impressive feat but the curiosity in this case was that Mrs Murphy had supposedly been found 'cold and dead' in her house by her husband when he returned from work. While it's certainly possible that he wasn't telling the truth, it appeared that his wife had taken her own life by swallowing poison at some point during the day. Unless there was some other indication that Dr Smith didn't mention at the inquest, it would have been all but impossible for him to have narrowed the time of death down to the previous thirty minutes before he arrived in the Murphy house.

---

[77] TNA: CRIM 1/10/1.
[78] *Kentish Mercury*, 30 April 1881.

Later in the same year, another medical practitioner, Dr John Astley Bloxham, also seemed to believe he could estimate the time of death from the body feeling warm. This was in the case of the death of Louisa Somes, a 33-year-old housemaid, who appears to have been struck by melancholy and took her own life in September 1881. The doctor said at the inquest that, 'The body was warm when I saw it, and I should think the deceased had not been dead more than an hour.'[79] Two months later, Frederick Gordon Brown, a surgeon, of 16 Finsbury Circus, was called to examine the body of Mrs Mary Davidson who had been found on the North London Railway line about a quarter of a mile from Broad Street Station, having apparently suffered from a fall. Dr Brown saw the body after it had been taken to the mortuary and felt that the body was warm, from which he concluded that, 'The woman must have been dead about an hour.'[80]

Despite all the literature saying that bodies could remain so warm it felt like they were alive for at least twenty-four hours, examiners were still saying that a warm body meant a very recent death. And, despite all the literature urging examiners to use a thermometer, they were still using their hands. The results of this were as random as they had always been. In January 1882, the medical officer at Morden College, Dr Cooper of Blackheath, was called to examine the body of an elderly man who had committed suicide by hanging himself on a beam. He said that, 'The body was warm, but the extremities were cold'. Even allowing for the fact that Professor Taylor had stated in 1863 that asphyxiated bodies can take longer to cool, from previous estimates given by medical examiners one might have expected that an estimate of time of death in the case of a largely warm body would be that it had occurred no more than four hours earlier but in this case the medical officer stated that the man 'had been dead seven or eight hours as far as he could judge.'[81]

When the murdered body of a young man called Charles Wagner, who had evidently been pushed off a cliff, was discovered at Ramsgate in the early hours of 2 April 1882, the coastguard who found it said that, 'it was quite warm'. Dr Liddon, who examined the body shortly afterwards also found that it was warm and, therefore, said at the inquest that, 'I concluded

---

[79] *Morning Post*, 12 September 1881.
[80] *Daily Telegraph*, 26 November 1881.
[81] *Kentish Mercury*, 21 January 1882.

that the man had not been dead more than a few hours – perhaps not so long.'[82] As an estimate on which a future jury could rely, it wasn't terribly helpful.

In the same year, Charles Meymott Tidy, Professor of Chemistry and of Medical Jurisprudence and Public Health at the London Hospital, and the author of *Legal Medicine*, was the latest authority to add his voice to the dangers of using one's hand to assess body temperature. Thus, he said in his 1882 book, 'All observations on temperature should be thermometric. The mere application of the hand to the body is not a sufficiently delicate test of temperature, so much depending on the relative warmth of the hand of the operator and of the body. To the cold hand of one person a body may appear warm, which to the hand of another might appear cold'. Still, no one in the medical profession whose job involved examining dead bodies at crime scenes seemed to be taking any notice.

At midnight on Saturday 29 December 1883, a prostitute called Emily Novell was last seen alive, the worse for drink, by a fellow prostitute, Charlotte Barnett or Barnard, outside a public house in Westminster. She was talking to her boyfriend, Frederick James Harris, with whom she lived in Artillery Square. At 12.30am, a fellow lodger heard Emily and an unknown man (not Harris) enter her apartment. She perceived there was some dispute between the pair about money. At 1.10am the man was heard to leave. Twenty minutes later Harris found Emily dead in her room. He immediately knocked on the door of Charlotte's house, which was also in Artillery Square, saying, 'Lottie, would you come and look at Emily, someone must have given her a cruel doing'. She went round and found her friend lying on her bed in a pool of blood. Dr George Toussaint Girdler, a physician and surgeon, was called to the scene at 3.30am. At the Police Court, where Harris was charged with the murder, Dr Girdler said, 'The body was warm. She had been dead two or three hours.'[83] The witness evidence was clearly that Emily had been murdered around 1am, two and a half hours earlier, so that must have been a correct estimate but, nevertheless, seemingly random on the basis of nothing more than the body being warm. Harris was cleared of the crime but the murderer was never found.

---

[82] *London Daily News*, 15 April 1882.
[83] *Morning Post*, 2 January 1884.

In September 1884, Dr James Finlayson reported in the *British Medical Journal* an interesting discovery in respect of rigor mortis, which had occurred shortly after midnight on 1 December 1883.[84] A young man, aged 22, who had been admitted to the Glasgow Western Infirmary suffering from Bright's Disease asked a nurse for a drink of water at 12.15am. When she brought it to him fifteen minutes late, he was dead. The sister who then examined the body found the arms quite rigid and the limbs slightly less so. As we have seen, Brown-Séquard had discovered rigor mortis in a corpse within a few minutes after death and Finlayson appeared to have corroborated this.

An interesting case from a medico-legal point view occurred in November 1885 regarding the brutal murder of nineteen-year-old Rachel Bailey, in Poplar. Although she was not married, her so-called 'husband', a cook called Harry Patrick, was seen to leave her room at 10am on Monday, 23 November 1885, and her body was discovered lying in a pool of blood in her lodgings at 11.15am, her throat having been cut. A local surgeon, Weston Erskine Wadley, arrived within fifteen minutes. At the inquest into Miss Bailey's death, held on 25 November 1885, Dr Wadley deposed that, 'The body was cold. She had been dead at least two or three hours.'[85] Given the precedent of the Gardner case where a cold body with some warmth supposedly indicated death at least four hours earlier (if not longer according to Professor Taylor), this might be considered surprising enough but, at the trial of Harry Patrick, who was arrested and convicted for Bailey's murder, held during the Old Bailey Sessions of 14 December 1885, Dr Wadley testified that, 'She was cold, and had been dead from an hour and a half to two hours'. Not only was this a fairly major shift in position but was the type of estimate that one would normally associate with a *warm* body, not a cold one. An explanation for Dr Wadley's amended testimony might be found in the witness evidence that the murder was likely to have been committed shortly before 10am (when Patrick was seen running away from the scene of the crime) which would mean that Miss Bailey could only have been dead for about an hour and a half when he examined her body at 11.30am. It looks like a classic

---

[84] 'Post Mortem Rigidity Within Fifteen Minutes of Death', *British Medical Journal*, 6 September 1884.
[85] *Globe*, 26 November 1885.

case of a medical witness modifying his evidence as to time of death in order to fit the non-medical witness evidence. In theory, Rachel Bailey could have been murdered any time after 11pm on the Sunday night and, from the fact of the body being cold alone, Dr Wadley could have given an estimate of time of death of anything between thirteen hours earlier and sixty minutes earlier had he so desired.

By way of contrast to Dr Wadley's testimony, we find another surgeon, George Richard Schmilt, testifying at an inquest in Swindon that he was called at 6am on Thursday, 18 November 1886, to see the body of 78-year-old Robert Simmonds who had died during the night while lying in bed next to his wife. According to Dr Schmilt, 'in his opinion he had been dead about an hour, the body being warm.'[86] It's impossible to understand from a medical point of view why some doctors, on being confronted with a warm body, were giving an estimate of death having occurred about an hour earlier while others were saying two or three hours. Yet, at the same time, a cold body can apparently mean that death occurred two or three hours earlier.

One of the nineteenth century's most infamous locked door mysteries occurred on Tuesday, 28 June, 1887, in a lodging house in Batty Street, Whitechapel. At 11am, Mrs Dina Angel, the mother-in-law of 22-year-old Miriam Angel hadn't seen Miriam that morning, which was unusual because she normally joined her for breakfast between 7.30 and 9am. She knocked at the door of her room but got no answer and the door appeared to be locked. She was quickly joined by some of her friends who attempted to help her. One of them looked through the keyhole and saw the key was in the hole, locking the door from the inside. Through a little glass window covered with a muslin curtain, Miriam could just about be seen lying on the bed. A decision was made to break open the door. As the women rushed in, they believed that Miriam had fainted and was unconscious but, oddly, she was lying with her nightdress pulled up to her breasts, exposing the lower part of her body.

John William Kay, a surgeon based at the corner of Batty Street, was sent for and arrived at about 11.45am.[87] He saw that Miriam was dead and

---

[86] *Swindon Advertiser*, 20 November 1886.
[87] He had been preceded about 15 minutes earlier by his assistant, William Piper, who made only a cursory examination at the scene.

immediately spotted marks of corrosive poison running from her mouth and on her hands. Her tongue and throat was also burnt with this fluid. She had a black eye and there were fist marks on her temple suggesting that she had been violently beaten around the head. Rather to the doctor's surprise, a young man was then discovered lying insensible under the bed. His mouth contained injuries caused by the same corrosive fluid as had been observed in Miriam's mouth. Dr Kay felt the man's pulse and realized he was still alive. When the man came round, the police were called and took him away, battling their way to Leman Street Police Station through a howling mob of about two thousand people who wanted the assumed murderer's blood. A bottle in which the poison was contained was then found at the foot of the bed. Dr Kay subsequently concluded that Miriam had died as a result of suffocation produced by the acid acting on the windpipe, closing the air passage.

Giving evidence at the inquest into Miriam's death, Dr Kay stated that when he conducted his examination shortly before midday, the body was 'not quite cold' and rigor mortis had not yet commenced.[88] On that basis, he testified, 'I think deceased had been dead from 3 or 4 hours', thus placing the time of death at somewhere between 7.30 and 8.30am which made perfect sense bearing in mind that this was when Miriam would have been expected to have come down for breakfast, had she then been alive.

The man pulled out from under the bed was Israel Lipski, a walking-stick maker and Polish born immigrant who had recently set up a small workshop in his room at 16 Batty Street. The cost of doing so had put him into financial difficulty. He had borrowed twenty-five shillings from the mother of his fiancée and had been trying to borrow another five shillings from his fellow lodgers during the morning of Miriam's death. Lipski's movements that morning were difficult to pin down due to the conflicts of timing in the evidence of two men and boy he had employed to assist him. The two men, Simon Rosenbloom and Isaac Schmuss, didn't speak English and the boy, Richard Pitman, was only fourteen years old, but Rosenbloom said he had last seen Lipski that morning at about 8.45am while Pitman, not regarded as a terribly reliable witness, said it was about 10am. An independent witness said he saw Lipski entering 16 Batty Street at 8.45am. It was clear, however that Lipski had been in and out of his

---

[88] TNA: CRIM 1/26/5.

workshop during the morning, apparently attempting to buy a sponge and a vice with the little money he possessed.

Lipski was charged with the murder and, at his trial at the Old Bailey, Dr Kay, perhaps aware that Lipski had been seen by witnesses in the street at 8.45am, now slightly modified his evidence to say of Miriam Angel that, 'I formed an opinion that she had been dead about three hours.' In doing so, he said, 'I have taken into consideration the state of the room and the weather and the condition of the body in forming my opinion as to the three hours.' He felt that, 'three hours must be pretty near the time.' As he stated the time of his examination as being 11.45am, he was evidently saying that the murder had occurred at about 8.45am.

Lipski's defence was that his two employees, Rosenbloom and Schmuss, had murdered Miriam and then attempted to kill him too, pouring nitric acid down his throat. He said they then threw him under Miriam's bed, leaving him for dead. He denied having murdered her himself.

Both Rosenbloom and Schmuss gave evidence during Lipski's trial and completely denied his version of events. Lipski was found guilty and sentenced to death on 30 July 1887. His solicitor, however, was convinced of his innocence and launched a persuasive campaign to save him from the gallows. He was allowed extra time by the Home Secretary to enable him to make further enquiries so that the execution was delayed by a week. Lipski had been a respectable young man and his story about being attacked and thrown under the bed seemed plausible. Schmuss was a locksmith by trade and his ability with locks could have explained why the door appeared to have been locked from the inside. Directed by the Home Office, Scotland Yard conducted an unusual but thorough re-investigation of the case after the trial. The *Lancet* commented in August that, 'Many points now being investigated ought, in our opinion, to have been cleared up at the time of the trial, instead of being considered during the respite of the prisoner, who has to linger in suspense, with the gallows ever present to his mental vision.' The *Pall Mall Gazette* took up the case and many were convinced in Lipski's innocence. The *Daily Telegraph* stated that, 'the case is now involved in far too much uncertainty to make the execution of the prisoner at all safe.'

With Lipski due to be hanged on 22 August, but the press asking all sorts of questions about the case, and even members of the jury having apparently changed their minds, many thought the Home Secretary would relent. However, after he stated on 20 August that he would refuse to interfere with the sentence, Lipski made a full confession. He said that he had gone into Miriam's room while she was asleep and locked the door from the inside. He intended to rob her but she awoke and cried out softly causing him to strike her on the head and seize her by the neck. He poured down her throat some nitric acid he had been carrying around with him, for the purpose of committing suicide, and took some himself. At this point he said he heard the voices of people coming up the stairs and he crawled under the bed. Crucially, he said, 'There was only a very short time from the moment of my entering the room until I was taken away.' This means, if true, that the murder must have been committed very shortly before 11am, much later than Dr Kay had estimated. As a correspondent in the *Pall Mall Gazette* of 22 August 1887 noted: 'The confession shows the medical testimony to be all wrong. The woman had been dead but half an hour, or at most three quarters of an hour, when Dr Kay examined her, and Lipski had only just murdered her when he was disturbed by knocking at the door and sought refuge under the bed…Why such an error in the exact science of forensic medicine should have been made it is hard to say.'

There was, however, a rather big problem with Lipski's confession. It failed to explain why Miriam hadn't appeared for breakfast that morning as she usually did before 9am. Why would she still have been asleep in bed at 11am? That part didn't make any sense. The authorities were, however, perfectly satisfied by Lipski's confession, so that Dr Kay's estimate has gone down in history as a rather major blunder.

In the same year as the Lipski case, Frederick Womack of St Bartholomew's Hospital published the paper which he had first read (in draft form) to the Abernethian Society two years' earlier.[89] Using the results of the experiments of Taylor and Wilks in 1863, and those of Niderkorn in 1872, he created a complicated mathematical formula to estimate time of death which was undoubtedly never used by any medical examiner due to its complexity. Nevertheless, Womack said that he tested it on the bodies of 118 dead patients whose exact time of death was presumably known (although he doesn't make this clear) and in only sixteen, he said, was the estimate in error by more than one hour. He put those sixteen errors down,

---

[89] 'The Rate of Cooling of the Body after Death'.

in the main, to abnormally high temperatures at death and, 'probably' a post-mortem rise in temperature. He didn't however, say how long after death the temperature readings on which those estimates were based were made, nor give any further details about them.

Although Womack appreciated that there were a number of factors which created difficulties in correctly estimating the time of death using his formula, he didn't think they were fatal, and he claimed that not definitely knowing the body temperature at time of death would 'not be likely to present any serious difficulty'. As we have seen, he had calculated that the average temperature of the abdomen at time of death was 93.1 degrees. While he accepted that using his formula would be problematic in the case of sick individuals whose temperatures were pathological, for most healthy individuals, he said, the range of temperature (of the abdomen) at time of death would not be greater than 3.6 degrees, which uncertainty 'would introduce at the most a possible error of one hour, and probably in general much less than this.' He accepted that there would be (small) temperature differences for well-nourished against poorly nourished individuals and for thin people against fat people but thought that such variations can 'to some extent be predicated (sic)', although he didn't explain precisely how.

The varying temperature of the atmosphere, noted Womack, was also a problem and any attempt to factor it into his equation meant that, 'The mathematical calculation becomes more complicated', but he felt that, unless the variation of temperature was more than eight to ten degrees, 'the discrepancy produced is not considerable'. A further problem, he accepted, was that a change in the covering of the body made at an unknown time after death 'would introduce an insuperable obstacle to the calculation'. Indeed, he said that, 'exposure of the naked body in an open space with a good current of air would cool it as much in an hour as would fall in six hours if covered with ordinary clothing'. This was a serious issue with the obvious potential to render any time of death estimates worthless but, rather optimistically, Womack said that it was 'improbable' that the covering of a body would be altered after death.

Also in 1887, a medical student at Edinburgh University called David Welsh presented his thesis for the degree of Doctor of Medicine which, borrowing from Burman, was entitled, 'On the Rate of Cooling of the Human Body after Death'. Observations were made by him on fifty recently deceased patients, presumably with the agreement of a hospital in Edinburgh, all of whom had died of some form of disease or illness, and involved twenty cases where the corpses remained covered up in bed and twenty cases where the corpses were left exposed. In these forty cases, half were stored in a room with a temperature of forty degrees and the other half in a room with a temperature of sixty degrees. The remaining ten cases were immersed in cold water. Temperature readings were taken with a thermometer inserted in the rectum every hour after death. Welsh claimed that the readings started at the time of death or, at least, no later than ten minutes after death.

By Welsh's calculations, the average rate of cooling for the twenty bodies covered in bedclothes was 1.06 degrees per hour which was somewhat different to Burman's finding of 1.6 degrees but that figure is misleading because, although Welsh didn't comment on it, his data shows that there was a much higher rate of cooling in the first twelve hours than in the second twelve hours which, in turn, was higher than the third twelve hour period. If one breaks it down into those periods, the average hourly rate of cooling for the first twelve hours after death was 1.6 degrees while the equivalent rate for the second twelve hours after death was 0.9 degrees. For the next period of twelve hours it then fell down to 0.8 degrees per hour and continued to fall thereafter. Consequently, the average body temperature for Welsh's covered corpses eleven hours after death was 80.5 degrees, which is almost exactly what Burman's formula would predict it should be, but it then starts to diverge after twelve hours as the rate of cooling decreases. Thus, after twenty-four hours, the average temperature in Welsh's experiment was 67.2 degrees compared with the 60 degrees that Burman's formula would have predicted, thus leading to an error of some four hours in the estimation of time of death. The coincidence is also less apparent four hours after death when the average for the covered corpses was 88.8 degrees compared to the 92 degrees which Burman's formula would have predicted.

When it came to the exposed corpses, Welsh calculated that the rate of cooling was 1.7 degrees per hour which, on the face of it, sounds very similar to the 1.6 degrees calculated by Burman for covered corpses. Again, however, this figure is very misleading. For the first twelve hours after death of the twenty uncovered corpses, the rate of cooling was 2.6

degrees per hour, one full degree higher than Burman had given as the rate of cooling for covered corpses. Consequently, the average temperature after death for the uncovered corpses during those first twelve hours was very different to what Burman's formula would have predicted. After four hours it was 85.1 degrees compared to 92 degrees for Burman's experiments, while after eleven hours it was only 68.8 degrees compared to the 80 degrees that Burman's formula provides, the equivalent of an error of seven hours in calculating time of death. It goes without saying that this means that Burman's formula certainly could not be applied to exposed corpses. As with Welsh's covered corpses, the rate of cooling fell dramatically for the second period of twelve hours, down to just one degree per hour.

Even these figures mask some major outlying temperatures for certain individual cases. One, for example, was a 40-year-old woman who died of tuberculosis (phthisis) and who was also described as 'emaciated' at the time of death. She was one of the exposed bodies, and Welsh recorded her temperature at the time of her death as being only 82 degrees. By four hours after her death, this had dropped to 75.5 degrees. After eleven hours it was down to 67 degrees. In the case of an exposed 25-year-old male suffering from tuberculosis, who was also described in the study as 'emaciated,' his temperature at the time of death was even lower, at 80 degrees, dropping to 76.5 degrees after only one hour. By four hours after death it was down to 70 degrees and, after eleven hours, was only 63 degrees. For another exposed female suffering from tuberculosis, but not in this case emaciated, we find that her temperature at time of death was 82 degrees but there was then a drop of five degrees in the first hour as it plunged down to 77 degrees. That it is almost impossible to make predictions of body temperature based on the cause of death can be seen from the fact that a thirteen-year-old emaciated boy who died of tuberculosis recorded a temperature of 102 degrees at the time of his death. This was followed by a seven degree drop down to 95 degrees within the first hour.

In respect of the ten cases placed in cold water, the falls were even steeper, with average temperature falls of 6 degrees and 8 degrees during the first and second hours after death respectively so that by four hours after death the temperature of those bodies had fallen, on average, to just over 70.5 degrees.

The Temperature of Death • 183

In his conclusion, Welsh stated that, in addition to the expected result of uncovered bodies cooling faster than covered ones, he had also discovered that, 'uncovered emaciated bodies cool faster than non-emaciated under the same conditions' while, in diseases such as tuberculosis, 'there is great loss of fat and consequently more rapid cooling.' His thesis, however, was unpublished and apparently unread by the majority of the medical profession. A copy was lodged in the British Library in London and was thus available for consultation by researchers but few appeared to have availed themselves of the opportunity. As a result, the information in Welsh's thesis wasn't widely known during 1888 which was when it might have been useful in estimating the time of death in at least one of the so-called 'Jack the Ripper' murders.

CHAPTER TEN

The Year of The Ripper

The Whitechapel of 'Jack the Ripper' is often dramatically portrayed in film and on television as being enshrouded in fog. While this wasn't actually true during the period of the murders, the first month of 1888 did indeed see London blanketed by a heavy fog. The London Correspondent of one regional newspaper noted in his London letter of 12 January 1888 that the fog was so thick that, 'Everyone is complaining of sore throat and headache...Persons suffering from asthma and other bronchial maladies are in great distress, and doctors are kept going night and day.'[90] London's doctors would soon be troubled by even more serious problems, as the mutilated bodies of murdered women were discovered in the eastern part of the city's streets and squares.

Police Constable John Neil needed the full use of his lamp to see blood oozing from the throat of a woman who was lying on the pavement of Buck's Row at about a quarter to four in the morning of 31 August 1888. A few minutes earlier, a couple of civilians had noticed her lying on the ground as they walked to work but it had been too dark for them to establish whether she was dead or drunk, even close up. They had continued on their route to work, notifying another constable at the end of the row of what they had seen, but, by this time, P.C. Neil had spotted the body as he walked his beat.

---

[90] *Newcastle Daily Journal*, 13 January 1888.

That constable had walked along Buck's Row half an hour earlier, so it would have been apparent to him that the woman, who turned out to be Mary Ann Nichols, had been alive at 3.15am and her throat had been cut after this time. Nevertheless, Henry Llewellyn, a surgeon based in Whitechapel Road, who was on the scene within fifteen minutes of the constable's discovery of the body, felt the need to provide an estimate of the time of death during the subsequent inquest. He would inform the coroner that, 'Her hands and wrists were cold, but the lower extremities were quite warm...I should say the deceased had not been dead more than half an hour'. In the context of evidence given by medical examiners in various courts of law during the nineteenth century, one would have thought that, from the hands and wrists being cold, Llewellyn would have concluded that the woman might have been dead for about two hours at least, bearing in mind how long after death the lower extremities could remain warm. Dr Llewellyn, however, might have factored into his thinking that a dead woman would have been unlikely to have lain in the pavement undiscovered for more than half an hour, especially as most main thoroughfares were patrolled by beat officers every half an hour, and the evidence of P.C. Neil would have confirmed this. Equally, it's possible that the doctor might have taken into consideration the fact that Nichols' wound was still oozing blood, although he himself did not say that was the case when he examined the body at 4am. He might, however, have been aware of P.C. Neil's observations about the oozing at 3.45am and decided that this would place the likely time of death at no earlier than 3.30.

Although there had been murders of women in the East End of London earlier in the year, the murder of Mary Ann Nichols, whose body suffered grotesque mutilations not found in the earlier murders, is considered by many to have been the first victim in the sequence of the 'Jack the Ripper' murders of 1888. The second such victim was Annie Chapman, and the estimate of the time of her death was one which was to prove rather controversial.

Chapman had last been seen alive at about two o'clock in the morning of 8 September 1888, four hours before her mutilated body was discovered in the back yard of a house at 29 Hanbury Street, Spitalfields, shortly before 6am. The medical examiner in this case was the experienced divisional surgeon of police, George Baxter Phillips, who was called at his residence at 2 Spital Square at 6.20am. Rushing to the scene of the crime, he arrived at 29 Hanbury Street about ten minutes later, at half-past six. A real question in the case was how long the body of Chapman had been lying in the yard. John Richardson had stood on the back steps of the house at about 4.40am, cutting leather off one of his boots, but despite him having been standing right next to where the body was found, he didn't see it. In his evidence to the coroner at the inquest, he would say that, while it wasn't yet light, he couldn't have failed to notice the body lying on the ground, had it been there. Dr Phillips, on the other hand, initially believed that the body simply must have been there at the time. When he carried out his examination of the body at shortly after 6.30am, he concluded that Chapman, 'had been dead at least two hours, and probably more', thus fixing the time of her death at no later than 4.30am. Assuming that Chapman was murdered and mutilated where her body was found, which the police believed was the case, this would mean that Richardson had completely missed her when he was looking into the yard ten minutes later.

A time of death of 4.30am, or earlier, would also mean that two witnesses who testified at the inquest were either mistaken, confused or lying. The first was Elizabeth Long who said she was walking along Hanbury Street at about 5.30am, to go to Spitalfields Market, and saw a woman who she later identified (in the mortuary) as Annie Chapman speaking to a man. She testified that she heard the man say 'Will you?' to which Chapman replied 'Yes.' The second witness was a carpenter called Albert Cadosch, a resident of 27 Hanbury Street, which was next door to number 29, who said he got out of bed at 5.15am and went out into the yard of his house where he heard a woman's voice, which he believed came from the yard next door, saying 'No' followed, a few minutes later by the sound of someone falling against the fence which divided his property from number 29. He did not, however, look over the fence to see what had caused the noise.

If Cadosch had heard Chapman being murdered in the yard of number 29 at about 5.20am then Elizabeth Long's story about seeing her in the street ten minutes later couldn't have been correct. Yet, Long stated that she was 'certain' of the time because she had heard the brewers' clock strike 5.30am when she passed number 29 (although that clock doesn't appear to have been tested for accuracy). Cadosch said that, after hearing the fall,

The Temperature of Death • 187

he left for work and passed Spitalfields Church at 5.32am, so there was an inconsistency in the timings that was hard to reconcile. Nevertheless, the coroner, Wynne Baxter, noting that it was 'not unusual to find inaccuracy in such details' felt that the 'variation was not very great or very important'. He thought that Cadosch was probably mistaken in his timings by fifteen minutes and thus concluded that Chapman was probably murdered at about 5.35am.

In reaching this conclusion, the coroner rejected the evidence of Dr Phillips that Chapman had been dead for a minimum of two hours when he saw her at about 6.30am. That evidence was essentially based on the fact that, according to Phillips, 'The body was cold, except that there was a certain remaining heat, under the intestines, in the body.'[91] As was all too common at the time, Phillips didn't take the body temperature of Chapman but relied on his hands to feel whether she was cold or warm. While it's not clear why Phillips said that there was heat 'under' the intestines, if, in detecting this heat, he plunged his bare hands into Chapman's exposed abdominal cavity, this would not normally have been done at the scene of a murder considering that the abdominal cavity was not normally exposed. One medical textbook published a few years after the murders stated that, 'The internal warmth of the body is often perceptible to the hand twenty-four hours after death; indeed in making a post-mortem examination twenty-four hours after death, you may find the viscera perceptibly warm', suggesting that checking the internal organs for warmth with one's hand was not uncommon practice during a post-mortem.[92]

Like so many medical examiners before him, Phillips didn't think that a body could become cold within an hour. Nevertheless, when giving his opinion to the coroner, he did add that, 'it is right to say that it was a fairly cold morning and that the body would be apt to cool rapidly from its having lost the greater portion of its blood'. The coroner clearly understood Phillips to mean that Chapman could indeed have been murdered at about 5.30am. When the foreman of the jury commented, after Elizabeth Long's evidence at the inquest, that what Long had said about seeing Chapman alive at 5.30am, 'was not consistent with that stated by the doctor', the coroner reminded him that, 'Dr. Phillips had since qualified

---

[91] *Daily Telegraph*, 14 September 1888.
[92] *A Treatise on Medical Jurisprudence* by George Vivian Poore MD, London, 1902.

that statement.' When summing up the evidence, the coroner said that, 'It was true that Dr. Phillips thought that when he saw the body at 6.30 the deceased had been dead at least two hours, but he admitted that the coldness of the morning and the great loss of blood might affect his opinion, and if the evidence of the other witnesses was correct, Dr. Phillips had miscalculated the effect of those forces.'

Had either Dr Phillips or the coroner been aware of the unpublished thesis of David Welsh, they might have added further reasons why the body of Annie Chapman could have become cold within an hour of her death. Welsh's study had found that the body temperatures of both emaciated people and those suffering from tuberculosis would fall faster than normal after death. Annie Chapman fell into *both* categories. Dr Phillips' post-mortem on Chapman's body revealed that, 'there were signs of great deprivation' and that she had been 'badly fed'. In addition, she was, 'far advanced in disease of the lungs and membranes of the brain' which is a strong indication that she was suffering from a wasting disease, such as tuberculosis, at the time of her murder. Either of these issues could have led to a more rapid cooling of a mutilated body lying out in the open on a cold September morning than Dr Phillips might have expected, either from his own experience or from the results in textbooks of experiments on bodies which had usually been covered or tested within a sheltered environment. Furthermore, as we have seen, Womack had noted in 1887 that 'exposure of the naked body in an open space with a good current of air would cool it as much in an hour as would fall in six hours if covered with ordinary clothing'. While Chapman wasn't entirely naked, her body had been mutilated and was thus partially exposed while lying in an open space.

In accepting that the body could have cooled more rapidly due to the coldness of the morning and loss of blood, Dr Phillips doesn't appear to have relied at all on the onset of rigor mortis in forming his estimate as to the time of death. As to this, his evidence was rather unusual. He said that, when he examined the body at 6.30am, the stiffness of the limbs was 'not marked', yet, at the same time, it was, he said, 'commencing', or 'evidently commencing' as the reporter from the *Times* newspaper recorded his evidence. In giving this evidence, Dr Phillips omitted to say precisely where on Chapman's body, other than the limbs, he believed the stiffness was commencing. Rigor mortis normally starts in the face and spreads down to the rest of the body.

The editor of the *Lancet* seemed to think that the doctor must have been factoring this 'commencing' rigor into his estimate of the time of death. In the issue of the *Lancet* of 29 September 1888, it was stated that, 'We confess to sharing Mr. Phillips' view that the coldness of the body and the commencing rigidity pointed to a far longer interval between death and discovery than [the evidence of Mrs Long suggested]' although, at the same time, it was accepted by the writer that, 'the almost total draining away of blood, added to the exposure in the cold morning air, may have hastened the cooling down of the body'. The idea of a cold body indicating 'a far longer interval' between death and discovery than one hour was, of course, a traditional view harking back to the Gardner case but, in 1862, as we have seen, the *Lancet* had excoriated the surgeon in the case (Sequeira), saying that he 'should have consulted some medical jurist before imperilling the life of a human being on the imperfect data he had at his disposal' and had stated that his opinion was nothing more than a guess. Despite the experiments conducted by Wilks and Taylor in 1863 and Rainy in 1869 it is difficult to see how the previously imperfect data had, by 1888, become perfect, enabling a medical examiner to rule out that death had occurred within an hour on the basis of feeling the body temperature of the victim and on the mere supposed commencement of stiffness.

There was one other potential indicator of time of death which was that, during his post-mortem examination, Dr Phillips found that the stomach contained 'a little food'.[93] The only food that Chapman was known to have eaten prior to her death was some baked potatoes which Timothy Donovan, the deputy of the common lodging house at which she was a resident, had observed her consume shortly before 2am. Even if she hadn't eaten anything else in the hours before her death (which is unknown), and even if one could rely on the belief that the stomach emptied in four hours (which Dr Phillips didn't mention in his evidence at the inquest), this wouldn't have been of much assistance because 'a little' of those potatoes could easily have remained in the stomach at 5.30am, thus not really helping one way or the other to fix the time of death. While it's true that, the more food eaten, the longer the process

---

[93] *Times*, 14 September 1888.

of stomach emptying would take, it's also the case that the time taken for stomach emptying varies amongst different people of different ages in different states of health so that one can't reach a definitive or reliable conclusion on the matter.

While the issue was ultimately academic, because no one was arrested for the murder of Chapman, had 'Jack the Ripper' been caught but had an alibi all night up to 5am, it would have been crucial for the prosecution to prove that Chapman could have been murdered long after 4.30am otherwise the killer might have got away with that murder at least.

During the night of the so-called 'double event', when the bodies of two women were found dead within a fifteen minute walk of each other in the East End, it wasn't difficult for even a layman to work out that Elizabeth Stride had been murdered very shortly before the crime was discovered at 1am on 30 September 1888, because a witness, Edward Spooner, saw that blood was still flowing from the dead woman's throat at that time. Dr Frederick Blackwell who arrived at Dutfield's Yard, where the body was lying, at 1.16am precisely, informed Wynne Baxter, the coroner at Stride's inquest, that, 'I do not think the deceased could have been dead more than twenty minutes, at the most half an hour'. Although Blackwell had put his hand inside Stride's dress and found that the body was 'quite warm', his reasoning on this score had nothing to do with his medical knowledge. He came to this conclusion because it had been a very wet night, yet Stride's clothing was dry. Had she been lying there since before 12.45, he deduced, her clothes would have been soaked. Hence, in his view, she must have been murdered since the rain had stopped, which had obviously been within the half an hour prior to his arrival at Dutfield's Yard. The coroner's theory in this case was that the murderer must have been disturbed in the act at 1am, 'for the death had only just taken place', and this would certainly explain why the killer did not mutilate Stride's body in the way that the bodies of the other victims had been mutilated.

Within forty-five minutes of the discovery of Stride's body, the dead body of Catherine Eddowes was found by a City Police constable in Mitre Square, Aldgate. That constable, Edward Watkins, had passed through Mitre Square fifteen minutes earlier so that it can be deduced that the murder and mutilation of Eddowes occurred between 1.30 and 1.45am.

Frederick Gordon Brown, the City of London Police Surgeon, reached Mitre Square at 2.18am and noted that, 'Body was quite warm – no death stiffening had taken place'. Consequently, said Dr Brown, 'She must have been dead most likely within the half an hour'. It's interesting that he thought death must have occurred within thirty minutes as opposed to one, two, three or more hours. It will be recalled that, in 1881, Dr Brown had said of the body of Mary Davidson, which was also warm when he examined it, that, 'The woman must have been dead about an hour'. Yet, with Eddowes, whose body was also warm, he felt he could say that she had died in half the time. It's possible that he was aware from a colleague who had arrived at the scene about fifteen minutes before him that the blood hadn't yet coagulated at that time. This was Dr George William Sequeira, the son of Henry, of nearby Jewry Street, who had been the first medical examiner on the scene, having been called at 1.55am. Brown only said in his evidence at the inquest that there was 'a quantity of clotted blood' on the pavement on the left side of the neck (although he did also note some 'fluid blood coloured serum' under the neck) and, when estimating the time of death, didn't say anything about the lack of coagulation of the blood being a factor in his estimate. Sequeira, who may well have noted that the blood hadn't coagulated when he first saw the body at about 2am, estimated that 'Life had not been extinct more than quarter of an hour'.[94] Dr Brown also noted, at a post-mortem examination of Eddowes, twelve hours later, at 2.30pm, that, 'rigor mortis was well marked, body not quite cold' but he didn't draw any conclusions from this.

When it comes to the fifth murder in the series, there was, and remains, real controversy surrounding the time of death. The discovery of Mary Jane Kelly's horrifically mutilated body was made by Thomas Bowyer at 10.45am on 9 November 1888. Knocking at Kelly's door, of her room in Millers Court, off Dorset Street, in order to collect the rent, but not getting an answer, he looked through a broken window and saw the gruesome sight of a barely recognizable woman lying on

---

[94] Some newspaper reports, e.g. *Daily Telegraph* of 1 October 1888, reported that, 'Both Mr. Sequeira and Mr. Gordon Brown found that the body was still warm, and the blood had not coagulated' but this might just have been the experience of Mr Sequeira given that it took Brown more than half an hour to reach the scene following the discovery of the body.

her bed. Although Dr Phillips was on the scene within half an hour of the discovery, entry wasn't made into the room until 1.30pm due to a canine mix-up. The Commissioner of the Metropolitan Police, Sir Charles Warren, had previously given instructions that bloodhounds should be used to try and track the killer in any future murder but had subsequently been unable to come to a final agreement for their use with the owner, causing them to be unavailable on the morning of the 9th. Unaware that the dogs weren't even in London, Dr Phillips advised the police officers at the scene not to effect immediate entry into Kelly's room in order to give the imminently expected bloodhounds the best chance of picking up the killer's scent. It wasn't until the arrival of a superintendent from Scotland Yard, who brought the news that the hounds weren't coming, that the door to Kelly's room was forced open.

As a result, almost three hours had passed since Thomas Boywer's gruesome discovery before Phillips had the opportunity to examine the victim. The extensive mutilations inflicted on Kelly's body could hardly have been performed in much less than forty-five minutes which means that the latest Kelly could have been murdered was 10am. She had been seen alive by a neighbour at 11.45pm the previous evening and had been heard singing by that same neighbour at about 1am (although another neighbour heard nothing). Assuming that Kelly did sing that night, the murder must have occurred in the nine-hour period between one and ten. Could the medical evidence shed any light on precisely when it had been?

At the inquest into Kelly's death, Dr Phillips wasn't asked to estimate the time of death.[95] A summary of a post-mortem carried out in Kelly's room in Millers Court commencing at 2pm on 9 November by Dr Thomas Bond, called in to assist Scotland Yard, however, survives, and he wrote this:

> Rigor mortis had set in, but increased during the progress of the examination. From this it is difficult to say with any degree of certainty the exact time that had elapsed since death as the period varies from 6 to 12 hours before rigidity sets in. The

---

[95] A report in the *Times* of 12 November 1888, prior to the inquest, stated that Dr Phillips was of the opinion that when he arrived at the scene, at 10.45am, Kelly 'had been dead some five or six hours', and was thus murdered at between 4.45am and 5.45am, but no reasons for this assessment were given.

The Temperature of Death • 193

body was comparatively cold at 2 o'clock and the remains of a recently taken meal were found in the stomach and scattered over the intestines. It is, therefore, pretty certain that the woman must have been dead about 12 hours and the partly digested food would indicate that death took place about 3 or 4 hours after the food was taken, so one or two o'clock in the morning would be the probable time of the murder.

Dr Bond's argument is hard to follow. His assertion that it was 'pretty certain' that the woman must have been dead about twelve hours is based on the setting in of rigor mortis and the comparative coldness of the body. As for the onset of rigor, however, he said himself that the period varies from six to twelve hours which surely means, on his own terms, that Kelly could have been murdered six hours prior to his 2pm examination or, in other words, at 8am. We've seen that no one would doubt that a body could be comparatively cold within six hours so it's very hard to know why Dr Bond concluded from the rigor and the temperature that Kelly had been dead for twelve hours instead of six.

Ultimately, the time of death arrived at by Dr Bond seems to have been based on the examination of the contents of the stomach. It had long been believed, as a rule of thumb, that the contents of a stomach take about four hours to empty. The *British Enyclopedia* published in 1809, for example, stated that, 'The time occupied by the digestive process must be expected to vary according to the constitution, age and health of the individual, and the nature of the aliment; but it may be stated, in general, at four hours.' Some, however, might say it would take five hours while others would say six or more (see Appendix B). On the basis of the partly digested food in the stomach, Dr Bond seems to have thought that Kelly had eaten three or four hours prior to her death, thus estimating her time of death as between about 1am and 2am. The extraordinary thing about this, however, is that there was literally no evidence available to him as to when Kelly had eaten her last meal. Dr Bond seems to have assumed that she would have eaten at about 10pm. This may or may not have been based on police enquiries as to when Kelly would normally have eaten but it could only have been speculation at best.

There was another indication that Kelly might have been murdered during the early hours of the morning. This was the evidence at the inquest of Elizabeth Prater, who lived in a room above Kelly's, that she was woken by a cry of 'murder!', seemingly coming from close by, at shortly after 4am. In a written statement prior to the inquest, Prater said that she heard 'screams of murder about two or three times in a female voice' but during her oral testimony at the inquest she seemed to change her mind, saying that the cry was a single one of 'oh! murder' which was 'in a faint voice'. She ignored the cry and went back to sleep, because, she said, 'it is nothing uncommon to hear cries of murder', and, 'I frequently hear such cries from the back of the lodging-house where the windows look into Millers Court.' Consequently, it is by no means certain that it was Kelly, in the process of being murdered, who was responsible for whatever sound was heard by Miss Prater.

It was a natural assumption to think that Kelly would have been murdered between midnight and four o'clock in the morning like the previous four victims but there was one witness at Kelly's inquest who claimed not only to have seen Kelly but also to have spoken to her at shortly after eight o'clock in the morning of 9 November, less than three hours before her dead body was discovered. This was Mrs Caroline Maxwell, the wife of the deputy of a nearby lodging house. Before she gave her evidence at the Shoreditch Town Hall, the coroner, Dr Roderick Macdonald, cautioned her by saying, 'You must be very careful about your evidence, because it is different to other people's.' This was quite unfair and most untrue. There was precisely no evidence produced by other witnesses as to the time of Kelly's death. Presumably the coroner had in mind the evidence of Elizabeth Prater about the cry of murder at 4am but she couldn't even identify that cry (if a sound made by a 'faint voice' can be described as a cry) as having been made by Kelly and she also testified as to it being a common occurrence to hear cries of murder in the district. It's possible that Macdonald was also thinking of the medical evidence, although at that stage of the proceedings, Dr Phillips had not yet testified and, even when he did, he didn't estimate any time of death.

Macdonald might have read a report by Dr Phillips in which he provided an estimate similar to that of Dr Bond but it's hard to see how it could be regarded as even reasonably accurate. It's perfectly clear that a body can become cold within four hours and in this case we are talking about a body with its insides horribly exposed so that there was barely a patch of undisturbed skin by which Kelly's temperature could have been felt by hand and there is no record of her temperature having been taken with a thermometer, despite the presence of at least five doctors in the room during her post-mortem examination. We've seen from the paper by Niderkorn that it was known that rigor mortis can set in within four hours (and, in fact, it can happen faster than that) so that, on the basis of body temperature and rigor, it would have been impossible for any competent medical examiner to have ruled out death having occurred between 8am and 10am that morning.

Mrs Maxwell's evidence was that she had been surprised to see Kelly up so early on Friday 9 November and was 'positive' that the time she saw her was between 8am and 8.30am. She asked her why she was up so early and Kelly replied, 'Oh! I do feel so bad! Oh Carrie I feel so bad'. She then asked her to have a drink but Kelly replied that she had just had a drink of ale and brought it up, motioning towards some vomit in the street. Maxwell said she then saw Kelly again at about 8.45am speaking to a man outside the Britannia Public House.

If Mrs Maxwell was correct, it's not impossible that Kelly then ate some breakfast which constituted the 'recently digested meal' referred to by Dr Bond. In his post-mortem notes he states that this was 'some partly digested food of fish and potatoes'. Although Dr Bond thought that he was seeing the results of three to four hours digestion, this is notoriously difficult to estimate accurately and it might have only been the result of an hour or two's digestion before Kelly was murdered. Alternatively, it might have reflected the results of a breakfast Kelly had taken before she had spoken to Mrs Maxwell at 8am. True, she had supposedly vomited some of this food up after drinking ale, but that might still have left some food in the stomach.

At any rate, this is a classic example of witness evidence conflicting with the medical testimony. Had someone been arrested for the murder, the time of death could have been a crucial factor in the case, either providing an alibi for the killer or condemning an innocent person to the gallows if it was wrongly estimated.

Aside from the Ripper cases, there had been a couple of other odd time of death estimates during 1888.

In April of that year, an inquest was held in Essex into the death of a three-month-old baby boy, Edward Claydon, who died suddenly in the presence of his mother and grandmother. The child, already delicate, became ill during the evening of 2 April and died at about a quarter past ten. There was no need, therefore, for the medical examiner, Dr Maybury, to provide an estimate for the time of death other than to corroborate the evidence of the family members who saw the baby die. Nevertheless, Dr Maybury, who examined the body at 1pm, testified that the baby, which he believed died of consumption, 'must then have been dead about two hours, the body being cold'.[96] He was, therefore, estimating the time of death at 11pm, which was some forty-five minutes later than the baby succumbed, but the curious element of this estimate was that he gave the impression that the conclusion that should be drawn from a cold body was that it had been dead for no more than two hours which was, of course, at odds with what other medical practitioners normally said.

Yet, only a few weeks later, in May 1888, another baby of about the same age died in Battersea and the medical practitioner in this case, Dr William Sewell, deposed at the inquest that, 'when I was called in the deceased had been dead about three hours, the body being cold'.[97] Not only was this inconsistent with what Dr Maybury had said regarding the death of Edward Claydon, but many doctors would say that a *warm* body indicated death having occurred within two or three hours. In other words, both a cold body *and* a warm body seemed to indicate to different medical examiners that death had occurred within about three hours making somewhat of a mockery of using an assessment of body temperature by hand to estimate time of death.

Another death in May 1888 was that of Mrs Frances Maria Wright, a woman with an existing heart disease, who died of shock or fright after two men entered her house attempting to rob her on 16 May. A neighbour saw the two men entering Mrs Wright's house at some point between 2.30 and 3pm followed by the sound of three cries after which the men left the house. The police were called and Mrs Wright's dead body was found at the foot

---

[96] *Essex Standard*, 7 April 1888.
[97] *South London Press*, 5 May 1888.

The Temperature of Death • 197

of the stairs lying partly in a sitting position with a mark below her left eye. Dr James Greenwood arrived at 3.05pm which was probably within half an hour of Mrs Wright's death. Giving evidence in October 1888 at the Old Bailey in the trial of Henry Glennie, who was charged with Mrs Wright's murder (but acquitted), Dr Greenwood told the judge that he found the skin 'cool' but, he said, 'on keeping my hand there I could feel the warmth under the skin'. He seems to have been unique in having this ability to detect warmth *beneath* the skin. The doctor also told the judge that, as a general rule, 'it would take nearly an hour for the body to get sensibly cold'.

CHAPTER ELEVEN

1889–1960s

A good example of the uncertainty within the medical profession about what inference could be drawn from a cold dead body occurred in the proceedings following the violent murder of George Gordon in September 1889.

On 26 September 1889, surgeon Robert Mitchell was summoned to a house in Bury at 12.45pm where he saw the fully dressed dead body of George Gordon lying on a kitchen table. Dr Mitchell later told the magistrate at Bury Police Court, on 2 October, that, 'The body was cold. The deceased must have been dead some hours'. When asked in cross-examination by the barrister instructed by the man accused of the murder to be more specific, he said that when he saw the body, 'deceased would have been dead from twelve to twenty hours' adding that, 'It was certainly more than twelve and might have been twenty'.[98] That range of eight hours wasn't terribly helpful in estimating the time of death but it wasn't until the trial at Manchester Assizes in December that Dr Mitchell said that not only was the body cold but that rigor mortis had set in. This doesn't appear to have had much influence on his estimate of time of death because, presumably based on what Taylor had stated as such in his 1873 textbook, *The Principles and Practice of Medical Jurisprudence*, he also said that he would expect rigor mortis to set in 'within five or six hours'.[99] Hence, the

---

[98] *Manchester Guardian*, 3 October 1889.
[99] *Manchester Guardian*, 6 December 1889.

rigor was irrelevant to his estimate which was evidently based on the fact that he didn't believe that a body would be 'cold' until at least twelve hours after death, in contrast to what almost every other medical examiner had testified about this, albeit that few referred to a body being 'stone' cold.

An admission of medical uncertainty in the matter of body cooling occurred at an inquest into the death of Ann Henderson in South Devon in December 1892. A local doctor, Dr Verity, said that he had been called to the home of the deceased woman at 9pm on 16 December when he found her to be quite cold, with a slight contused wound on her left eye. Her husband, Thomas, said he had found the body at 8.15pm. The couple had apparently had a quarrel and there was a suspicion of foul play (although the jury eventually found that Mrs Henderson died of excitement as a result of the quarrel, with insufficient evidence to show that violence had been used against her). Asked by the coroner how long Mrs Henderson had been dead, Dr Verity said, 'I should certainly think she had been dead twelve hours…She may have been dead one hour and forward up to twelve hours.' The coroner expressed surprise that she could have been dead as long as twelve hours to which Dr Verity replied, 'I express my opinion because I [do] not know the circumstances and I wish to be correct.' In other words, he didn't have any clues provided by independent witness testimony as to when Mrs Henderson had last been seen alive or when she had died. Asked by a juror what the maximum time was for a body to get cold after death, Dr Verity frankly replied that, 'Science has not yet been able to fix that maximum'.[100]

Two years earlier, on 1 January 1890, Dr Edward Fountain had been called at noon to a house in Chiswick where a 39-year-old woman, Margaret Louise Bryden, was lying dead on her bed, her nightdress case having been placed firmly in her mouth. In what appeared to the inquest jury to be a case of murder which was never solved, her false teeth were in her stomach. Dr Fountain told the coroner that, 'The body was warm', and he said he thought that death had occurred 'about five hours before.'[101] By contrast, in the case of a suicide by shooting in April 1894, when Dr Henry Fraser Stokes examined the body of William Oldham Hughes he found that, 'The body was warm' but concluded from this that, 'death must have

---

[100] *Devon and Exeter Daily Gazette*, 21 December 1892.
[101] *Reynolds's Newspaper*, 2 February 1890.

taken place about an hour [earlier]'.[102] Two years after this, in a case of murder at the Old Bailey, Dr William Henry Kempster said in his evidence at the trial of Alice St John, who was eventually acquitted of murder, that, when he examined the dead body of her violent husband Frederick Charles St John at about 6am, he found that, 'it was perfectly cold; rigor mortis had set in – I should say he had been dead about six hours'. That estimate was fundamentally different, despite the same apparent temperature and existence of rigor mortis, to the 'twelve to twenty hours' estimate of Dr Mitchell in the case of George Gordon a mere seven years earlier. In the St John case, however, neighbours had heard slapping noises coming from the couple's room at about 11pm of the night before and that might have been a clue for Dr Kempster when forming his estimate.

Five or six hours had, however, become somewhat of a benchmark for bodies found cold and rigid. It was the estimate given by Dr James Gurney Curruthers at 4am on 3 June 1898 when examining the body of a policeman, William George Traske, whose body had been found on the line at Northwood Junction, thus placing the time of death at around 10 or 11pm of 2 June.[103] Without rigidity but feeling a body to be cold, one might expect an estimate of two or three hours, which was the estimate offered by Dr Cundell following the death of Walter Thomas Jones, a builder, whose cold body was found near the gates of Kew Gardens in September 1899.[104] But three, four or five hours was equally possible. At the same time, a body found warm could also produce an estimate of death having occurred within a few hours, easily two or three but sometimes half an hour or, more often, 'recently'.

Moving into the twentieth century, 1902 saw the publication of *A Treatise on Medical Jurisprudence* by Dr George Vivian Poore. Noting that some medical textbooks were saying that the body cools at a rate of one degree Fahrenheit per hour, Poore commented laconically, 'That is so easy to remember that it is a pity it is not true'. He cautioned that the rate of cooling of a body depends on circumstances, especially the temperature of the surrounding air, while the temperature after death sometimes rises, and the message to his student readers and colleagues was that, 'I warn you

---

[102] *Islington Gazette*, 30 April 1894.
[103] *Croydon Times*, 4 June 1898.
[104] *Kentish Mercury*, 15 September 1899.

when you go into courts of law not to attempt to be precise where precision is really impossible'. He added that, 'If you try to lay down the rules of that kind you will, with the best of intentions, more often deceive the jury and yourselves than you will do good.' Despite this, when it came to discussing the Gardner case, Poore, misled by Taylor into thinking that only the lower part of the abdomen had been found to be warm, felt the need to defend the medical profession by saying that Mrs Gardner had been dead 'very likely ten hours' when her 'cold and stiff' body was discovered at 8am (which would place the time of death as 10pm the night before) so that, 'everybody was justified in saying that the time was more than four hours'. Given that there was no evidence about the temperature of the surrounding air of the room in which Gardner was found, it is surprising that Poore felt able to make this statement, especially in view of his own warnings about the difficulty of precision. As we know, it is also highly misleading to say that Mrs Gardner's body was found to be cold and stiff at 8am. Some of it was still warm and there was no evidence of stiffness at 8am, suggesting that Poore had deceived himself and his readers.

Also in 1902, James Glaister, Professor of Forensic Medicine and Public Health at the University of Glasgow, published *A Text-Book of Medical Jurisprudence*. According to Glaister, when it came to body temperature after death, generally speaking, 'the rate of loss may be estimated at about one degree an hour on the average of time taken by the body to fall to the temperature of the surrounding medium, but relatively, the temperature falls most rapidly immediately after death, and more slowly the nearer it approaches the temperature of the medium'.[105] He estimated that the cooling process may usually be reckoned as taking between eight and twelve hours, subject to the condition of the body, the medium in which the body is placed and the kind of death. Citing Nysten, he claimed the suffocated bodies retained heat for a longer time. In respect of rigor, while making clear that he could only speak in a general way because so many factors determined the result, Glaister said that, on average, stiffening will likely have begun in the neck and jaw and face about five or six hours after death and 'will definitely be present in the upper part of the body after 10

---

[105] In later editions after Glaister's death, edited by Glaister's son, this was modified to an average loss of 1.5 degrees per hour, which formed the basis of a formula to estimate the time of death assuming a rectal temperature at time of death of 98.4 degrees.

hours, and will be present all over the body between 12 and 18 hours; and it will in all likelihood have passed off in the bulk of cases by the end of 36 hours'. He did, however, concede that it may appear 'unusually early' and cited the examples noted by Brown-Séquard and Finlayson where it had commenced in a matter of minutes after death.

One of the first major murder cases of the new century to deal with time of death involved the murder of Emily Farmer, an unmarried newsagent in her sixties who was battered to death in her shop in Commercial Road, Stepney, at some point during the early hours 12 October 1904.

At the inquest into Emily's death, held on 13 October 1904 before Wynne Baxter, Dr Charles Graham Grant, who was called by police to examine the body at 8.15am on 12 October, testified that, 'Rigor mortis was not present, but she was getting cold on the chest'.[106] From this, he concluded that, 'She had died within half an hour of my seeing her.' It was known that Emily had been alive at 5.45am because she had received a bundle of newspapers from a delivery boy at that time and two men, Conrad Donovan and Charles Wade, were seen coming out of her shop at about 6.30am. Locals noted at about 6.45am that Emily had gone missing from her shop and her body was discovered, lying in her bedroom above the shop, at about 8am. She had been bound and gagged and there were obvious signs of a burglary.

Donovan and Wade were arrested on suspicion of murder but there was an obvious problem. If, as Dr Grant, believed, Emily had died at some point after 7.45am, i.e. within half an hour of his examination at 8.15am, how could Donovan and Wade have been responsible for her death if they had left her shop at 6.30am? The answer couldn't have been that Emily took more than an hour to die because Dr Grant said at the Thames Police Court on 25 October that she must have died very quickly after violence had been inflicted against her, and certainly no longer than thirty minutes after being attacked. The situation was somewhat confused by a couple of lay witnesses, Cecilia Baker and Constable James Hooper, who said they felt Emily's heart beating at 8am but this was dismissed as impossible by Dr Grant who believed that they had simply felt the pulsation of their own fingers. At the Police Court, Dr Grant repeated his evidence from the

---

[106] TNA: CRIM 1/96/1.

inquest, saying that, 'half an hour would probably be the longest between death and my seeing her.'

If Emily couldn't have been alive for more than thirty minutes after being attacked, and she had been dead within half an hour of Dr Grant's examination at 8.15, this would have caused a serious problem for the prosecution at their trial because it would have meant that Donovan and Wade couldn't have committed the murder. Somewhat predictably, at the Old Bailey on 19 November, we find Dr Grant changing his mind as to his estimate of time of death when giving evidence for the prosecution. After having said that, when he examined Emily's body at 8.15am, 'her chest felt colder than one would expect if she were alive and was losing temperature', the doctor went on to say, 'I formed the erroneous opinion at the time that she had been dead within half an hour, but on maturer consideration of the facts, and on looking up the authorities, I was reluctantly compelled to alter that opinion; I think she had been dead then over half an hour but I would not like to say how much over.'

A clearer case of a medical witness changing his evidence to fit the prosecution case one would be hard pressed to find. It was actually his second change of mind for, at the magistrate's court, Dr Grant had been recalled after his initial evidence and said under cross-examination that instead of having died within half an hour, he now thought Ms Farmer had been dead, 'over an hour' when he saw her that morning. By way of explanation, he said that he had noticed at the time, 'a certain flexion in the limbs, both arms and legs' and that, 'The body was also slightly bent at the hips'. Factoring into the equation a rarely used and uncertain indicator of time of death, he also drew attention to the fact that, 'The eyes had lost their tension and transparency'. In addition, he now told the magistrate, 'The chest felt colder to me than would be consistent with very recent death'. Furthermore, he attempted to deny what he had actually said at the inquest, claiming that, 'It is an error to say that my evidence was that she died half an hour before I saw her. It was impossible for anyone to be so specific as that'. Yet, he agreed that he had read the written deposition of his evidence before he signed it at the inquest. As we've seen, when the case reached the Old Bailey, Dr Grant did accept that he had originally been of the opinion that Farmer had died within half an hour.

One of the reasons for Dr Grant's change of mind was that the police had instructed Professor Augustus Joseph Pepper to examine the evidence in the case. Pepper testified to the magistrate on 9 November 1904, which he repeated at the Old Bailey, that, from his understanding of the evidence, Emily must have been dead 'over an hour' when Dr Grant had arrived at 8.15am. As he explained at the Old Bailey, 'my grounds are, in the first place the temperature of the body which was spoken to by Dr Grant – the front of the chest was cool – the death was clearly from suffocation, which is one of the causes of slow cooling of a body – it was in a room, as I understand...where the windows were closed and had not been opened – that was the room in which the woman had slept that night, so it would be comparatively warm, which would tend to prevent the cooling of the body – Dr Grant deposed that the eyeballs had lost their tension – in death from asphyxiation the eyeballs as a rule are prominent and the flaccidity comes on slowly – I do not lay much stress on the transparency, the tension is more important – it takes time for the tension to alter in cases of suffocation – I do not place much stress on the dark blue colour, round where the ligatures had been on the wrist – I think that would form very quickly after death – I think death ensued within ten minutes of these injuries being received'.

Another medical man, Dr John Charles Anderson, was also consulted and he said at the Old Bailey, 'it is extremely difficult to place the time of the death; I should say it had taken place certainly over an hour, perhaps two hours...I thought the deceased had been dead for a couple of hours, from the cooling of the body and the ligature marks round the wrist, which were very marked, being of a dark blue colour with no surrounding area of redness or inflammation.' Anderson, however, had initially told the magistrate a few days earlier that he thought Emily had been dead for *three* hours, which would have placed her death some time before she had last been seen alive at 5.45. Under cross-examination at the Old Bailey by defence Counsel, he said, 'I was asked by the Magistrate, not knowing the facts of the case, how long should I say she had been dead, and I said three hours – I did not form any definite opinion, when I first saw the body, as to how long she had been dead, but I formed the opinion that nobody could say exactly'. This is as close to an admission that he was tailoring his medical opinion to fit witness evidence as it is possible to find. Cross-examined further, Dr Anderson agreed that he had thought it was 'an important matter' when he gave his first estimate of three hours and went on to admit that, 'it is very difficult to decide the exact moment when death took place'.

Naturally Dr Grant was also cross-examined hard on his change of mind by the defence Counsel at the Old Bailey. His evidence under cross-examination was recorded thus in the Old Bailey proceedings:

> Mistakes are made by skilled persons as well – I am not quite certain as to the date when I altered my opinion as to how long the deceased had been dead, but I think I said at the Police Court that it was half an hour; whether you cross-examined me or not I cannot say – my opinion was not founded on the gag, but upon the condition of the body, the set eyes, and the losing temperature – one strong point to tell how long a body has been dead is the eye losing its tension – I am not an expert like Professor Pepper, and I did not mention the fact of the eye losing its tension at the inquest – I know Professor Pepper said that this was such an important point that I ought to have mentioned it — the fact is not down in my report of the *post-mortem* examination – I did not take the eyes sufficiently into consideration until after I gave my evidence at the Police Court — the uncovered parts of a body would cool more rapidly than the parts that are not exposed – I do not know sufficiently to give an opinion whether a dead body cools more rapidly at first than later on; if an authority said it was the general rule, I should disagree; it depends on what was the cause of death – I heard that Professor Pepper, Dr. Anderson, and myself are all at variance as to the exact time the deceased had been dead – I can assure the jury, with the greatest possible confidence, that Miss Baker and the policeman could have mistaken a body that had been dead for two or three hours for a living one – it is extremely difficult, by placing the hand upon the heart of a person lying on their back, to tell whether the heart is beating or not, even if it be a healthy one – in forming the opinion that the body had been dead half-an-hour, I was not aware that the eye is more brilliant after asphyxia than it is before – of course,

skilled persons on looking at the eye of a dead person would make different remarks to unskilled persons – I do not know what conclusion Professor Pepper has arrived at as to how long the deceased lived after the gag had been inserted; I cannot say without seeing the gag in the mouth.

Questioned by the jury about the onset of rigor mortis, Dr Grant said that it 'sets in more rapidly in some deaths than others.'

Professor Pepper also didn't have an easy ride under cross-examination. He agreed that Professor Taylor was an authority on body cooling and that 'he [Taylor] says in some cases of asphyxiation a body has been observed to cool as rapidly as in death from other causes, and that is so; there is no fixed rule.' Taylor had stated in the 1865 edition of the *Principles and Practice of Medical Jurisprudence* that, 'the bodies of persons who have died of asphyxia, by hanging or suffocation…do not cool, *caeteris paribus*, until from twenty-four to forty-eight hours after death…'. However, it was also stated in the next sentence that, 'Too much importance must not be attached to this statement, since in some cases of fatal asphyxia, the body has been observed to cool just as rapidly as in death from other causes'. This caveat had been retained in subsequent editions of his book published after his death, as edited by Dr Thomas Stevenson. Pepper also agreed that, if anything turns upon the temperature of the body, a thermometer would be more accurate but, he confessed, 'it is not usually used'. He further said that, 'it is extremely difficult to place the time of death; I should say it had taken place certainly over an hour, perhaps two hours – I cannot say nearer than that'. Under re-examination, the professor said: 'In the majority of cases where death is due to suffocation, the body cools more slowly than it does in ordinary circumstances. There are cases where temperature rises after death.'

During closing speeches, Percival Hughes, in behalf of the defence, said to the jury that, 'The question as to when death took place was of vital importance in the case'. He also questioned the evidence as to the identification of his clients but all to no avail as Donovan and Wade were found guilty of murder and sentenced to death, being executed on 13 December 1904. Wade said nothing before the sentence was carried out, but Donovan basically confessed to the crime by saying to the prison chaplain, 'No murder was intended.'[107]

In 1905, a new edition of Taylor's book was published, edited by Dr Frederick John Smith, who modified the passage on asphyxial death by saying that, while the cause was 'not clear', asphyxia could delay body cooling, probably as a result of 'the loading of the tissues with oxidisable materials combined with slackening of the circulation before death'. At the same time, Smith followed this by repeating the warning that 'too much importance should not be attached to this statement', because, as Taylor had said, 'in some cases of fatal asphyxia the body has been observed to cool just as rapidly as in death from other causes'. The 1905 edition also contained a revised warning about estimating time of death by simply feeling a corpse, as follows:

> A caution must be here inserted with regard to the exact meaning of the cooling of the body and how it is to be determined. It is customary to judge of the coldness by placing the hand on the skin: this is very fallacious, inasmuch as it depends, first of all, upon the warmth of the observer's hand, a corpse may feel cold to the warm hand and warm to a cold one; and secondly the warmth of the skin of a corpse is not a good criterion of the warmth of the viscera.

As usual, the medical profession didn't appear to be paying attention. We have already seen that in the important murder case of Miss Farmer a year earlier no thermometer had been used at the crime scene.

Another major twentieth century case where the time of death formed a central feature was the murder of Emily 'Phyllis' Dimmock in Camden Town in 1907. Dimmock was a prostitute whose throat was cut while she was in bed at some point during the night of 11/12 September 1907. The first police report on the case noted that the divisional surgeon had concluded that Dimmock had been 'dead for some hours' when her 'cold and rigid' body was examined at about 1pm on 12 September. As usual, no temperature appears to have been taken. At the inquest into Dimmock's death, Dr Thompson stated his belief that she had been dead for seven or eight hours, thus placing the time of death at between 5 and 6am. A

---

[107] *Times*, 14 December 1904.

subsequent attempt was made to include an examination of Dimmock's stomach contents into the estimate but there was no evidence as to when she had taken her last meal. Nevertheless, when factoring the stomach contents into his estimate, on the basis of an *assumed* meal at 11pm, Dr Thompson amended his estimate to the murder having occurred at about 3am, although he amended it again under cross-examination, ultimately plumping for 4am. This estimated time of death caused huge problems for the prosecution during the trial of Robert Wood, the man suspected of having committed the murder, for he had been seen to have returned to his home near King's Cross at midnight, following a known meeting with Dimmock in a public house in Camden Town earlier that evening. On the basis of the doctor's estimated time of death, the prosecution had to rely on a theory that Wood had gone back out again and returned to Dimmock's house in Camden Town to commit the murder. There was, however, no evidence to support this theory and Wood was acquitted to rapturous public applause.

On 27 December 1911, Dr Percy Goodman of Brick Lane was called in the early hours of the morning to a kosher restaurant and illicit gambling den in Hanbury Street where owner Solomon Milstein and his wife Annie had both been violently attacked with a knife and were lying dead on the floor. At the inquest into the two deaths, Dr Goodman stated that due to 'the body being cold', but no rigor mortis having set in, Solomon 'might have been dead about an hour'.[108] This unusually short time period for a body becoming cold might have been influenced by the fact that Annie's body was still warm (and Dr Goodman thought that *she* had been dead for only about thirty to forty-five minutes). It was also the case that a resident in a flat above the restaurant had heard groaning at about 2.30am which lasted from about thirty to forty-five minutes, followed by a smell of burning (as some bedding had been burnt) at which point he called the police. Myer Abramovitch, a costermonger who had lost all his money gambling that night, confessed to the murder of the couple and was convicted at the Old Bailey and sentenced to death.

If, in 1912, you were to refer to a medical textbook for the time taken for onset of rigor mortis after death you would probably have learnt that, 'it generally commences within five or six hours after death, while the body is

---

[108] *Leeds Mercury*, 30 December 1911.

engaged in the act of cooling'.[109] While Glaister, as we have seen, had noted some recorded examples of very fast onset of rigor in his 1902 textbook, most of the leading textbooks of the early twentieth century ignored them, and it wasn't until 1968 that Professor Francis E. Camps included an entry in the second edition of *Gradwohl's Legal Medicine* saying that, 'sometimes rigor is seen within 30 minutes of death'. A practical example of fast onset of rigor can be found much earlier than this, though, in the case of Stephen Titus who fired a revolver at barmaid Esther May Towers in a central London hotel at shortly after 11am on 27 September 1912, killing her, after which he then shot a number of members of the public who attempted to detain him. Dr Thomas Rose, divisional surgeon, was quick on the scene, arriving at about 11.45am, and noted in his evidence at the Old Bailey trial of Titus that Miss Towers, 'had been dead some forty-five minutes, the body was beginning to stiffen'. This obviously meant that rigor mortis could commence within forty-five minutes of death. Titus was found guilty but insane and ordered to be detained at His Majesty's pleasure.

One of the heroes of the day on 27 September 1912 was John Starchfield, a newspaper vendor, who tackled Titus as he tried to flee the scene but was shot in the abdomen. Within two years Starchfield was back in the news after his young son, Willie, was abducted and strangled on 8 January 1914. Having gone missing at about 12.50pm, the boy's dead body was found on a train some three and a half hours later. John Starchfield was initially arrested for the crime and, at the police court proceedings, Dr Edward Garrett, the police divisional surgeon, who examined the boy's body at 4.40pm, stated his opinion that Willie had been murdered at between 2.30 and 3pm based on some 'slight warmth' he had felt between the thighs and armpits. Cross-examined by Starchfield's Counsel, Mr Margetts, Dr Garrett accepted that he hadn't used a thermometer but refused to agree that time of death could be extended to 3.30pm (at which time Starchfield had an alibi) although he accepted that it could have been earlier than 2.30pm.[110] Starchfield was tried at the Old Bailey but discharged when the case against him was withdrawn at the suggestion of the judge.

---

[109] *The Principles and Practice of Medical Jurisprudence* by Alfred Swaine Taylor, 1905, ed. Fred J. Smith, p.267.

[110] *Manchester Courier*, 24 February 1914.

During the trial of Jack Field and William Gray for the shocking murder of London typist Irene Munro on the Eastbourne Crumbles in August 1920 while she was on holiday at the seaside resort, the prosecution medical witnesses managed to contradict themselves over the issue of the time of death in a way which set up a ground of appeal of the conviction.

Munro's battered but clothed body had been found by a young boy buried under a pile of shingles on the Crumbles, about 800 yards from the sea, between 3 and 4pm on Friday, 20 August 1920. It took a few hours for the news of the discovery to be reported to the police so that it wasn't until after 8pm that an inspector arrived on the scene, although it was still light at this time. After a further delay, the police surgeon for Westham, Dr Ernest Cadman, was summoned at 10.25pm and arrived at about 11pm by which time it was dark, but the doctor had brought a strong acetylene bicycle lamp with him. It was noted by the doctor that the body was cold to the touch, although no external or internal temperature was taken, and that rigor mortis was well established, with the limbs not able to be moved (although this rigor had relaxed by the time of the post-mortem examination which occurred during the afternoon of the following day). Cadman formed an immediate opinion that the woman had been murdered between twelve and twenty-four hours earlier. He wrote in his report to the coroner that the body was 'not more than 24 hours dead' at the time he saw it, so that death could not, in his opinion, have occurred before 11pm on Thursday 19 August. This conclusion wasn't based so much on the body temperature, although it appears to have been a factor, but more on the rigidity of the limbs and the fact that, when the body was moved, 'blood ran out of the left nostril'. It was from these facts that Dr Cadman considered that the time of death 'would not be more than 24 hours [earlier]'. He stuck to this opinion during the inquest and committal proceedings and wouldn't budge from it.

This caused a major problem for the prosecution because it was soon established by the police from witness evidence that Irene must have been murdered by Field and Gray between 3pm and 5pm on Thursday, 19 August. Any significantly later time than this meant that both men would have had solid alibis and could not have been responsible.

Fortunately for the prosecution, the Home Office had instructed Dr Reginald Elworthy of the West London Hospital to conduct an

The Temperature of Death • 211

independent examination of the body on 25 August. Although this didn't provide any new information, he told the coroner during the inquest that, on the basis of what Dr Cadman had observed, death could have occurred thirty hours earlier, although that would only have taken it to 5pm on Thursday afternoon. Without committing to a specific time, he said it was 'quite possible' that death could have occurred on the Thursday afternoon. When giving evidence before the magistrate, Elworthy began by saying that: 'The timing of death is not a mathematical speculation… but under ordinary circumstances it is accepted that a body does not get cold earlier than twelve hours and later than twenty-four'. Having explained that there were various factors which needed to be taken into account when estimating death based on body temperature, namely the suddenness of death, the amount of exposure, the amount of ventilation, the temperature of the atmosphere to which the body is exposed after death and the health of the deceased during life, he said, 'It is quite impossible when a body is cold to say how long death has taken place by studying the temperature alone'. Nevertheless, from the fact that Irene Munro was strong and healthy and had died suddenly, he concluded that, 'I should say it took not twelve hours, but twenty-four in a case like this'. He tried to explain why he preferred twenty-four hours over twelve by saying incomprehensibly that, 'there are certain reasons for the body to lose its heat…there are certain conditions in this case for the body to get cold… No-one could tell how long she had been cold; there is no medical way.' After suggesting a time of death of twenty-four hours 'plus any number of hours', Elworthy came round to a helpful answer from the prosecution's point of view that, after taking into consideration the conditions in which the body was found, 'I should say from eighteen to thirty-six hours when Dr Cadman saw the body.'

When cross-examined by defence counsel, Elworthy said that, 'There is a stage in the cooling of a body when it would be described as cold, up to that it would be a matter of degree' but he conceded that, 'In ordinary cases this would take twenty to twenty-four hours'. He nevertheless insisted that it all depended on the temperature of the night and the nature of the contact with the earth, which made any precise calculation impossible. In the end, he stuck with an estimate of death having occurred between eighteen and thirty-six hours prior to Dr Cadman's initial examination, thus between 11am on Thursday and 3am on Friday.

A couple of weeks before the trial was due to begin, Dr Elworthy was asked to provide his views on Dr Cadman's opinion for the benefit of prosecuting counsel. In a written report, he agreed with Dr Cadman that the limit of the time usually taken by a body to become absolutely cold and stiff was from twelve to twenty-four hours but said that both the cooling of the body and the onset of rigor mortis was 'usually delayed in healthy subjects who have been killed suddenly without having been subjected to fatigue beforehand'. While this was helpful for the prosecution, it is unclear what scientific basis Dr Elworthy had for saying it. He also suggested that another factor which might delay cooling was burial with clothes on in summer time, as had happened with Irene Munro. Having found rigor mortis still persisting in his own examination on 25 August, and believing that there was 'well supported observation' that 'the longer rigor mortis takes in appearing, the longer it tends to persist', he repeated his conclusion from the magistrate's hearing that the lowest time limit for death to have occurred was 18 hours prior to Dr Cadman's examination at 11pm on Friday night, and 36 hours at the outside, taking the possible time of death back to 11am on Thursday, although he said it could have been even earlier because 'the body remained fresh a fairly long time'.

In this case, the famous Bernard Spilsbury, lecturer in special pathology at St Bartholomew's Hospital, was asked for his written opinion, which he provided on 6 December 1920, a week before the trial of Field and Gray was due to commence. Noting that the body was cold when examined by Dr Cadman at 11pm on 20 August, he said that, taking into account the conditions in which the body remained after death, the clothing, the covering with shingle and the climactic conditions, he was of the opinion that the body would have been cold on external examination in from twelve to eighteen hours. Noting that rigor mortis was also complete, he claimed that, 'In cases of rapidly fatal injuries inflicted upon healthy persons the onset of rigor mortis tends to be delayed unless the person is exhausted by a struggle prior to death'. He felt that the onset of rigor might have been delayed in this case, 'and might not be complete until ten hours after death or even a little longer'. At the same time, he was aware of cases where the duration of the rigor might be greatly increased and be present for as much as seven days after death. His ultimate conclusion was that death occurred 'not less than twelve hours before the examination by Dr Cadman on Friday night', which wasn't entirely helpful for the prosecution, but he added that, 'the condition of the body at that time is consistent with death having occurred on the afternoon of the previous day'. In the end, Spilsbury wasn't called as an expert witness at the trial, as had been intended. The evidence of Dr Elsworthy, who had actually examined the body, albeit some days after Dr Cadman, appears to have been regarded as sufficient to put the time of death back to Thursday afternoon.

During the trial at Lewes County Hall during December 1920, Dr Cadman was asked by, James Cassels, Counsel for Jack Field, if he would confirm that twenty-four hours was the extreme limit for the time it would take for a body left out in the open covered with clothing and by shingle to cool. To this question he surprisingly, and perhaps evasively, asked the barrister to tell him when Irene Munro had eaten her last full meal. This was curious because there was no good scientific reason to think that the time of her last meal would have impacted upon the body cooling. He was nevertheless asked by Mr Cassels to assume that she had eaten within four hours of her death. Although he had been asked about body cooling, Dr Cadman's answer was that, in this event, rigor mortis would come on in about six hours from the time of death and would relax in twenty-four hours. When pressed further about how long it takes for rigor mortis to relax, he said that rigor had not been a special subject for him to study and that he could only refer Counsel to the authorities on the subject. Returning to the subject of body cooling, he agreed that the atmosphere has a considerable effect on the cooling of a body but, as he had no information about the atmosphere on the night he examined the body other than that it was a fine night and very dark, he couldn't say any more about it.

Although Dr Cadman stuck firmly to his belief that death could not have occurred more than twenty-four hours before his examination at 11pm on Friday night, he gave an unexpected answer when asked by Mr Cassels if the condition of the body was consistent with death having taken place late on Thursday night or during the early hours of the morning. Bafflingly, he said, 'I should say Thursday afternoon'. He was then asked if he meant to say that the condition in which he found the body was inconsistent with death having taken place on Thursday night or the early hours of Friday morning, to which he replied, 'I could not give a definite opinion with regard to that because rigor mortis is so indefinite, and you cannot state positive times except the times I have given'. He repeated that rigor mortis would set in six hours after death and would relax in twenty-four hours.

Edward Marshall Hall, on behalf of William Gray, then attempted to try and clarify the confusion about what the doctor was saying regarding the time of death. Cadman agreed with the famous barrister that he had told both the coroner and the magistrate that 'the limit of time of death' was, in his opinion, twenty-four hours and that this opinion, which he had first formed on the Friday night, had been entirely independent and impartial. Asked if he still retained this opinion, he confirmed that he did retain it and, when Marshall Hall said that this must mean that he would agree that eleven o'clock on Thursday night was 'the earliest time at which this poor girl could have been done to death,' he responded, 'Decidedly'.

Mr Justice Avory then attempted to clarify what the doctor was saying about the time of death. He reminded him that he had told Mr Cassels that the conditions in which the body had been found were consistent with death on the Thursday afternoon. Cadman replied mystifyingly, 'I do not wish to withdraw that because it is so'. The judge pressed him and asked: 'When you say that you retain the opinion now that the limit of time of death was 24 hours from 11 o'clock on Friday night will you tell me what you would have expected to find different from what you did find if death had taken place on the Thursday afternoon instead of Thursday night?'. The doctor's confusing response was, 'Well, I can only say my Lord, that when we moved the body round, the blood that came out of the left nostril was not congealed; it flowed out and if it had been longer I should have expected the blood to have been coagulated'. That seemed to be saying that the victim could *not* have been murdered as early as Thursday afternoon but, at this point, Dr Cadman was allowed to step down from the witness box without anyone really quite knowing what his concluded view of the matter was.

Had this been the only evidence about the time of death, Field and Gray might have had a chance of acquittal but, as mentioned, the police and prosecution had already anticipated the problem and had called for a second opinion from Dr Elworthy. Before he testified, however, the jury heard from the police surgeon for Eastbourne, Dr James Adams, who, together with Dr Cadman, had conducted the post-mortem examination at 2.30pm on Saturday afternoon. He wasn't asked anything by the prosecution about the time of death, and had never previously expressed an opinion on the subject, but Marshall Hall somewhat recklessly asked him if the effusion of blood from the nostril observed by Dr Cadman at the crime scene on Friday night wasn't a 'curious symptom' if Munro had been dead at any time between 3 and 5pm on Thursday afternoon. The barrister obviously assumed that Dr Adams would agree with Dr Cadman about this but Adams said that there is sometimes a little blood like that when the body is moved. Putting Dr Cadman's opinion to Dr Adams that twenty-four hours would be the maximum time for the blood to run, because he would have expected it to have already coagulated, Adams replied, 'No, I do not agree that the condition of the blood would determine the hour of death'. Asked if it would be a factor in determining it, Adams said that, 'It is so uncertain, it is so variable'. Further, he said, 'When the body is moved you will often get a bloody discharge and it is not very often blood but it is a very fine serum and it looks like blood'. In respect of the onset of rigor mortis, by contrast to Dr Cadman, Dr Adams said it can commence, 'At any time from an hour to six hours after death' and that it could last for a week.

Dr Adams' answers had been helpful to the prosecution and Mr Gill wanted to press home his advantage in re-examination when he asked the doctor if the fact that Irene Munro had been a healthy well-nourished young woman whose organs were healthy throughout the body but who had been killed suddenly would not have 'a considerable bearing' on the question of rigor mortis. Dr Adams' reply was, 'Well, some bearing, they would have some bearing.' He added that, 'in the case of a violent death it would come on more rapidly, and there is no rule as to rigor mortis.' He also confirmed that it was common for 'moisture of some kind' to come from the nostrils after death and that one might see after twenty-four hours, 'what I call coloured serum oozing from the coagulated clot'.

With much of the damage caused by Dr Cadman's testimony repaired, the prosecution called Dr Elworthy who stated that, when he had examined the body on 25 August: 'As soon as the body was tilted out of the shell blood came out of the nostrils'. He said he had observed such a thing very frequently when there was a head injury. With respect to rigor mortis, he told the jury that it was 'impossible' to say exactly when it had set in or how long it had lasted, and that: 'It will last sometimes for a considerable period when the body has been killed suddenly and the tissues are healthy.' For that reason, in this case, he agreed that rigor mortis could have lasted 'a considerable time'. Asked by the judge if he could put any limit on it, he said it largely depended on the external temperature but he had seen some cases lasting six or eight days.

When cross-examined by Mr Cassels, Dr Elworthy admitted that there was nothing he had discovered in his own post-mortem examination which enabled him to say anything of value as to the time of death. Asked if Dr Cadman was in the best position to form an opinion as to the time of death, being the first doctor called on the scene, Elworthy's cautious reply was, 'He should have been'. He accepted that Cadman would have been able to establish that the body was cold to the touch and that rigor mortis was well pronounced. Asked if the internal temperature of the body should have been taken, Elworthy said, 'It would have thrown much more light on the matter'.

Asked further about body cooling, Dr Elworthy said that a clothed body brought into a mortuary from the street would lose all signs of superficial heat in twenty-four hours but that, in the conditions in which the body of Irene Munro had been found buried in shingle, it would cool a little quicker. While he agreed that twenty-four hours would be the outside limit for coagulation of blood, there might still be liquid blood or serum in the body. Pressed with regard to Dr Cadman's estimate of the time of death, Elworthy said that the relaxation of the rigor mortis observed during the post-mortem was of no value in forming a view about it. While he accepted that there was nothing inconsistent in the medical evidence with death having occurred between 9.30pm on Thursday night and 2am on Friday morning, he said that the same factors could mean that death had occurred on Thursday afternoon and that there would be no difference in the body temperature or rigor mortis. During re-examination, he confirmed that the conditions observed by Dr Cadman were 'quite consistent' with death having taken place between 3.30 and 5pm on the Thursday.

In his summing up to the jury, Mr Justice Avory said: 'A great deal of argument has been properly addressed to you on the medical evidence in this case which it is said points, or at least is consistent with the fact of this murder having been committed about 11 o'clock at night on the 19th August. If the only evidence as to the time at which it was committed were that of the medical men, and you found by the other evidence in the case that it was impossible that the prisoners could have been at that spot at 11 o'clock that night, of course your duty would be plain. You would say that the Crown had not established the case against them.' In summarizing the evidence of Dr Cadman, the judge said, 'It is true that Doctor Cadman, the doctor who was called to the spot…on the night of the 20th, formed an opinion at the time that the body had probably been dead at the most for 24 hours…Having formed that opinion he has adhered to it, but he says quite frankly that having regard to everything he now knows, everything that he saw and found is consistent with the death having taken place between 3 and 5 o'clock on the afternoon of the 19th August.' This was a rather generous interpretation of Dr Cadman's evidence in which he had appeared to say two entirely inconsistent things but, if he *had* switched to agreeing that death had occurred during Thursday afternoon (which was far from clear), it can only have been factors other than medical ones which had influenced him. The judge concluded his summary of the medical evidence by saying that this evidence was 'all consistent, everything is consistent with the death having taken place on the afternoon of the 19th'.

With overwhelming circumstantial evidence that Field and Gray had murdered Irene Munro, the two men were found guilty and sentenced to death. When filing his Grounds of Appeal, Jack Field stated as one of his grounds that: 'The Doctor who was the first to see the dead body, gave as his opinion as a practised medical man, that the girl had not been dead, more than 24 hours, which means not earlier than 11pm on Thursday August 19 at which time it is proved that I was in Eastbourne'. By the time of the hearing of the appeal itself, however, he changed his story and admitted that the murder must have occurred at about the time the prosecution said it did, except that he claimed he was not present, having left Gray with Irene Munro on the Crumbles. It was too late for this sort of story and both men were executed at Wandsworth Prison on 4 February 1921.

The failure of the medical profession to have established a method to ascertain a reliable time of death was clearly demonstrated by the Wallace case in 1931. Julia Wallace was murdered in her home in Wolverton Street, Liverpool, during the evening of 20 January 1931 while her husband, William, was on a wild goose chase, supposedly trying to find the home of a Mr R.M. Qualtrough at a non-existent 25 Menlove Gardens East. The evidence showed that Wallace must have left his house shortly after 6.45pm. He returned two hours later when his wife was lying dead on the floor of the front parlour. John Edward Whitely McFall, Professor of Forensic Medicine at Liverpool University, and police surgeon, arrived at Wallace's house at shortly before 10pm. He noted that the hands of Mrs Wallace 'were quite cold' as were the lower arms, 'but the upper arm and body were warm'. He also noted that, 'Rigor mortis was present in the upper part of the left arm and in the neck'. On the basis of the body temperature (by feel) and the rigor, he stated in his evidence at the trial of Wallace, who was charged with his wife's murder, that death had occurred four hours earlier, at 6pm.[111]

There was, however, evidence from a milk delivery boy who testified that he had spoken to Mrs Wallace at about 6.30pm, in which case she couldn't possibly have been murdered at 6pm. To the professor's credit, he refused to be swayed by this witness's evidence (which could, of course, have been mistaken) and stuck to his guns. On the other hand, he refused to admit that he could have been wrong. During cross-examination by Wallace's Counsel, Mr Hemmerde (who had, as it happens, represented John Starchfield at his trial), Professor McFall stated that, because the rigor had progressed to the neck and arm, the margin of error 'could not possibly in this case be more than an hour', but, somewhat perversely, he would only accept that this margin of error meant that death could have occurred

---

[111] TNA: HO 144/17938. The professor also argued that his opinion was corroborated by the fact that when he examined the body there was a small amount of serum exudation from the blood. He claimed that very little serum exudes from the blood during 'the first few hours' after death so that the fact that there was *some* serum seemed to him to support his estimate of at least four hours. At the same time, he didn't actually rule out the notion that the same amount of serum could have been exuded in three hours rather than four, and he didn't really seem to place much reliance on this point in any case. The judge described the evidence on this point as 'obscure'.

an hour earlier at 5pm, not in the other direction at 7pm. During cross-examination, the professor got himself into a tangle by refusing to accept that rigor would likely have come on more quickly than normal in this case due to Mrs Wallace having been a frail woman, despite agreeing that the speed of rigor depended on the muscularity of the person, a position that confused the judge.

Another witness for the prosecution was Dr Hugh Pierce who arrived at the Wallace house a couple of hours after Professor McFall. Asked what conclusion he came to as to the time of death, he said: 'Well the fact that the hands and feet were cold proved to me that death had been for some few hours previous to that'. Asked what he meant by 'some few hours', he said, 'Taking all things into consideration, I thought death had taken place about 6 o'clock or, it may be, after'. Pressed as to what the limits were to this estimate he said, 'I would give two hours limit on either side' and he agreed that this would place the time of death anywhere between 4pm and 8pm. All he felt able to say positively was: 'I would say definitely it could not have occurred after 8 o'clock'. He accepted that no temperature of the corpse had been taken nor had any detailed notes of the rigor mortis been made. Asked whether the tests on which he relied were not flimsy, he said, 'I took the age of the woman into account. Extremes of age bring it [rigor] on quicker. In middle age it will come on from 4 to 6 to 8 hours after death…the extremities, the legs and arms, were cold when I arrived. That means that death with the cooling and the rigor would make death about 6 o'clock'. The judge, who was having problems with this evidence, commented, 'I want to know what your view is in this case. You have said so many things it is difficult to follow what it is you have [said] or not. So far you put it at 6 or perhaps later, but with a margin of error two hours either way which I thought referred to this particular case, otherwise what is the use of saying of it?'. Dr Pierce then confirmed that the margin of error of of two hours either way did apply in the case.

Giving evidence for the defence, Jason Henry Dible, Professor of Pathology at Liverpool University testified that rigor mortis, taken by itself, was 'a very unreliable and inaccurate guide to the exact time of death'. He said that if he had been in Professor McFall's position he would have estimated time of death as possibly before 6pm but also possibly after 7pm. He added that, 'It is an enormously difficult subject full of pitfalls' and that it wasn't possible to come to an estimate with any degree of certainty. He agreed that the temperature of the body should have been taken but, of course, this hadn't been done.

It isn't surprising that, summing up the evidence of the three doctors to the jury, the judge said, 'With these conflicting views you may well think that you can derive no help from the medical evidence…You may think that is evidence from which you derive no assistance in considering that aspect of it, and you must act upon other considerations'. This was a devastating commentary on the state of medical knowledge regarding the estimation of time of death in the second quarter of the twentieth century. In a Home Office memo dated 19 May 1931, at a time when Wallace, who had been found guilty of the murder of his wife, was appealing the jury's verdict, Sir Ernley Blackwell, the government's chief legal advisor, having reviewed the transcripts of the trial, recorded his view that, 'The evidence of the medical men called with regard to the time at which the woman had been killed appears to me to be quite useless'. Wallace's conviction was overturned by the Court of Criminal Appeal.

Although neither Professor McCall nor Dr Pierce had taken the temperature of Mrs Wallace with a thermometer, we can say that some medical examiners did carry thermometers with them, and were prepared to use them, at crime scenes during the 1930s. Professor Keith Simpson tells us in his memoir, *Forty Years of Murder*, how he used his thermometer to take the rectal temperature of the first murder victim he examined on behalf of Scotland Yard, which he said occurred in 1934, at a hotel opposite Waterloo Station. He recognized that, 'timing is almost more important to the police than how the murder was committed'. In his book, he recounts that he was confused at that first murder case to find that the body temperature of the murder victim was 102 degrees until the detective in charge mentioned that she had obviously died of asphyxia. Simpson's reaction was to think, 'Of course. The body temperature rises in deaths from asphyxia'. He had, he said, been told that the woman had booked into the hotel the night before with a man who had been seen running down the hotel steps and over to Waterloo Station at 9am. In the finest traditions of pathologists who basically guessed at the time of death, Simpson told the detective, 'She can't have died long before that young man ran out at 9am…Early this morning'.

The case Simpson was referring to was, in fact, the 1939 murder by strangulation and suffocation of Peggy Pentecost, aged seventeen, in a private hotel in York Road, near Waterloo Station, for which her fiancé, 38-year-old Harry Armstrong, was convicted and hanged. Upon examination of the facts, what actually happened in this case didn't reflect quite as favourably upon Professor Simpson as he portrayed in his book.

Peggy's body was found by the hotel staff lying in bed in her room at 8.30am on 2 January 1939 but her rectal temperature wasn't anything close to 102 degrees when Simpson carried out his examination in the hotel room at 12pm on the same day. It was, in fact, only 72 degrees Fahrenheit, an assumed post-mortem drop of 26 degrees (from an assumed 98 degrees Fahrenheit). On that basis, and apparently assuming a fall in temperature of just over 2 degrees an hour, Simpson initially estimated in his post-mortem report that death had taken place 'a little over 12 hours before this examination', or 'shortly before midnight' on 1 January.[112] When giving evidence at Tower Bridge magistrate's court, however, he modified this and said, 'I estimated death to have taken place about 13 hours previously, that is about 11pm on January 1st'. While this had the mathematical advantage over his previous estimate in assuming a fall in temperature of exactly 2 degrees an hour, it also conveniently placed the time of death at precisely the same time as the hotel manager had heard a door being shut, supporting the police theory that Armstrong had run out of the hotel at this time, having just committed the murder. When giving evidence for the prosecution at the Old Bailey during Armstrong's trial, Simpson repeated his belief that Peggy's death had occurred at about 11pm. To the surprise of everyone at the Old Bailey, however, it turned out that Armstrong had a solid alibi from about 9.30pm on 1 January until the time Peggy's body was found the following morning. He revealed for the first time in the witness box that he had left Peggy alone in their hotel room at 9.30pm and, after having a drink in bar in Waterloo, met a woman in a café in Westminster Bridge Road at shortly after 10pm with whom he spent the night. This woman, who was a prostitute, did exist and corroborated his story. The proprietor of the café also confirmed seeing Armstrong that night.

Suddenly, the possibility of Peggy having been murdered by a stranger at 11pm needed to be considered. In this respect, the key to the hotel

---

[112] TNA: MEPO 3/1738.

room was missing and was never found, the room having been locked when the body was discovered. Armstrong said he had left it in the lock when he departed at 9.30pm, so, if that was true, it seemed possible that a stranger could have entered Peggy's room and taken the key away with him. The police had also traced and accounted for all fingerprints on a bottle of sherry in the hotel room except for a single print which couldn't be explained. The police were reportedly 'mystified' by this.[113] Now that Armstrong appeared to have a solid alibi for the time of the murder, there seemed to be a reasonable chance that he would be acquitted.

With the prosecution in disarray, the judge recalled Dr Simpson to the witness box to ask him within what limits the time of death of the murdered woman should be fixed. It was only at this point in the proceedings that Simpson mentioned that the temperature of people dying of asphyxia might rise as much as six degrees after death so that her temperature *could* have reached as high as 104 degrees. Allowing for a rate of cooling of 2 degrees an hour, it now occurred to Simpson that Peggy might have been murdered as much as 16 hours before his 12pm examination, although he plumped for 15 hours, presumably on the basis of an *assumed* body temperature of 102 degrees at the time of her death (or immediately afterwards), due to asphyxiation, and he helpfully told the judge that he could say 'with probable confidence' that Peggy had died somewhere between 9 and 11.30pm on the night of 1 January, thus destroying Armstrong's alibi.[114] This was particularly fortunate for the prosecution because, had Simpson said that death could not have occurred at any significant time after 9.30pm, Armstrong would have been in the clear. In the end, Armstrong was found guilty although, after the verdict was announced, he told the jury, 'In spite of your verdict, I am not guilty of the murder'. Nevertheless he was hanged at Wandsworth Prison on 21 March 1939.

While there was never any direct evidence presented that Armstrong was the killer, he did behave oddly after his arrest when he told the police that he would neither confirm nor deny that he had murdered Peggy. It was a rather strange way of exercising his right to silence. He also had a long criminal record, including an attempted murder of a young woman with

---

[113] *Sunday Mirror*, 12 March 1939.
[114] *The Journal of Criminal Law*, vol.2, 1939.

whom he was in a relationship by stabbing her in the throat following a quarrel some fourteen years earlier, although the charge had disgracefully been reduced to one of unlawful wounding. The Home Office files on the case reveal that Armstrong confessed his guilt to the murder of his fiancée to a prison officer, explaining that he killed Peggy because he had suspicions she had feelings for another man.[115] He presumably did so at about 9.30pm and fled the hotel in an attempt to establish an alibi. He must have thrown the key away – perhaps in the Thames - so that it was never found. There doesn't seem to be any good reason to doubt the verdict in this case, especially in light of the confession, although Dr Simpson's estimate as to the time of the murder, into which he factored an assumed rise in body temperature after Peggy's death, and an hourly rate of body cooling unsupported by scientific data, doesn't really assist. Throughout his career, Simpson seemed to have been convinced that body temperature did indeed always rise after death for victims of asphyxia, despite Professor Taylor's uncertainty, and he appears to have estimated the time of death accordingly. This seems to have been based on anecdotal evidence rather than any scientific studies.

Five years after the Wallace case, another clash between experts occurred during the trial at the Sussex Assizes of Arthur Cyril Jefferson Peake, a former sportsman accused of murdering Arthur George Noyce, a young chauffeur with whom he had enjoyed a sexual relationship. Noyce was found by his wife to be dead from strangulation in his Brighton flat at 1.45pm on 9 October 1936. Peake and Noyce had been seen together in bed by a maid but Peake claimed he had left the flat at 10am to make a telephone call and then returned to find Noyce dead, causing him to use the gas stove in a failed attempt to kill himself. Dr Binning examined the body of Noyce at 2.45pm and estimated the time of death as being twelve hours previously, i.e. 2.45am, with a range of error of two or three hours either way: so no later than 5.45am. Another medical examiner, Dr Crawford of Hove, however, gave his opinion on behalf of the defence that, on the basis of the temperature of the body and the presence of rigor mortis, Noyce had died between 8.30 and 10.30am, which was consistent with Peake's evidence about the time of death. He said that the

---

[115] TNA: HO 144/21220.

estimate put forward by Dr Binning was, 'Quite impossible.'[116] Peake was nevertheless found guilty and sentenced to death although he was reprieved by the Home Secretary and sent to Broadmoor.

On 2 February 1946, Charles Greeney's parents left home in Liverpool for a social visit at 8.30pm. When they arrived back home at about 10.20pm they discovered to their immense distress that their house had not only been broken into but their eleven-year-old son was hanging by his neck from the clothes rack in the kitchen. Four men were tried for his murder in what the police regarded as a burglary gone wrong. The electric clock wire had been pulled out and stopped at 10.03pm which gave a guide as to the time of the burglary, although it was believed that the clock was about seven or eight minutes fast. Dr George Patterson Read, the house surgeon at Liverpool Royal Infirmary, where Charles was brought at shortly after 11pm, said that, on the basis of the fall in temperature in the body, he deduced that the boy had died, 'somewhere in the region of an hour before he was admitted'. In view of all the circumstances, he put the time of death at anywhere between 9.30 and 10pm. Questioned by defence Counsel during the trial, Dr Reed agreed that many factors could add to the difficulties of gauging the time of death but, 'in the present instance he thought he could estimate time of death within half an hour'.[117] A prosecution expert, Dr W.H. Grace, lecturer in pathology and forensic medicine at Liverpool University also testified that he thought that Charles had died between 9.30 and 10pm but said that this was based on the fact that another witness who saw the body at 10.15pm, a few minutes before his parents returned home, had stated in evidence that the boy's face was white. Based on goodness knows what, Dr Grace said that 'the whiteness of the face showed the state of shock which comes shortly after death' and he, therefore, concluded that the witness must have seen the body very shortly after death. At the same time, Dr Grace also conceded that such a white pallor could last several hours after death and this moved the trial judge to interject by saying, 'I know you are anxious to be fair. Do you really feel confident to say to the jury from what you know of the facts that death might not have occurred at, say, nine o'clock?' This brought

---

[116] *Illustrated Police News*, 12 November 1936.
[117] *Liverpool Echo*, 29 April 1946 et seq.

Dr Grace to his senses and he told the judge, 'No, I don't think one could draw conclusions as to the time of death with very complete accuracy.'

For the defence, Dr John Glaister, Professor of Forensic Medicine at Glasgow University, said that death could have occurred some three or four hours prior to Dr Reed's examination, thus placing the time of death at any point after 7pm, making the entire process meaningless bearing in mind that it was known that Charles was still alive at 8.30pm. In a surprising verdict, all the defendants were acquitted of both murder and manslaughter even though there was medical evidence that Charles had received a blow on the side of the head with considerable force prior to his death. However, the men all pleaded guilty to burglary for which they received prison sentences.

In a 1947 textbook entitled *Forensic Medicine* by Keith Simpson, then a lecturer at Guy's Hospital, it was stated that, 'Under average conditions the clothed body will cool in air at the rate of about 2.5 degrees an hour for the first six hours and average a loss of 1.5 to 2 degrees for the first twelve'. It's not entirely clear where Simpson obtained these figures, which became known as 'the Simpson formula' and no source was given. After noting that the body will lose heat more slowly as the temperature comes nearer to its surroundings, Simpson said that the body, 'should feel cold in about twelve hours' but he didn't define what he meant by 'cold' and, clearly, medical examiners were informing coroners that bodies were feeling cold much sooner than this. Simpson did, however, state that cooling when naked was fifty percent faster than when clothed and twice as fast in water.

A 1956 study of forty-one executed prisoners in Sri Lanka recorded the temperatures in the rectum of hanged criminals.[118] The authors of the study found that temperatures taken immediately after execution varied from between 97.8 to 100.8 degrees and that, for the first forty-five minutes after death, there was no lowering of the core body temperature. The explanation for this was that, 'it is necessary for the body surface to first drop in temperature and establish a temperature gradient before cooling can effect the internal body temperature'. Their study was, however, conducted in a hot climate so this might have contributed to the body surface not dropping as fast as it might have done in a cooler climate and

---

[118] G.S.W. De Sarem, G. Webster, N. Kathirgamatamby, 'Post-mortem temperature and the time of death' *Journal of Criminal Law and Criminology*, 46 (1956) 562.

thus allowing the core temperature to cool. Once that initial lag was over, though, 'the temperatures of almost all bodies, where temperatures have been recorded for the full period, show a rapid fall over the first few hours gradually slowing down onwards as the body temperature approximates to that of the atmosphere'.

Still no one had managed to produce an accurate formula to calculate the time of death. At the Third International Meeting in Forensic Immunology, Medicine, Pathology and Toxicology in 1963 the chairman, Dr Frank Cleveland of Ohio remarked that, 'all forensic pathologists were fascinated by our apparent inability to determine the precise time of death, and work continued on this problem.'

An interesting experiment was conducted during the winter of 1963 and summer of 1964 by two pathologists, James and Knight (the latter being Bernard Knight), who examined one hundred bodies, each with a supposedly known time of death within a range of twenty minutes to seventy-five hours earlier, in order to estimate the time of death in each case. The pathologists were not told the real time of death so that they were working blind. The bodies were brought from domestic homes, from the street or from hospitals, some wearing normal clothes, some wearing their nightclothes and others being naked. The known times of death were obtained from police officers, ambulance drivers and doctors. Only bodies where there was certainty as to the time of death were used in the experiment.

The results were that of the one hundred bodies, the correct time of death was estimated in only eleven cases, with under-estimation in fifty-two cases and over-estimation in thirty-two. In most cases, the error was greater than 10% with an error of 100% in two of the cases. James and Knight said that a significant problem they encountered, occurring in seven cases, was with bodies having rectal temperatures at or above 98.6 degrees Fahrenheit up to four hours after death.

CHAPTER TWELVE

1960s-Present

In the 1967 film *In the Heat of the Night,* Detective Virgil Tibbs, played by Sidney Poitier, corrects the local medical examiner's estimate as to the time of death of a body which had been discovered lying in the street at 3am. Whereas the medical examiner estimated death, from a brief visual examination, as having occurred between thirty minutes and an hour before the body had been discovered, Tibbs finds, during his own examination of the body at 4.45am, that rigor had commenced in the face and jaw, with post-mortem lividity in the legs, so that the time of death must have been much earlier, at about 12.30am. This clears the prime suspect who was known to have been playing pool at that time. From a forensic point of view, post-mortem lividity, which occurs when blood in the body settles as a result of gravity, can commence within half an hour to two hours after death, so it's hard to see how Tibbs could have come up with a time of death more than four hours earlier based on the lividity. The same is true of rigor. In the film, Tibbs says that he would be able to pinpoint the time of death with even more accuracy as soon as he gets hold of a thermometer because, 'loss of heat from the brain is the most reliable way of determining death'. Naturally, the temperature reading confirms his estimate. Scenes like this helped to establish the notion that a medical examiner could very quickly and easily calculate the time of death from just a few indicators. Subsequent detective dramas would often feature a medical examiner speedily calculating a time of death which would invariably be sufficiently accurate to enable the police to catch the murderer.

By 1971 this notion was so well established in the minds of the general public that an episode of *Columbo*, 'Suitable for Framing', involved the great detective in a case where the murderer, a well-known art critic called Dale Kingston, played by Ross Martin, shoots his uncle with a revolver at what must have been about 9 or 10pm during the evening then wraps the dead body in an electric blanket, thus fooling the Los Angeles Police medical examiner who, on the basis of the warmth of the body, subsequently provides a remarkably specific estimate for the time of death as 11pm, at which precise time the murderer had arranged for his female accomplice to fire a shot in his uncle's house which was heard by a security guard while, at the same time, giving himself a cast iron alibi by attending an art exhibition. That it was believed by the writers of the episode, and by implication its viewers, who were all potential jury members, that a medical examiner could realistically provide a precise estimate of the time of death in a murder case to the nearest hour based on the temperature of a dead body, to the extent that a police investigation could potentially be fooled by an artificial attempt to manipulate that temperature (although Lieutenant Columbo saw through it!), shows the widespread belief and confidence in the almost mystical abilities of a medical examiner.

The reality, though, was very different, as can be seen from the Confait case. At 1.30am on 22 April 1972, the dead body of Maxwell Confait, also known as Michelle, a transvestite prostitute, who had been strangled with a ligature, was found by two firemen from Lewisham Fire Brigade while they tackled a blaze at his house in Catford. One of them described it as 'cold and stiff'.[119] When the police surgeon, Dr Angus Bain, examined the body at 2am, however, he noted that parts of it, including the abdomen, 'felt quite warm to the touch' but agreed that there was stiffness, feeling that 'rigor mortis was complete', and, on that basis, concluded that Confait had been strangled between 8 and 10pm the previous evening. A pathologist, Dr James Cameron, Professor of Forensic Medicine at the London Hospital, arrived at 3.45am and, feeling the body to be 'cold', estimated the time of death as between 7.45 and 11.45pm (which he later revised to between 6.30 and 10pm), although his view was that rigor was 'commencing' during

---

[119] TNA: HO 253/1.

his examination![120] Neither man took Confait's rectal temperature due to the belief that he might have 'indulged in unnatural practices' and they didn't want to interfere with his rectum in order to preserve evidence of any sexual activity.

The police initially had a suspect in Confait's landlord, William Goode, but he was soon forgotten after three teenage boys, who were known to have started small fires in the area, were arrested and helpfully confessed to the murder. They also confessed to starting the fire in Confait's house to remove traces of their fingerprints. The problem was that one of the boys had a watertight alibi from 7.30pm until midnight on 21 April. If they had jointly committed the murder, it had to have been after midnight, which conflicted with the medical estimates based largely on the appearance of rigor mortis. The evidence of the fire experts was that the fire had been started at about 1.10am, much later than the estimated time of the strangulation, yet the confession of the boys placed the two events much closer together.

During the boys' trial, Dr Bain stated that rigor mortis 'normally starts in about six hours after death' but he also said that 'it has been known to start as shortly after death as an hour'. The prosecution, relying on the murder having been committed at 1am, managed to introduce a number of elements of doubt about the doctor's longer estimate, such as the notion that rigor can accelerate in conditions of great heat, like a fire. The possibility of cadaveric spasm was also mentioned. Dr Cameron, helpfully for the prosecution, slightly modified his own evidence during the trial to say that, 'death could even have been extended up to the region of midnight' but, more crucially, he suggested that the heat of the fire could have acted as an accelerator of rigor. As a result of the confusion surrounding the time of death, the alibi evidence, according to Christopher Price and Jonathan Caplan, authors of a 1977 book entitled, *The Confait Confessions*, 'became devalued to the point of worthlessness'. The three boys were convicted of the crime at the Old Bailey in November 1972 with leave to appeal refused.

In May 1974, however, William Goode, the original suspect, committed suicide which drew attention to the possibility of him being

---

[120] He would later explain that he didn't mean rigor was only *just* commencing, simply that it wasn't complete.

the real culprit. Campaigners, who believed that the boys' confessions had been manipulated out of them by the police, obtained expert evidence from Professor Keith Simpson which discounted the possibility of rigor mortis having been accelerated by the heat of the fire or by cadaveric spasm. The Home Secretary referred the case to the Court of Appeal which conducted a hearing in October 1975. Giving evidence for the appellants, Professor Donald Teare, a leading pathologist, completely ruled out the possibility of heat or any factor having accelerated rigor mortis in the case. He estimated that the time of death was between 8 and 10pm, as Dr Bain had originally stated, and discounted the possibility of it having occurred after 10pm. He accepted that rigor mortis could start within two hours but said, 'I have never seen it.' He strongly denied, however, that rigor could commence within an hour, thus not only conflicting with the opinion of Professor Camps from 1968 but with the evidence from 1912 in the Titus case. Professor Keith Simpson provided a statement in which he said that, 'all the evidence is most consistent with Confait being killed at least six hours before 3.45am', adding that he 'could not possibly accept' that death could have taken place around or after midnight. Professor Cameron also gave evidence at the appeal to the effect that death could not have been as late as 1am.

As a result of the new medical evidence, Counsel for the prosecution accepted that the boys could not have killed Confait because at least one of them had a solid alibi for the time that the murder must have been committed. Subsequently, the Court of Appeal accepted that a miscarriage of justice had occurred and the boys' convictions were overturned. The widow of William Goode gave an interview to the *Daily Mirror* in which she claimed that her husband had committed the murder. There were good reasons to think that Goode was responsible for the crime but, equally, it's difficult to see how the medical experts could have categorically ruled out the possibility of Confait having been murdered after midnight on the basis of stiffness of his body at 1.30am when it is known that rigor can commence within an hour.

An inquiry into the case conducted by Sir Henry Fisher in 1976 took testimony from Professor Gilbert Forbes of Glasgow University, as well as Professor Cameron and Dr Bain, which led Fisher to conclude in his report published in December 1977 that Confait could not have died after midnight of 21/22 April 1972, and probably died before 10.30pm on 21 April.[121] In reaching this conclusion, Fisher appears to have placed considerable weight on evidence of hypostasis, or coagulation and accumulation of blood, whereby red colouration on the side of Confait's neck and down his back was visible in photographs taken at about 6.30am on the morning of the fire. According to Fisher, these photographs, which hadn't been seen by the experts prior to his inquiry, indicated that death had occurred not less than eight hours earlier, or not later than about 10.30pm. Fisher dismissed attempts at estimating time of death from both external body temperature and rigor mortis as being unreliable, at least on their own. The Commissioner of Metropolitan Police submitted, in what Fisher described as a 'powerful and sustained argument', that it wasn't possible to reach any reliable conclusion as to the time of death, but Fisher was satisfied that the evidence that death couldn't have occurred after midnight was 'solid'.

In a rather extraordinary twist to the story, a fresh investigation by John Fryer, the assistant chief constable of West Mercia, concluded in 1980 that Confait had died *48 hours* before the fire and was killed by two men known to the police, one of whom returned to the scene to set fire to the house.[122] However, the evidence in the case is that Confait had been seen alive by three witnesses between 3 and 4pm on 21 April which leaves that conclusion in some doubt.[123]

An interesting feature of the appeal hearing in the Confait case is that Professor Teare was asked by Counsel for the prosecution, Mr Hawser, what he was talking about when he spoke of a body 'being cold' to which he replied, 'Round about 80 degrees Fahrenheit'. The two men might have been speaking at cross purposes, however, with the professor referring to the core body temperature rather than the external surface temperature, which appears to have been what Counsel was asking about. Thus, Teare went on to say that the body cools at a rate of 2.5 degrees an hour for the first two or three hours after death, then slows off so that, overall, it takes

---

[121] TNA: HO 253/1.
[122] *Times*, 5 August 1980.
[123] A statement was also taken from a married couple that they saw Confait in a pub between 6.45 and 7.45pm on 21 April but there is some reason to doubt its accuracy (Fisher Report, pp.146-147).

about twelve hours to get down to 80 degrees under average conditions. But, as a dead body can obviously feel cold to the touch much sooner than twelve hours after death, it seems that Professor Teare didn't really answer the question. We may also note that Professor Teare was asked if he drew any distinction between a layman's touch of a body in finding it cold and that of a highly skilled professional expert. He said he did draw such a distinction, not because there was any special technique employed by the expert for feeling body temperature, but because the expert would be 'touching it to find out' whereas the layman would be making 'just a casual observation.'

Sir Henry Fisher also dealt with these matters in his 1977 report. Based on what he had been told by the expert witnesses who gave evidence at his inquiry, he noted that, 'Judgments formed on the basis of external body temperature felt by the hand are unreliable since they will depend on the temperature of the hand of the person who feels the body.' He also said that, 'the temperature which different people will describe as 'hot' and 'cold' will not necessarily be the same.' Contrasting the apparent belief of Professor Teare that the temperature of a 'cold' body - as Confait's body was described by Professor Cameron - would be around 80 degrees Fahrenheit (which, interestingly, was also the view of Professor Simpson who said it would be 80 to 85 degrees), Fisher recorded that Professor Forbes told him that a body would not feel cold until it was down to 65 degrees, which Forbes had said would take twelve hours after death, compared to six to eight hours to reach 80 degrees. The experts couldn't seem to agree on an apparently simple matter such as what 'cold' meant in respect of the temperature of a dead body.

A 1974 paper entitled 'Body temperature as a means of estimating the time of death' by A. Brown and T.K. Marshall followed Womack from 1887 by offering a formula which medical examiners could use to determine time of death by a single rectal temperature reading but it assumed a rectal temperature at time of death of 99 degrees, a constant ambient air temperature and a naked body lying on its back. Given these specific elements, the formula couldn't be applied to most cases and was largely ignored. Three years later, a group of Danish doctors took temperature readings from twenty cases with known times of death and concluded that 'the determination of the time of death will always be encumbered with great uncertainty'.[124] In particular, they identified the impossibility of knowing an individual's body temperature at the moment of death about which, they said, 'All investigations show that it may vary enormously'. While Womack had said in 1887 that the range in body temperature would not vary by more than 3.6 degrees, this Danish study showed variation of between five and eight degrees. Thus, they concluded, with the fall in temperature after death being in the region of 1.8 degrees per hour, even the most accurate reading of post-mortem body temperature would be liable to wide inaccuracy.

In 1978, K.S. Narayan Reddy's *Essentials of Forensic Medicine* advised that, 'The rectum is the ideal place to record temperature except in cases of sodomy' and stated that for the first forty-five minutes after death the rectal temperature remains constant with slow cooling for the first three to five hours following which there is 'a fairly rapid fall to the temperature of the surroundings' with body heat lost by conduction, convection and radiation. However, Reddy warned that, 'It cannot be assumed that body temperature is normal at time of death'. In many cases of asphyxia amongst other things, 'a sharp rise in temperature occurs'. It's unclear where this belief came from because there don't appear to have been any studies on the subject. He might have been relying on the 1956 version of Taylor's *Principles and Practice of Medical Jurisprudence* edited by Sir Sydney Smith, assisted by Keith Simpson, in which it was stated that deaths of violence, involving a struggle, and 'sometimes in death from asphyxia as in suffocation' could lead to the body temperature being 'above normal at the time of death' but no evidence was referred to in support of this. Nevertheless, there is no doubt that, for whatever reason, there is a real possibility of an increase in temperature after death and Reddy said that, largely as a result of this, 'an accurate formula cannot be devised to define the rate of heat loss.'

Professor Keith Simpson's *Forty Years of Murder* was also published in 1978 in which the famous pathologist described five or six cases in which he claimed to have accurately estimated the time of death on the basis of the victim's rectal temperature, presumably based on 'the Simpson formula' set out in his 1947 textbook. Whether he was really able to do so or not, or

---

[124] Simonsen, Voigt, Jeppesen, 'Determination of the Time of Death by Continuous Post-Morten Temperature Measurements, 1977, *Medicine, Science and the Law*, 2, p. 112.

was right by chance, this would have confirmed in the public's mind what they saw in dramas on television about the ability of the medical profession to assist the police in this way. Yet, in major modern police investigations, one repeatedly finds a lack of evidence to support this portrayal.

When police found three adults and two children massacred in White House Farm in Essex early one morning in August 1985, not only did no one check to feel by hand the body temperatures of the victims but their temperatures weren't taken with thermometers either. In her book, *The Murders at White House Farm*, Carol Ann Lee explains that Dr Ian Craig, the attending medical examiner, wasn't required to take body temperatures unless specifically asked to do so by the police and that it wasn't the general practice of Essex Police to estimate times of death based on that method (not, at least, without first consulting a pathologist). During the trial of Jeremy Bamber, Dr Craig said that, due to the difficulty in establishing time of death, the murders could have occurred 'any time during that night'. This was effectively an admission that the medical profession is unable to do what most people probably still believe they can do very easily.

The year 1985 also saw the publication of a paper by G.M. Hutchings who had found that body temperatures taken at the rectum at the earliest feasible time after death of twenty hospital patients were higher than expected.[125] In these cases the rectal temperatures had been recorded while the individuals were still alive so that it was possible to compare the pre-mortem temperatures with those taken after death. Hutchings said that his results 'suggest that there is an initial postmortem elevation in body temperature as measured rectally, probably as a result of continuing tissue and bacterial metabolism in the absence of the usual heat-dispersal mechanisms'. Any such increase of temperature was undoubtedly going to frustrate any calculations to estimate time of death based on the assumption of a steady decline in temperature after death.

The Brighton Babes in the Wood case was one where confusion over the estimated time of death had disastrous consequences.

The strangled bodies of two missing young girls, Nicola Fellows and Karen Hadaway, were found in a Brighton park by a search party at about 4pm on 10 October 1986, their bodies being 'absolutely stone cold,

---

[125] Hutchings, G.M. 'Body temperature is elevated in the post-mortem period', *Human Pathology*, vol. 76, 1985.

like marble', according to the first constable on the scene.[126] The police called in Home Office Pathologist Dr Iain West who could see from just looking at the two bodies that they had been dead 'for quite a number of hours'. As daylight was fast fading, and worried about damaging evidence, West decided to postpone taking the body temperature until the body was removed to the Brighton mortuary, a slight delay which made no appreciable difference but proved very controversial. West found that the livers of the murdered girls, when measured at the mortuary through an incision in the abdomen, were at 'environmental temperature' which only told him that they had been dead for some time.[127] As he explained it: 'Environmental temperature is not as useful an indicator as some people think...for the outdoors scene, temperature measurements are notoriously unreliable because environmental conditions vary so much...So it becomes a much more difficult scientific experiment'.[128] He couldn't, as a result, offer any precise estimate of the time of death but, at the trial of Russell Bishop who was accused of the murders, the prosecution's case was that the girls had been murdered between 5.15 and 6.30pm on 9 October 1986. This was based not on anything the pathologist had said but on Bishop's movements; he had been seen entering and leaving the park between these times. There was, however, witness evidence that the two girls were alive, eating chips, at around 6.30pm. Bishop's barrister strongly criticized the failure of the pathologist to take the body temperatures of the girls at the crime scene, implying that, had he done so, it would have been possible to accurately estimate the time of death (and thus prove the innocence of his client due to him having been seen leaving the park at 6.30pm). The judge directed the jury that unless they were sure the girls were dead by 6.30pm they should acquit Bishop, which is exactly what they did. At liberty, Bishop went on to attack, sexually assault and suffocate another young girl he left for dead on the South Downs, a crime for which he was, on this occasion, convicted and sentenced to life imprisonment. In 2018, after the presentation of new forensic evidence, Bishop was finally convicted in a re-trial of the 1986 murders of the two girls, during which the prosecution

---

[126] Constable Paul Smith speaking on 'The Babes in the Wood Murders', Channel 5 documentary, 2021.
[127] *Dr. Iain West's Casebook* by Chester Stern, 1997, Warner Books.
[128] Ibid.

suggested a revised time of death of some point *after* 6.30pm. The judge in his sentencing remarks confirmed that Bishop lured the two girls into the woods 'at around 6.30pm' which must have been just after they'd been seen eating chips, meaning that Bishop must have returned with the girls to the park that he'd just left.

In his 1991 book, *Forensic Pathology*, Professor Bernard Knight, a consultant forensic pathologist to the Home Office, having previously conducted a thorough analysis of the history of the estimation of the time of death from body temperature in a 1988 paper entitled, 'The Evolution of Methods for Estimating Time of Death from Body Temperature', conceded that, 'accuracy in estimating the time since death from temperature remains elusive'. Referring to the old rule of thumb that body temperature falls at about one and half degrees Fahrenheit per hour, Knight said that the only confidence that could be placed in this rule was that it was 'always wrong'. Nevertheless, Knight advised pathologists to feel the skin of a dead body to assess the temperature at a crime scene once photographs had been taken and with the permission of investigating officers, saying: 'The general warmth or coolness of the hands and face can be assessed by touch and the degree of rigor felt by gently testing the limbs'. He described these 'crude methods' as 'a useful first manoeuvre at the scene of death' and that, 'A hand placed on the forehead, face or exposed hand may give a first impression of whether death has occurred recently or not'. However, he cautioned that, 'if these exposed areas are feeling cold, feeling inside the clothing to touch the chest, abdomen or axilla may detect some heat, as may sliding a hand under the body where it is in contact with the supporting surface.' Although he said that 'conditions vary enormously' he nevertheless felt able to advise that 'a body indoors will feel cold on exposed areas in two to four hours and in protected areas after some six to eight hours'. He didn't offer any advice on bodies found outdoors.

Interestingly, Knight advised against taking the rectal temperature with a thermometer at the crime scene in most cases, absent pressing reasons to do so, due the fact that it would involve disturbing clothing and would potentially contaminate the rectum and perineum. He suggested either using a place other than the rectum or waiting until the body was at the mortuary.

When the murdered bodies of Nicole Simpson and Ron Goldman were discovered in Simpson's Los Angeles home shortly after midnight on 13 June 1994, none of the attending members of the emergency services bothered to take the opportunity to feel whether their corpses were warm or cold. It wasn't until shortly before 11am that an electronic thermometer was used to take the liver temperatures of the bodies, by which time rigor mortis was fully established, and the estimated time of death based on those temperatures was so wide, covering a near four-hour period from 9pm on 12 June to 12.45am on 13 June, that it included a fifty-minute period when the couple were known to have been alive, and also a forty-five minute period when they were known to have been dead, and was useless for investigative purposes. The prosecution at the trial of Nicole's former husband, O.J. Simpson, needed the murder to have occurred prior to 11pm on 12 June, at which time Simpson was known to have been driven in a limousine from his house to Los Angeles International Airport for a flight to Chicago but the uncertainty meant that the murder could have occurred for almost two hours after this, according to the official time estimate, and, in the end, Simpson was famously acquitted.

A 1996 publication by Greater Manchester Police entitled 'Principles of Forensic Medicine' authored by Stephen P. Robinson stated that, if asked by an investigating officer to give a time of death, a police forensic medical examiner should always ask 'why does it need to be known?' and he advised that, if it's not important, the body should not be interfered with until a forensic pathologist has had a chance to inspect the unadulterated scene. Interestingly, after noting that rigor mortis may be a useful indicator, Robinson said that, 'Other factors are often more helpful with estimating the approximate time of death' and he referred in this regard to when the deceased was last seen alive, what was on their calendar and other indications such as newspaper and milk deliveries or what time their curtains were normally opened, none of which, of course, require any specialist medical knowledge. In doing so, he was unwittingly harking back to the advice of Dr Male from 1816 that 'we should also inquire by whom [the deceased] was last seen'. Not too much had changed in 180 years. Regarding the use of a thermometer for the taking of the rectal temperature, this was discouraged by Robinson not just because it might contaminate the evidence in cases of sexual assault but also because there were question marks over its reliability.

It would undoubtedly have been useful to have known what time Stuart Lubbock died while attending a party at the comedian Michael Barrymore's home in March 2001. Hours after his death, a rectal temperature reading was taken (something which, it was later suggested, almost certainly wrongly, might have caused the serious anal injuries found in Lubbock's rectum). However, as Lubbock had been fished out of a swimming pool, and the effect of water on body temperature after death was known to distort the normal calculations for estimating time of death, no reliable estimate was ever produced.

A 2004 paper by Joshua A. Perper, 'Time of Death and Changes after Death' looked at all possible methods for estimating time of death and concluded that, 'none of the methods used...are totally reliable and mathematically precise' so that 'pinpoint accuracy in this matter is not achievable'.[129] In respect of using the temperature of the skin, Perper said that, 'The skin, as the closest organ to the environmental air, cools quite rapidly and is not useful for sequential temperature measurements.' With reference to the body's core temperature, and reminiscent of 'Simpson's Formula', he said that, 'Under average conditions, the body cools at a rate of 2.0° F to 2.5° F per hour during the first hours and slower thereafter, with an average loss of 1.5° F to 2° F during the first twelve hours, and 1° F for the next twelve to eighteen hours.' However, he accepted Bernard Knight's conclusion that 'the level of accuracy remains low' and said that measurements of postmortem temperature 'should be cautiously interpreted in view of variables affecting postmortem cooling'.

In a 2009 paper entitled 'Early postmortem changes and time of death', after reviewing the literature on estimating time of death, the author, Dr William Cox noted that if you, as a medical examiner, stuck to the known formulas it would 'consistently guarantee you making a fool of yourself'. He stated that, while it is important to take the core body temperature as well as the air temperature, 'What is also important is to gather all

---

[129] Perper, J. A. 'Time of Death and Changes after Death—Part 1. Anatomical considerations' in: Spitz, W. V., ed. Medicolegal *Investigation of Death. Guidelines for the Application of Pathology to Crime Investigation*. Charles C.Thomas, Springfield, IL, pp. 14–64, 1993.

other objective information (witness statements, cell phone and land-line phone records, e-mail records, mail, newspaper, stomach contents and postmortem chemistries)'. With the exception of the last two, obtaining them doesn't require any medical training so that Cox was admitting that the time of death cannot reliably be established on medical grounds alone. His advice to gather witness statements again rather echoes the advice of Dr Male from 1816 to establish by whom the deceased had last been seen. The same is true of a formulation used in his evidence at criminal trials by the pathologist Professor Alan Usher, recalled by Paul Worsley QC, that he could confidently tell the jury that the time of death was 'between the victim being last seen alive and the discovery of the body'.[130]

Given Professor Keith Simpson's reliance in many cases on the temperature of murder victims in estimating the time of death, it is somewhat ironic that the thirteenth edition of *Simpson's Forensic Medicine*, published in 2011, states that, due to the number of variables involved, 'the sensible forensic pathologist will be reluctant to make any pronouncement on the time of death based on the body temperature alone'. The so-called 'Simpson formula' has apparently been abandoned. Harking back to the time when hands rather than thermometers were used, the authors of the book also state that, 'Sometimes the perceived warmth of the body to touch is mentioned in court as an indicator of the time of death; this assessment is so unreliable as to be useless...'. Thus was more than one hundred years of medical practice at crime scenes dismissed as just as likely to result in a miscarriage of justice than lead police to the murderer.

In place of Simpson's formula in the modern age is a 'rectal temperature time of death nonogram' developed in the 1980s by the German forensic expert Claus Henssge and which can be done online by a layperson once the relevant temperature readings (body and air), and information about the deceased, are entered into its calculator. Its main limitation, other than the fact that the underlying basis for its calculations seem to be unproven, is that it assumes a temperature at the time of death of 98.96 degrees so that if that is not, in fact, the case, it could provide significantly inaccurate results. Even Henssge has conceded that his nonogram isn't suitable for every case.

---

[130] Paul Worsley QC, *The Postcard Murder: A Judge's Tale* (pp. 277-278), Pilot Production, Kindle Edition, 2019.

Guidance issued by the Forensic Science Regulator and the Royal College of Pathologists in the United Kingdom in 2014 stated that, when providing a time of death estimate based on heat loss from the body, the pathologist, 'must make clear the estimate is only an estimate and the accuracy cannot be determined' and must also explain that 'the death could have occurred outside the estimated period and, perhaps, a significant period outside it'.[131]

We didn't really travel very far in two hundred years.

---

[131] 'The Use of Time of Death Estimates Based on Heat Loss from the Body'.

CONCLUSION

We will never know what information was available to medical examiners throughout history when they conducted their initial examinations of dead bodies at crime scenes but the suspicion in most cases must be that they learned certain facts from friends, neighbours or relatives of the victims, or from police officers in attendance, which guided them in their estimates of the time of death. If they were told when the victim had last been seen alive, or of any suspicious activity – the sound of violence or a scream for example – that kind of thing would ensure that they could tailor their estimate to match the time when those clues indicated that death had occurred. This would certainly explain why some examiners were saying that a primarily cold body indicated that death had occurred two or three hours earlier while others were saying the same thing about a primarily warm body. It would equally explain why some examiners would say that a totally cold body indicated death had occurred within, say, four hours, while others would say it indicated a much longer period since death.

On occasions, we have seen clear evidence of examiners changing their estimates when they learnt of other non-medical evidence in respect of the time of death. Sometimes this might be information as to when the victim was last seen alive, or when they had been found dead, but much worse was when their estimate was tailored to fit the prosecution case as to when death had occurred. Dr Grant's change of evidence in the Farmer murder proceedings is a good example, whereby it seemed that he could have said virtually anything in the end, as long it matched the prosecution case. Indeed, a medical examiner giving evidence could say pretty much whatever they wanted if they claimed that their assessment was based on their own experience, which could be kept as vague as possible, while introducing all kinds of hard to disprove elements into their assessment. The way that Dr Grant brought in the concept of eye tension to support his revised time estimate is a good example of this, and was something that was almost impossible for anyone to challenge due to its vague and obscure nature. It's hard not to conclude that the practice of estimating time of death has been essentially a pseudoscience, based on very little hard data.

The Irene Munro murder case is very instructive because this was one instance where the medical examiner gave an early opinion as to time of death which certainly wasn't influenced by any witness evidence (because there wasn't any available at the time). Even though he bravely, if foolishly, stuck to his guns about the time of death during the inquest and committal proceedings, Dr Cadman ended up getting himself in a complete muddle during the trial, when he said inconsistent things, clearly aware that the murder must have happened some hours before he said it must have done. The poor man obviously didn't want to destroy the prosecution's case but equally didn't want to contradict his own opinion on grounds other than medical or scientific ones. In the end, it seems that the medical evidence wasn't required to provide an actual estimated time of death but to simply state that the police and prosecution's estimated time of death, based on witness evidence, wasn't inconsistent with the medical evidence. When one adopts that kind of approach, there will hardly be any occasion when the police and prosecution theory will be disproved but one would have to question the value of the medical evidence in such cases.

Perhaps the clearest case of evidence being tailored to fit a prosecution case was Keith Simpson's dramatic change of mind as to when Peggy Pentecost had died. In his biography, Simpson recounts how he impressed the officer in charge of the case with his methodical approach, thus causing his services to be called on again by Scotland Yard, but it was more likely due to the smooth way he changed the estimate of time of death in the witness box upon being recalled and, thinking on his feet, was able to provide the judge with an explanation of a supposed increase in body temperature after death due to asphyxia which he had somehow omitted to include in his initial calculation set out in the post-mortem report as well as in his evidence before the magistrate and his evidence-in-chief at the Old Bailey trial. If we assume no increase, and we also assume that Peggy's internal body temperature before she died was 98 degrees Fahrenheit, then, if she was murdered at about 9.30pm, it took about 14.5 hours for her body temperature to drop 26 degrees to 72 degrees Fahrenheit, which is roughly an average drop of 1.8 degrees an hour. That would seem to be perfectly normal, and in line with experiments conducted during the nineteenth century, with no reason to assume that there was a post-mortem increase in her temperature due to asphyxiation.

If we were to use Burman's formula to calculate the time of Peggy's death, we would divide the 26 degrees by 1.6 which would indicate that her death had occurred a little over 16 hours prior to the examination, i.e. at 8pm on the evening of 1 January, something which was not impossible, although it was likely to have been closer to 9.30pm. Yet Simpson initially chose midnight as his estimate of time of death which he subsequently changed without explanation to 11pm, presumably when he learnt that the hotel manager had heard a door shut at this time. It was only when Harry Armstrong produced an alibi for 11pm that Simpson extended the possible period for time of death back to 9pm based on an increase in temperature after death which he hadn't factored into his calculation prior to that point.

It's particularly interesting that when Simpson told the story of the case many years later in his book, albeit not providing specific details, such as the name of the victim or perpetrator, or even the correct year of the murder, he made it seem like Peggy's body temperature had risen to 102 degrees *at the time of his examination*, seemingly confirming that there had been an increase after death due to asphyxiation, and that he could thereby inform the police that she had been murdered only a few hours earlier that very morning (although he was vague in his book as to what time of day his examination was supposed to have taken place). The truth, as we have seen, was very different. There had been no increase in temperature and he had placed the time of the murder as having been committed the previous evening. Can Professor Simpson really have forgotten the true facts involving his dramatic change of evidence in the witness box in his first murder case, which ensured Armstrong's conviction? It seems unlikely, so that he would appear to have been deliberately misleading his readers.

The Pentecost case involved a medical examiner actually taking a rectal temperature reading, which they had been told they were supposed to do since at least the 1860s, yet there was no way to avoid ending up with a relatively wide range of at least four hours, between 8pm and midnight, when it could reasonably be said the murder is likely to have occurred, based on the state of knowledge of body cooling in the 1930s. The situation was far worse when the only information available was whether a body felt warm or cold. As we've seen, with some dead bodies feeling warm many hours after death and others feeling cold at the moment of death, it was almost impossible for medical examiners to provide an accurate and reliable estimate of time of death from this information alone. Even if we add in other factors such as the commencement or completion of rigor mortis or the contents of the stomach, the variables are so great as to make any estimate almost worthless.

By way of example, the average height of men in the United Kingdom is said to be five feet, nine inches and the average height of women is, apparently, five feet, three inches. On the law of averages, one might think that this means that when any British person leaves their home, the first man they see in the street should be five feet, nine inches and the first woman they see should be five feet, three inches. No one would be surprised, however, if the first men and women they see on any given day are smaller or taller than these average heights. Not every man is five foot, nine inches, after all, and not every woman is five feet, three inches.

The same principle is true for a medical examiner attempting to estimate the time a person has died from clues provided by their dead body. Medical textbooks might say that the body temperature *of an average person* cools by a certain amount every hour in certain conditions, so that, in theory, their temperature reading after so many hours should reveal exactly when they died, but what if one is not dealing with *an average person*? If some people cool faster, some slower, that difference in cooling times would surely affect the results. The same is true of any other test. If everyone is different, or at least if *some* people are different, there is an obvious problem with using average timings to reach a conclusion of this nature. One can, however, easily fall into the trap of thinking that the average *always* applies in every individual case.

While this may seem obvious, it's surprising how many times a medical examiner, faced with the pressing need to provide the police or a coroner, or some other form of judicial enquiry, with a time of death, has relied on what happened to an average person after death. On the law of averages, or the law of probability, they will be right most of the time but, almost inevitably, wrong some of the time.

When tracing the evolution of the medical world's understanding of how the temperature of corpses could be used to estimate time of death, we have seen how pivotal to that understanding the Gardner case of 1862 was. Before that time there was very little scientific knowledge about how long precisely it would take for a body to become cold after death, with the medical textbooks barely saying a word on the subject. The Gardner case set off a flurry of research activity in order to rectify this deficiency but it's important to appreciate that some of that research was being conducted with a bias in order to defend the verdict. At the very least, the Gardner case explains why Taylor and Wilks' experiments involved taking the temperature of the abdomen, which seems to have puzzled modern day readers. I also believe I have revealed for the first time that Taylor and Wilks had misunderstood the evidence in the Gardner case, thinking that the area of Mrs Gardner's abdomen was partly cold, whereas it was entirely warm when her body was found.

Even during the 1870s it seemed to be widely appreciated that body temperature was a very unreliable indicator as to when death occurred, something which was thrown into focus by the Gulliver case even though that was about the very different issue of whether a warm body temperature after death pointed to foul play. By the 1880s, however, the doubts seem to have been forgotten. We've seen how the *Lancet* from 1862 was fully aware of the difficulties in estimating time of death from a 'cold' body but in 1888 it fully supported the estimate of Dr Phillips in the Chapman case even though this was based on no more than feeling the cold body of a sick and emaciated woman out of doors with the addition of the extremely vague supposed commencement of rigor. Perhaps by this time it was believed that science could answer all questions and that medical experts really could now identify when someone had died, even if there was no new scientific data available. That might explain why there were no significant developments in the subject during the next forty years and we can see the result in the Wallace case where the medical evidence was in disarray, with different experts saying different things, confusing the judge and jury, and being dismissed in its entirety by Home Office officials.

We've seen how Dr Bennett Dowler mentioned the unpleasant nature of research into the temperature of corpses after death yet it is still somewhat surprising, considering the importance of the subject for murder cases, that so few experiments have been carried out. This may be explained by the difficulty of having access to dead bodies, especially those of otherwise normal, healthy people at the time of death, in circumstances where it is known precisely when they died. One might have thought that during the First and Second World Wars there would have been ample opportunities to conduct such experiments but, of course, the priorities for doctors during this time would have been saving lives, not taking temperatures of dead bodies, and society would have had other priorities in any case, such as basic survival from attack.

Taking the temperatures of dead bodies in experiments is one thing but that information is worthless if medical examiners are relying on their hands to assess whether a corpse is cold or warm or just not making any effort to take the temperature at all. Even in modern day murder investigations, we find the body temperature not taken by medical examiners at crime scenes, either because they don't want to interfere with the corpse or because it's not policy for them to do so. Given the variables and lack of certainty in any formula to calculate the estimated time of death, this is probably not so surprising. As we've seen, even with an accurate temperature reading, this still doesn't enable a calculation of the time of death to be made with any degree of certainty sufficient to convict or acquit someone of the murder.

APPENDIX A

The Gardner Blood Marks

Sergeant Mobbs first described the discovery of the blood marks in his evidence at the inquest on 24 September 1862. He said it occurred on Thursday 18 September (which was three days after the death of Mrs Gardner). As reported, his evidence was: 'I examined the parlour, and on the top window-curtain I noticed a slight stain of blood. There was a bloody finger mark on the shutters which was shut. Gardner remarked to me that these spots had not been there the day before.' In this account, therefore, Mobbs spotted the blood himself. On going up to the first floor he said that he then saw various spots of blood in the bedroom, some of which were not quite dry, at which point, 'I remarked to Gardner that the wall, the cornice, and the bedstead had no blood upon them when I searched the house before, upon which Gardner replied that the spots of blood might have been caused by the wet cloth with which the body was washed.' From this it would seem that Mobbs also spotted the blood in the bedroom himself but, in fact, he also said, 'I would have noticed the new spots of blood but Gardner pointed them out to me'. So, in this account, Mobbs appears to have himself spotted the blood on the curtain and shutter in the first floor parlour but the upstairs blood was drawn to his attention by Gardner who then suggested that the bloody wet cloth might have been responsible for it. Nothing seems to have been said about the source of the blood in the parlour. Crucially, when Mobbs said that he hadn't noticed the blood when the house had been searched previously he must have been referring to searches on Monday and Tuesday.

There was then said to have been a further examination the following day. Thus: 'On Friday they went again and Gardner was in the parlour…'. Gardner was then supposed to have pointed to the window on this occasion and said: 'She opened the window that morning'. According to Mobbs: 'They had searched three days before, most minutely, and there was no blood then'. This is confusing if there was supposed to have been a search the previous day. Mobbs also stated that, 'The cornice on which coagulated blood was found could not have received it while the body was being washed'.

When Mobbs next told the story, at the Mansion House Police Court on 7 October, it had changed significantly. He said that he had searched Gardner's house on Thursday, 18 September, with Detective Monger and the Ward Beadle but he didn't mention finding anything on that day. He now said that the discovery of the blood occurred on Friday, 19 September, when he returned with Detective Monger to search the house again. In this version of events, the officers were downstairs when Gardner mentioned to them that there were spots of blood upstairs, so the three of them went up the stairs to the first floor bedroom and saw the various splashes of blood around the room. Mobbs said that he told Gardner that, 'neither the splashes on the wall nor the board were there when we previously examined the premises'. In response to this, Gardner suggested that it might have happened when the corpse was washed. It will be recalled that, when Mobbs first told the story, the blood in the downstairs parlour was discovered first, followed by the upstairs blood, but now he said that, 'We then went downstairs and Gardner, having pointed to the front window on the ground floor, I saw a slight stain, apparently of blood, on the top of the window curtain, and on opening the window a finger mark in blood was visible on the inside of the shutter'. Mobbs said, 'I again told Gardner we had examined these places before, and the blood was not then visible. Gardner made no reply.' The significance of this change of story is that the previous searches that Mobbs was referring to in which no blood had been seen must have been the searches carried out on the previous day (i.e. Thursday), which was after the body had been washed, whereas in his original story he could only have been referring to searches carried out on Monday and Tuesday, prior to the body being washed.

When it came to the trial, Sergeant Mobbs continued to state that the blood was first seen by him on the Friday but this simply couldn't have been possible. The reason for this is that the evidence of the Ward Beadle, Thomas Pallet, was that he was present at the time of the discovery of these blood marks and he didn't visit the house on the Friday. He was clear that the blood was discovered on Thursday. Thus, he said in his evidence, 'I was present when the interior of the room, on the first-floor, was examined by Mobbs on the Tuesday, and again on the Thursday after the inquest had taken place — I did not examine the wall of the room on the first-floor — there were spots on the wall which the sergeant cut out with his pen-knife — that was on Thursday, 18th September — I had not examined the wall particularly on the Tuesday, my attention not having been at all called to it — I was present when the room below was examined by Mobbs on that Thursday, the 18th — the prisoner was there — I looked at the short curtain at the window on the ground-floor — the prisoner said, "Look here; here are some marks of blood here" — that was on the curtain; and he also remarked, "And here appears like the marks of a bloody hand" — that was across the outside window shutter, on the inside of the outer window shutter—that was the same day that the paper was cut off the wall — it was on Thursday — my attention had never been directed to the window curtain or the shutters on any day previous to that Thursday'. In cross-examination, Pallet further stated, 'I was present, and examined the room on the Monday and on the Tuesday, with the constable — he and I examined together — the prisoner was present, and rendered every assistance — he saw us examining — we examined together on the Thursday — the prisoner accompanied us in the same way — he offered no kind of obstruction; in fact, he gave every assistance, and produced all his clothes — he said, "Here is a spot of blood on the curtain, and marks of blood on the window-shutter" — it was a white curtain — it was not a very large spot of blood — it was small, not the size of a half-crown; it would be nearer the size of a sixpence'. Pallet, therefore, was saying he was present when the blood was discovered in both the ground floor and first floor rooms on the Thursday. He doesn't, however, appear to have heard Gardner being asked where the blood came from.

That the blood was discovered on the Thursday was confirmed by the evidence of Detective Monger at the trial but there was no indication by the detective (as there wasn't by the Ward Beadle) that the blood in the room on the first floor was pointed out to him by Gardner. On the contrary, he gave the impression that he saw it himself. Thus, he said, 'I went to the prisoner's house on Thursday, 18th September — I went up to the room on the first-floor, and made a search there in company with Sergeant Mobbs and Mr. Pallet — I saw some blood on the wall, some at the head of the bed, some at the side, and some by the foot.' Monger then went on to say that, 'after that we proceeded downstairs, and Gardner showed us a mark on the curtain of the window, something like a thumb or finger mark, and also on the shutter'. So, once again, we have evidence that the blood was first spotted by the police on Thursday in the first floor room *after which* Gardner directed the police's attention to the blood marks in the ground floor parlour.

The account of Sergeant Mobbs at the trial of the discovery of the blood (which he said happened on the Friday) was, 'I saw the prisoner on the ground-floor — he then said he had seen several spots of blood on the wall upstairs — I went upstairs, and found several spots of blood on the wall at the head of the bed — they were small spots, sprinkles, as if it had been thrown against the wall, and also at the side of the bed several other spots, and on the wall near the feet, a large splash, and across the rail at the foot of the bedstead...I am positive that this was not on the wall when I searched it previously, nor were the spots on the wall by the side of the head, and on the head — on the rail along the foot of the bedstead there were the appearances of a wet bloody cloth having been drawn across it — it was dry on the rail, on a piece of cornice standing at the head of the bed there was a large splash of clotted blood, not quite dry — the greatest portion of it was wet — that was the cornice I have spoken of as having examined before — it was not there then — when I discovered it, I turned to Gardner and said, "There were none of these, neither on the wall, bedstead, or board, when we searched the premises before" — he then said, "Perhaps it might be done in washing the body" — the body was washed, I believe, some time on the Wednesday...we then went downstairs on the ground-floor — Gardner pointed to the short curtain on the window — I then saw a stain of blood on the top of it — he said, "She opened the window that morning" — I then opened the window, and on the shutter, on the inside, I saw a mark of blood, apparently of a person with the finger doubled as if it had been splashed on; as if a finger had been doubled up in that way, and put it on in a heap; it was as if done with a knuckle — I then turned to Gardner, and told him that I had examined it seven or eight times previously, and was positive it was not there even the day before — he made me no answer…I had examined the shutters eight or nine times previously, for we had been there daily — the blood was on the inside'. While the precise sequence of events may not be of critical importance it can be seen that Mobbs' account here reverses the sequence in his original story in which the blood in the ground floor parlour was found first after which the upstairs blood was spotted.

After the trial, the bloody knife and the bloodstained paper taken by the police from the wall were sent for testing to the Medical Officer of Health for the City of London, Dr Henry Letherby. His tentative conclusion was that the blood on the knife had come directly from a living body and had coagulated and set whereas the other blood he tested (on the wallpaper and the cornice) had partially coagulated or set before reaching the paper and did not look like blood which had come directly from a living body. That didn't seem to take matters much further but it was perhaps surprising that such tests were not carried out before a man had been sentenced to death.

APPENDIX B

Time Of Death From Stomach Contents

On 6 June 1822 a young Canadian called Alexis St. Martin, fighting in Michigan, was wounded by the discharge of a musket which perforated his stomach. The hole in his stomach never healed and this gave Dr William Beaumont of the US army the opportunity to visually study the rate of digestion within St. Martin's stomach. In a paper published in 1834 entitled 'Experiments and Observations on the Gastric Juice and the Physiology of Digestion', Beaumont showed digestion rates of various foods eaten by St. Martin ranging from one and a half to four and a half hours. While St. Martin's medical condition afforded a unique opportunity to study digestion, he was only one individual. Two years after Beaumont's paper, Dr C.H. Schultz, a professor of Physiology at the University of Berlin, published a paper in the *Edinburgh Medical and Surgical Journal* entitled 'Observations and Experiments upon the Function of the Coecum' in which he said, 'It is generally admitted that a man digests a moderate meal within three or four hours. My experiments, however, upon carnivorous animals, which digest much more quickly than the omnivorous, to which class man belongs, show that six or seven hours are requisite for the digestion of a moderate meal'. According to Schulz, 'it may be safely assumed that six hours are necessary for perfect digestion'.

The potential for using gastric emptying as evidence in murder cases was recognised, and a paper by Dr Gustav Liebmann was published in the *Boston Medical and Surgical Journal* in 1895 entitled 'The Stomach Test in Murder Trials'. Dr Liebmann noted that it was assumed that a stomach would empty in five hours but the stomachs of some individuals empty faster or slower than others so that, in cases where a person's stomach empties faster than normal, 'the possibility arises, that the test may lead us astray…in that the time of death would be fixed at a later time than warranted by the facts'. Liebmann explained that when a stomach was found empty in a corpse this would normally mean that, 'the time of death is put down as having occurred at least five hours after the last meal, while in point of fact the emptying of that organ might have been complete three hours after that meal.' He added that while such cases are not the rule, 'they are on record, and should be reckoned with.' His conclusion was that, 'it would appear that this so-called stomach test, as applied at present to determine the time of death is not alone inexact, but that there is even a great question whether it is approximately correct'.

Professor Alfred Swaine Taylor never mentioned gastric emptying as being of assistance in establishing time of death nor, indeed, did Professor Keith Simpson in his 1947 book, *Forensic Medicine*. Yet Simpson testified in a major murder case hearing in Canada to support the idea that it was possible to establish the time of death based on gastric emptying. When questioned about the omission of this important piece of information from his book, Simpson said that it was written for medical students 'and was not intended to be comprehensive'. It was a somewhat curious answer because if medical students are not told that one can rely on stomach contents to determine the time of death how would they ever know about it? Nevertheless, Simpson said in this Canadian case that, 'The exact time of death was as vital a piece of evidence in this case as in any I had known in thirty years practice'.

The case being referred to by Professor Simpson was that of Steven Truscott who had been convicted in June 1959, when he was aged fourteen, for the murder of his friend, Lynne Harper, whose body was found two days after Truscott had been seen giving her a ride on his bicycle. She had been sexually assaulted and strangled. At Truscott's trial, the prosecution argued that, based on the amount of food in the dead girl's stomach, she was unlikely to have been murdered more than two hours after her last meal. As it was known that she had eaten at 5.45pm on 9 June 1959 (the day she went missing), it was estimated that death could not have occurred later than 7.45pm which was about twenty minutes after Truscott and Harper had been seen together, thus putting Truscott very much in the frame for the murder. Truscott was convicted but a 1966 book on the case, which suggested a miscarriage of justice had occurred, led to what was effectively a retrial in that year (and was described as such by Simpson, albeit technically an appeal) before eleven judges in the Canadian Supreme Court at which Professor Simpson gave evidence supporting the estimate of the original pathologist as to the time of death based on the amount of food in the stomach. He told the court that, 'in the absence of any evidence to the contrary, it must be assumed that Lynne Harper was an average subject whose stomach emptied at the normal rate.' A pathologist called by Truscott's defence team, however, argued that, due to the uncertainties over the rate of gastric emptying, Harper, 'could have died within an hour – or up to nine or ten' and that reliance on the stomach contents could be 'dangerously misleading'. In the end, the judges rejected Truscott's claims of innocence, deciding that there had been no miscarriage of justice, and it seemed that the medical evidence was reliable after all. Simpson certainly had no doubt about this at the time he published his memoir in 1978.

In Canada, however, further investigations led to the case being referred back to the Ontario Court of Appeal in 2006 and several medical experts testified that it was now widely accepted that it wasn't possible to reliably estimate the time of death based on stomach contents due to the fact that the rate of gastric emptying can fluctuate widely for different individuals. Other evidence presented to the Court of Appeal suggested that Lynne Harper's murder might have occurred on 10 June 1959, the *day after* Truscott had been seen with her. On 28 August 2007, Truscott's conviction was quashed and he received an apology from the Attorney General of Ontario along with $6.5 million in damages for a wrongful conviction. Simpson, convinced of Truscott's guilt to the last, must have turned in his grave when that happened.

The limits of estimating time of death from stomach contents can be seen from the investigation into the murder of six-year-old Rikki Neave in November 1994. After having breakfast at around 9am in the morning of

Monday, 28 November, Rikki left his house in Peterborough for school, from which he played truant, and never returned home. His concerned mother contacted the police at 6pm and a search for the boy was instituted but he wasn't found until lunchtime of the next day when his naked body was discovered in woodland a few minutes walk from his home. A forensic pathologist was unable to estimate the time of Rikki's death based on his body temperature but he thought that he was so cold that he must have been lying outside for at least 12 hours. There had been sightings of Rikki on the estate in which he lived throughout the day of 28 November up to as late as the time his mother called the police in the early evening. The police at the time ignored a post-mortem report which stated that Weetabix found in the boy's stomach was of such a 'fresh appearance' that it seemed there had been 'a very short time of digestion' of '1 hour or so'. They concluded that he had, in fact, been murdered by his mother during the late afternoon. She was charged with the murder but acquitted. It wasn't until 27 years later, following a cold case review by Cambridgeshire police, that James Watson, who had been 13 years old at the time, was convicted of the murder. Watson had been seen with Rikki by a local resident outside her house at between 12.30 and 1.20pm and it was believed by the police that he had taken Rikki to the woodland and strangled him shortly thereafter, so that the witness sightings of the young boy after this time were all mistaken. While this theory was broadly consistent with the pathologist report as to stomach contents, it would mean that Rikki was killed three or four hours after his breakfast, not one hour as the pathologist report had suggested.

In 2011, postmaster Dr Robin Garbutt was convicted of murdering his wife on 23 March 2010, by hitting her over the head with an iron bar while she was sleeping, largely on the basis of a time of death determined from an analysis of his wife's stomach contents. An ambulance arrived at the scene of death, the village post office in Melonsby, North Yorkshire, at 8.45am, and Garbutt had a solid alibi from 4.30am but, primarily on the basis of the stomach contents, the prosecution pathologist testified that the murder had occurred in the two hours before that. A subsequent review of the evidence by former Home Office pathologist Dr David Rouse concluded that the prosecution's expert had been 'incorrect' and that death might have occurred after 6.45am which would have corroborated Garbutt's evidence that his wife had been murdered by an armed robber who took £16,000 from the safe. At time of writing Garbutt, supported by *Private Eye*, is challenging his conviction in a case which goes to show that potential miscarriages of justice based on dubious estimates of time of death continue unabated.

Ingram Content Group UK Ltd.
Milton Keynes UK
UKHW020805310523
422635UK00011B/253